GOOD BANDITS, WARRIOR

APR 1 3 2011

GOOD BANDITS,
WARRIOR WOMEN,
AND
REVOLUTIONARIES
IN
HISPANIC CULTURE

edited by

Gary Francisco Keller

Bilingual Press/Editorial Bilingüe

TEMPE, ARIZONA

Published in cooperation with the

International Association of Inter-American Studies

www.interamericanstudies.net

Library of Congress Cataloging-in-Publication Data

Good bandits, warrior women, and revolutionaries in Hispanic culture / edited by Gary Francisco Keller.
    p. cm.
  In English and Spanish.
  "Published in cooperation with the International Association of Inter-American Studies."
  "Most of the articles in this volume were presented at the Bold Caballeros and Noble Bandidas conference, which took place April 16-18, 2009, at Arizona State University."
    Includes bibliographical references.
    ISBN 978-1-931010-71-9 (alk. paper)
  1. Outlaws in popular culture—Latin America. 2. Outlaws—Latin America—History. 3. Revolutionaries—Latin America—History. 4. Latin Americans in literature. 5. Latin Americans in motion pictures. I. Keller, Gary Francisco.
  HV6543.L29G66 2010
  364.3098—dc22

2010027678

Front cover art: María Félix with Rifle *(2002) by Héctor Silva*
Cover and interior design by John Wincek

Acknowledgments

The Hispanic Research Center gratefully acknowledges Arizona State University Executive Vice President and Provost Elizabeth D. Capaldi for her ongoing financial support of the Arizona International Latina/o Arts Festival (AILAF), from which this publication emerged. Most of the articles in this volume were presented at the Bold Caballeros and Noble Bandidas conference, which took place April 16-18, 2009, at Arizona State University's Downtown Phoenix campus. We would also like to acknowledge the staff members and student assistants of the Hispanic Research Center for their contributions to the success of this conference, particularly Ana María Regalado, Concepción Biebrich, Brian Ellis Cassity, Brandon M. Ortega, and Santiago A. Moratto.

Additional visual material to illustrate this book may be seen online at
http://noblebandits.asu.edu/Topics/GoodBandits2009.html

Table of Contents

*Additional visual material to illustrate this book may be seen online at
http://noblebandits.asu.edu/Topics/GoodBandits2009.html*

O Tempora, O Mores, OMG!
ENORMOUS CHANGES AT THE LAST MINUTE

Gary Francisco Keller

ARIZONA STATE UNIVERSITY

THE BEAT GOES ON!

The Bilingual Press/Editorial Bilingüe is pleased to publish this newest component of the Hispanic Research Center's ongoing project Bold Caballeros and Noble Bandidas. This project primarily treats Latin@ noble bandits in Iberoamerican culture (Spain, Latin America, the United States, and elsewhere) but also provides, to a lesser degree, textual and visual information on banditry in antiquity and in other nations and cultures, including the Far East, the Middle East, Oceania, Africa, Europe, and elsewhere. We expect the project to run for decades and to undergo extensive development by a national and worldwide community interested in noble bandits in popular culture as well as in the related social science construct of "social banditry."

This volume is one of a number of project components.

The Bold Caballeros and Noble Bandidas Web site

This Web site (at http://noblebandits.asu.edu/Intro.html) has been online for several years and has a broad and rich variety of entries from Hammurabi to Salma Hayek. Although it provides a variety of information from various time frames and locations, like the overall project itself, the Web site seeks to capture or recapture the image of the good-bad Hispanic bandit and to contrast her or him with the simple degenerate or unregenerate bad Hispanic bandit. At times the image is, alternately—and occasionally simultaneously—good, bad, ugly, beautiful, banal. Above all it is bounteous.

We have had a wealth of images to work with, albeit only a fraction of those originally created, and even most of what remains with respect to early cinema is in less than optimal condition. We have worked hard to recapture a partially lost culture and its imagery. There are Cisco and Zorro, the bold caballeros and the gay caballeros, and their counterparts who include the "athletic but feminine" or "avenging spitfire" females.

We have profiled generations of Cisco and Zorro characters who have been represented in an extensive literary style. Other real life, rather than literary, social bandits have received extensive folkloric treatment as well: Joaquín Murrieta, Gregorio Cortez, Elfego Baca, and Tiburcio Vásquez. We have made a determined effort to cover women of history and popular fancy, including Zorro's Black Whip; Anita Delgado, the Avenging Arrow; Lasca of the Rio Grande; and the daughter of

Don Q. We cover popular history, legend, and folklore; journalistic accounts; and what Miguel de Unamuno termed the "intrahistoria," and his contemporary Carl Jung called the "collective unconscious" of the good-bad bandit mythos.

Now that we approach the centennial of the Mexican Revolution of 1910, the Web site as well as the book introduced here focus on the heroes, the good-bad, and the irredeemably bad players of that profound transformation. These include archetypes such as la Negra Angustias, la Adelita, la Valentina, and la Cucaracha, all modeled on real people, the real *generalas* and *coronelas* of the Mexican Revolution of 1910 such as Margarita Neri, and, of course, Felipe Ángeles, Pascual Orozco, Pancho Villa, and Emiliano Zapata.

On the other end of the spectrum it covers the stereotyping of Latinos/as in film and advertising, examples of which are the Frito Bandito and Speedy Gonzalez. Carlos Bedoya as Gold Hat proclaims, "Badges? . . . I don't have to show you no stinking badges." It waters at the way stations of "gringoized" parodies and Chicanoized parodies, or even parodies of the parodies, as in *I Don't Have to Show You No Stinking Badges!* (1986), set in California during Ronald Reagan's presidency. It samples the inspirational image of the Latino good bandit in contemporary Latina/o art and cinema, to the point that Hispanics can say not only that the "Cisco Kid was a friend of mine," but claim him legitimately as a fellow traveler, *un compañero* to break bread with and to serve as a model for the community and for youth. It addresses the issue of mixed heritage and mixed bloodlines, the nature of those termed "half-breeds" or even less attractive epithets at the time of the birth of Cisco and Zorro. A good place to review this is the introduction to the Web site.

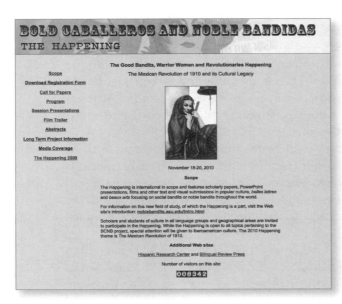 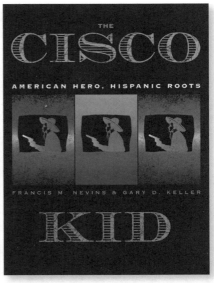

Left: The Bold Caballeros and Noble Bandidas Web site. *Right: The Cisco Kid: American Hero, Hispanic Roots*, by Francis M. Nevins and Gary D. Keller, Bilingual Press, 2008. *Facing page:* the Bold Caballeros y Noble Bandidas exhibition at the Autry National Center, Los Angeles, California. *Following page:* Exhibit entry close-up.

The Cisco Kid Book

In *The Cisco Kid: American Hero, Hispanic Roots* (2008), Frances M. Nevins and Gary D. Keller review the Cisco phenomenon in literature, film, radio, television, and popular culture. Despite the Cisco Kid's initial creation outside the Hispanic world by such mainstream writers and filmmakers as O. Henry and Webster Cullison, by 1929 with the first Cisco sound film, *In Old Arizona,* the character was endowed with a Latino persona that it has retained in both Hispanic and mainstream American culture. This visually rich book, which includes film stills, lobby cards, and posters, recounts the history and *genio y figura* of a fictional figure who has taken on legendary proportions. It also provides a good deal of coverage of other noble bandits and revolutionary figures, including warrior women, especially during the Mexican Revolution of 1910. It looks at historical figures such as María de la Luz Espinosa Barrera, Margarita Neri, Francisco "Pancho" Villa, and Emiliano Zapata, and also at fictional personages of literature and film, including the characters played by María Félix, Pedro Armendáriz, Silvia Pinal, Jorge Negrete, and many others.

The Joint Arizona State University and Autry National Center Exhibition

The attention gained by the Bold Caballeros and Noble Bandidas Web site and publication of *The Cisco Kid: American Hero, Hispanic Roots* led to the mounting of a major exhibition in Los Angeles. The joint Arizona State University and Autry National Center exhibition on *Bold Caballeros y Noble Bandidas*, which ran from October 31, 2008 through May 10, 2009, became a

BOLD CABALLEROS Y NOBLE BANDIDAS

TIERRA Y LIBERTAD

OCTOBER 31, 2008 – MAY 10, 2009

great favorite in Los Angeles County and Southern California, and it brought in tens of thousands of school children to learn about good bandits and warrior women. Once again, the looming centenary of the Mexican Revolution of 1910 took center stage and, in addition to art, material items, photographs, and posters, it included brief film clips dedicated to María Félix, revolutionaries in Mexican culture sometimes interpreted in the United States as "banditos" (yes, the preferred spelling by gringos), and a brief history of the Mexican Revolution using historical footage between 1906 and 1924. There was also plenty of coverage of the Bandit Queen, Cisco and Zorro, Zorro's Black Whip (a female counterpart), and the Chicana and Chicano art of good bandits.

As the sales pitch goes, "but that's not all!" In addition to the exhibit, other events included a film festival with the likes of movies such as *Viva Zapata!* (1952, director Elia Kazan, with Marlon Brando, Anthony Quinn, and Jean Peters) and *Como agua para chocolate* (1992, director Alfonso Arau, with Lumi Cavazos and Marco Leonardi). For the youngsters, puppet performances ran once a month. Who wouldn't want to make a Pancho Puppet? For the musically inclined, the exhibition offered a wide sampling of Mexican *corridos de la Revolución*.

The April 2009 Happening in Downtown Phoenix

Fed by these accomplishments, the April 2009 Happening dedicated to *Bold Caballeros and Noble Bandidas/Bandidas y Bandidos Valientes y Generosos* was next in line. At the Downtown Phoenix campus of Arizona State University, the Happening offered in great meals, papers, visual presentations, and about sixteen hours of film clips from dozens of movies and songs, which we divided into eight separate themes:

> Selections from the María Félix Warrior and Vamp Films
> Project Films Produced by the Hispanic Research Center
> What Do Women Want? From Revolutions of Course!
> Great Novels and Other Narratives and Their Filmic Adaptations
> Revolution from the Radical Left to the Far Right
> Athletic Outlaws: Lights, Camera, Action!
> Music of the Revolution, Revolution in Music
> Gringo Interpretations: The Good, the Bad, the Ugly

Good Bandits, Warrior Women, and Revolutionaries in Hispanic Culture

The book before you, *Good Bandits, Warrior Women, and Revolutionaries in Hispanic Culture* is the fruit of the 2009 Happening. The papers included here follow the trail of the project itself. The first section is dedicated to good, good-bad, and bad people across Hispanic culture. Arizona State University Regents' Professor David William Foster traces the history in film, literature, and popular culture of gay caballeros in both senses of that semanteme: "gay" in its earlier meaning of "devil may care," and "gay" as a synonym for "queer." As Prof. Foster effectively documents, both meanings are often intertwined. Carlo Gaberscek, a prolific independent scholar who is affiliated with the University of Udine and with Le Giornate del Cinema Muto, both in Northern Italy, discusses an interesting Italian "spaghetti" western phenomenon: Zapata Westerns. Contrary to expectations, these don't need to treat Emiliano Zapata; they are a designation in Italian film culture. Columbia University Gonzalo Sobejano reviews different types in *Don Quixote de la Mancha,* including *bandoleros*, *aventureros*, *guerrilleros*, and *bandidos generosos*.

The second section hones in on the popular culture and novel of the Mexican Revolution of 1910. Prof. Santiago Daydí-Tolson at the University of Texas, San Antonio has two contributions. Both deal with *Los de abajo*: the one on Demetrio Macías as a heroic bandit who sets things right, and the other on the elements of race and social class in Azuela's depiction of the bandido. The novel *La negra Angustias* by Francisco Rojas González, which won the Premio Nacional de Literatura in 1944, is reputed to be the first novel of the Mexican Revolution that has a female warrior as the main protagonist, coronela Angustias Farrera. The film, *La negra Angustias* (1950, director, Matilde Landeta), is not easy to find. We are privileged to have in this volume two papers related to *La negra Angustias*. Prof. Laura Kanost at Kansas State University exercises a valuable analysis of how identities are developed in the novel, screenplay, and film versions of *La negra Angustias*. Prof. Margarita López López, of Los Angeles Valley College, analyzes the Afro-Mexican element in the novel. Robert McKee Irwin, at the University of California, Davis develops the relationship of the renowned, iconic, "Santa popular," Teresa de Cabora with her villainous sister Jovita. Prof. Emil Volek, of Arizona State University, analyzes the memories of a *soldadera* from Madero to the *cristeros* as they are depicted in Elena Poniatowska's *Hasta no verte, Jesús mío. Y de pilón,* Prof. Kristín Guðrún Jónsdóttir at the University of Iceland highlights the impact of the bandido Pancho Villa as a blessed religious hero of the people to whom they plead for intercession.

1910-1929: Revolution and Its Culture and the 2010 Happening in Tempe, Arizona

The educational documentary *1910-1929: Revolution and Its Culture* debuted in San Antonio on January 21, 2010. It will be presented as an educational event in selected cities and culminating at our 2010 Happening in Tempe, which will take place *justo en el centenario de la Revolución de 1910:* 18-20 November 2010. The 2010 Happening in Tempe will operate along the lines of the 2009 event, with film and food and presentations both textual and visual, and, of course, excited and exciting discussions. After all, this is revolution! To learn more, see: http://noblebandits.asu.edu/Topics/ConfIntro.php

In early 2012, we expect to produce another book that collects the research production of the 2010 event.

To communicate your interest in collaborating in this project, use the following contact information:

Gary Francisco Keller, Regents' Professor
Hispanic Research Center
PO Box 875303
Arizona State University
Tempe, AZ 85287-5303

E-mail: gary.keller@asu.edu
Fax: 480-965-0315
General HRC telephone: 480-965-3990
Web site: http://www.asu.edu/clas/hrc/

IT'S ALL ABOUT ALGO

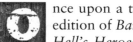nce upon a time in wild and spiritual Italy, Eric Hobsbawm's latest edition of *Bandits* firmly in hand, the silent version of William Wyler's *Hell's Heroes* stirring my imagination, an idea began to take hold. I was attending Le Giornate del Cinema Muto in Pordenone, a festival of restoration and screening of silent films from around the world. This idea emerged from the fertile womb of a movie theater, the Cinema Verdi (constructed in art deco in the "fascist period," according to my dear departed friend and profes-

sor of Italian, Gino Rizzo). Le Giornate takes place each October in the Friuli region in the foothills of the Dolomites, about half the distance between Cortina d'Ampezzo, home of the first Pink Panther film and La Serenissima Repubblica di Venezia in its lagoon on the Adriatic.

The serendipitous idea joins two separate strands within the brain. On the left side was housed Hobsbawm's *Bandits,* the observation that launched it, and its systematic development within a Marxian framework (by Hobsbawm but not by me). The thesis began with the empirical conclusion based on extensive research across cultures worldwide "that exactly the same stories and myths were told about certain types of bandits as bringers of justice and social redistributors all over Europe; indeed, as became increasingly clear, all over the globe" (*Bandits* 2000, ix). Hobsbawm began exploring this observation in 1959 and a new line of research emerged from it. Hobsbawm coined the phrase "social bandits" and this notion has proved to be both controversial and enduring. At the center of the controversy is the historical veracity of what goes by "social bandit." In Hobsbawm's analysis, social bandits transcend the label of "criminals"; they are robbers and outlaws elevated to the status of avengers and champions of social justice. Some, such as Robin Hood, Rob Roy, Jesse James, and Francisco "Pancho" Villa, are famous throughout the world, the stuff of story and myth. Others, from Balkan *haiduks* and Indian *dacoits* to Brazilian *cangaceiros,* are known primarily by their own countries' people.

On the right side, my brain was awash in an unforgettable, thrilling experience. At the end of *Hell's Heroes,* the silent and subsequently sound Ur-version of the countless "Three Godfathers" films, out of the uppermost balcony of the Teatro Verdi, an Italian chorus appeared miraculously and played the Christmas song that climaxes the movie.

Left side, right side. It grew on me that there hasn't been a popular culture history of good or noble bandits. At the heart of the social science research is the issue of the historical accuracy or legitimacy of specific social bandits. Thus, much historical and anthropological work has been devoted to whether a certain figure, for example Jesse James (1847-82) or Pancho Villa (1878-1923), was legitimately a social bandit, or whether, because of the aggrandizing effects of popular culture, that figure had undergone a transformation. However, putting the issues of veracity in Husserlian brackets, it occurred to me that popular culture had the potential to make a huge contribution to noble bandit research. It seemed that the aggrandizing dynamic of popular culture was the defining agent of all of these figures. The historical ones documented to have existed, the semi-historical, pseudo-historical, or composite figures, the totally fictional ones such as Cisco and Zorro, all have undergone transformation into legendary entities, which is an operation within the province of popular culture. Consider the conventions of film, a most powerful medium of popular culture. One such convention is that "Movies are life with the boring parts cut out."

Or consider what Shakespeare tells us in *The Tempest,*

> "We are such stuff
> As dreams are made on . . ."

Similarly Bogie tells us in *The Maltese Falcon,* "It's the stuff that dreams are made of."

Carly Simon sings in "The Stuff that Dreams Are Made Of,"

What if the prince on the horse in your fairytale
Is right here in disguise
And what if the stars you've been reaching so high for
Are shining in his eyes

It's the stuff that dreams are made of
It's the slow and steady fire
It's the stuff that dreams are made of
It's your heart and soul's desire
It's the stuff that dreams are made of

This project addresses a great need, which is to develop the history of the transformation of historical figures by the forces of popular culture, the projecting of legendary figures from a shred of reality, or the creation of a Zorro or other personage simply out of whole cloth.

Once upon an earlier, medieval time lived individuals of stature. Their unit of measure was *algo.* In Spain, they were called "hidalgos," a shortened form of *hijos de algo.* The hidalgos were the heirs of substance, literally the sons of something. Their status was not earned by dint of deed; it was ascribed. Either you were born with and have *algo* or you were not born with it and you have naught. At the polar opposite in the great chain of social status, were the lowly *hideputas*, a shortened form of *hijos de putas.* They were the heirs of whoredom, of illegitimacy, literally the sons of whores. Hidalgos and *hideputas* were the poles in the great medieval chain of being, the outermost limits of the social set.

If humans were measured by *algo,* what was *algo*'s unit of measure? If language be our refuge, it was the horse. In days of old when knights were bold, a Latin gentleman, a Latin hidalgo, a Latin knight was a man on a horse: *un caballero, un chevalier, un cavaliere,* a cavalier. This measure of Latin quiddity persisted through the Renaissance, the Enlightenment, the nineteenth century, not without changes. In the nineteenth century the Iron Horse began to confound the indigenous peoples on their pintos.

The process of degradation of the hidalgo, of the caballero, makes a quantum leap during the Spanish Siglo de Oro. This is splendidly indexed by Miguel de Cervantes's masterpiece, *El ingenioso hidalgo don Quixote de la Mancha.* The Cisco Kid and Pancho owe much to Don Quixote and Sancho Panza. They all do: the bold caballeros and noble bandidas of this project on popular culture. The sort of hidalgo that interested Don Quixote was the medieval knight-errant, the *caballero andante,* the *cavaliere errante,* the *chevalier errant,* namely the sort of knight who travels the land in search of adventures that will prove his military skills, prowess, and generosity.

Don Quixote, of course, is not played "straight." It is infused with parody, irony, and satire and reflects the world's evolution from the middle ages to the rise of cities, trading companies, and banks, the European discovery of the so-called New World, and the compact between the king and the *villanos* that led to the weakening of the aristocracy and the centralization of power by the Spanish Hapsburg monarchs such as Carlos I (Charles V of the Holy Roman Empire), Felipe II, and Felipe III. Don Quixote represents a petty noble, *venido a menos.* The type is ubiquitous in the culture of the period: The hidalgo who has his name but few other resources. Don Quixote looks backwards; his aspirations stem from the nostalgic memory of past nobility. Not the historical account of nobility, mind you, but its fictional elaboration. Enamored of these knights-errant, he debates such weighty questions as whether the Amadís de Gaula or Palmerín de Inglaterra is the better *caballero andante.*

By the late sixteenth and early seventeenth centuries (first and second parts of Don Quixote respectively) the *algo* unit of measure had changed. It had become democratized, or if you are nostalgic, degraded. It certainly was no longer ascribed. More and more it could be earned by actions. And eventually, *algo,* "the right stuff," would not only be assessed on the basis of behavior, but the assessors would be commonfolk, moviegoers, or other characters in the film or novel.

Don Quixote is not a *novela de caballería* but is considered the first modern novel and one that in part is a comic satire against the chivalric romances. Cervantes does not confound the chivalric ideals, the nobility of *caballería,* but does transfigure them, and that is one of the reasons the novel is neither wholly tragic nor wholly comic, but tragicomic. The elderly, idealistic hidalgo in his own warped mind sets out on his nag, Rocinante, to seek adventure, and the materialistic squire Sancho Panza ("Panza" means "belly" in Spanish) accompanies him on his ass from one failure to another. Although they argue arduously, ultimately in their debates, as Miguel de Unamuno, the existentialist philosopher of the early twentieth century, masterfully explains, they gradually take on some of each other's attributes, the "sanchification" of Quixote, and the "quixotization" of Sancho. This means that the Quixote is somewhat brought down and Sancho is built up. He has his own aspirations for *algo.* He'd like to govern an *ínsula* (island), although he's never heard of the word and can only validate the wish through his hidalgo master. It's democratization.

The dichotomy between past and present, between chivalric idealism and modern materialism, between the nobility of aristocracy and the power of the people, between nostalgia and satire, between comedy and pathos is set up from the very start. Before the novel itself, Cervantes establishes this tension masterfully in his *versos comendatorios,* such as the different *sonetos* from the Amadís de Gaula, from Solisdán, and from Orlando Furioso to Don Quixote de la Mancha, la señora Oriana to Dulcinea del Toboso, from Gandalín, the squire of Amadís, to Sancho Panza, Don Quixote's squire.

Let's stay in the saddle and sample the discourse in sonnet form between Babieca, the great warhorse of the Castilian knight, El Cid, and Rocinante in order to get an inkling of this.

DIÁLOGO ENTRE BABIECA Y ROCINANTE

Soneto

B.   ¿Cómo estáis, Rocinante, tan delgado?
R. Porque nunca se come, y se trabaja.
B. Pues ¿qué es de la cebada y de la paja?
R. No me deja mi amo ni un bocado.

B.   Andá, señor, que estáis muy mal criado,
pues vuestra lengua de asno al amo ultraja.
R. Asno se es de la cuna a la mortaja.
¿Queréislo ver? Miraldo enamorado.

B.   ¿Es necedad amar? R. No es gran prudencia.
B. Metafísico estáis. R. Es que no como.
B. Quejaos del escudero. R. No es bastante.

      ¿Cómo me he de quejar en mi dolencia,
si el amo y escudero o mayordomo
son tan rocines como Rocinante?

B. How comes it, Rocinante, you're so lean?
R. I'm underfed, with overwork I'm worn.
B. But what becomes of all the hay and corn?
R. My master gives me none; he's much too mean.

B.   Come, come, you show ill-breeding, sir, I ween;
'Tis like an ass your master thus to scorn.
R. He is an ass, will die an ass, an ass was born;
Why, he's in love; what's plainer to be seen?

B.   To be in love is folly? R. No great sense.
B. You're metaphysical. R. From want of food.
B. Rail at the squire, then. R. Why, what's the good?
    I might indeed complain of him, I grant ye,
But, squire or master, where's the difference?
They're both as sorry hacks as Rocinante.

From translation of Don Quixote *by John Ormsby, London, 1885*

Verily, if the *caballo* were once the golden *algo* of the caballero, truly by the time of the Quixote, the substance has been debased to the lowly copper of the *asno.* Conversely, the lowborn can now aspire to rise in this world by force of their deeds. They can be contenders. It's all in the *algo,* and its measure keeps evolving. Keeping up with the *algo* is part of what this project in popular culture studies is about.

Language certified the horse as the measure of man, of the *hidalgo.* It was a sensible unit of measure for the medieval world and way beyond that. Pancho Villa's corrido "La cucaracha" expresses the turning point, the obsolescence of the *caballo* as the defining asset of the caballero. "La Cucaracha," the most famous corrido of the Revolution of 1910, was originally about the *fotingo* (Ford automobile) of the Centauro del Norte.

La cucaracha, la cucaracha
Ya no puede caminar
Porque le falta, porque le falta . . .

The damn *cucaracha* was all show and it never did *caminar*. Where's the gasoline? It needs a tune-up! The tire is bad, the axle is broken . . . and Pancho Villa's *dorados* had to drag it over land and running water with horses. But it was there, even if just for show. It was a good show. By 1923 it had become the very reliable vehicle that carried Pancho Villa to his death in Parral, Chihuahua.

Pancho Villa's Model T Ford

Now the whole caballero concept has changed, and its original meaning has been compromised. The caballero has been democratized; that is the democratic way of looking at it. The aristocrat, the traditional heir to substance, may think of the trajectory as one of degradation. Democratized or degraded, the caballero now can be any old guy. It is simply the sign on the door of the men's room.

The Wild Bunch, set around 1913 or 1914, takes the measure of goodness and nobility a step further. It is partially about the hard fact that these bandit gunslingers have outlived their time, at least in the United States. In Mexico, however, they can return to a past decade or two and assume a heroic, revolutionary function by serving the campesino. The Wild Bunch realize at some level that they are has-beens, and this issue comes up several times. With respect to the horse as a measure of man's worth, they come upon and are confronted by a shiny red car (the devil's spawn, evil Mapache's "showhorse") and they look at it with awe. And the airplane, while not seen, assumes a mind-boggling status in the mind's eye. The oldest wild buncher marvels about an airplane and he is ridiculed as a fool. It's just a balloon. No, the character played by William Holden says, it is an airplane and it goes sixty miles per hour. The times they are a-changin'.

GOOD, GOOD-BAD, BAD

In the bandit and revolutionary film genre, and ergo in this book, there exists a paradigm along the axes of good and bad. Section I of the book sums up the categories: good, bad, good-bad. A well-known process of popular culture is the dichotomization of characters into good and bad, and of course, characters can be simultaneously or alternately good-bad. However, if you have a two-by-two set, what about the missing category? Bad-good?

Good
Good-bad
Bad-good?
Bad

The Cisco Kid cycle participates in all three of the confirmed categories. In different periods and with different actors, Cisco has alternately been bad, good, and good-bad. He was bad with just a touch of redeeming Latin generosity as portrayed by Warner Baxter in *In Old Arizona*. He was good in a manner evoking a highly effective, virile protector of the oppressed who is respectful of señoritas in the manner of Don Quixote in the Duncan Renaldo and Leo Carrillo period. He was a good-bad do-gooder in the Gilbert Roland cycle. In the end, he always did the right thing.

Sam Peckinpah's *The Wild Bunch* provides another array of characters useful for validating this paradigm. At the top of the moral pyramid is Don José, played by Mexican director Chano Urueta in his twilight years. Urueta is known for directing a host of films including the Blue Demon wrestling movies. Here, Don José and the other villagers, dressed in white campesino clothes, are deserving and brave, but oppressed and without weapons to defend themselves. When they obtain these weapons, they use them for good purposes. The best of the good-bad men is Ángel. Fulfilling his name, Ángel is a fallen angel trying to reform himself, especially with his efforts to help the village where he was born. However, he is a victim of Latino passions, particularly with regard to the opposite sex. The characters played by William Holden and Ernest Borgnine are very interesting and I will profile them later. At the bottom of the heap is General Mapache, played by world-recognized director and actor Emilio "El Indio" Fernández. He is totally, irredeemably bad: a drunk, sadist, murderer, and lecher. Mapache, to use a category borrowed from *Dungeons and Dragons*, incarnates lawful evil, while Alfonso Bedoya as Gold Hat in *Treasure of the Sierra Madre* represents chaotic evil.

Who is good?

The Cisco starring Duncan Renaldo is a lighthearted, clean-cut hero who is frequently mistaken for a bandit, but is instead a carefree adventurer whose exploits generally center on his ardor for beautiful señoritas. Despite this key motivation, in seven films Renaldo's Cisco kisses a woman only once, in *The Daring Adventurer*, also known as *The Cisco Kid Returns*, as his gentlemanly code of conduct means that he habitually restricts himself to courtly praise of female beauty. One line specifically is repeated throughout the films, "You are the most beautiful señorita in all the world. On my heart, I swear it." Both Duncan Renaldo and Leo Carrillo make a conscious effort to emulate the characters of Don Quixote and Sancho Panza.

Some other good characters are included in the consolidated paradigm, as well as good-bad, and bad ones.

Who is good-bad?

The conventional American Western was straightforward in its depiction of good and bad. The good cowboys wore white hats, shot straight, and practiced a sort of gallantry that, in a different and "fallen" Spanish seventeenth century, Don Quixote attempted to recover. The bad cowboys wore black hats, were lousy shots, and were cheats, often shrewd, lewd, and cynical ones. Nevertheless, there was always a subgenre of the Western that amalgamated the good and the bad within the same cowboy and occasionally cowgirl.

Perhaps the most interesting characters of popular culture have been the good-bad ones, and one frequent observation by both analysts and aficionados over 100 years and more of Westerns and other film genres, such as detective films, is that many of its "heroes" are good-bad. The good-bad protagonist emerged from the earliest days of the Western such as the Broncho (later Bronco) Billy films and the characterizations of Thomas S. Hart. Four years before his appearance as Zorro (1920), Douglas Fairbanks Sr. starred in a film where good-bad was the highlight of the title, *The Good Bad Man* (1916, director Allan Dwan).

Gilbert Roland's Cisco, in contrast to Renaldo's perfectly turned out, pure, and gentlemanly character, is more in the mold of a traditional Western gunslinger. He is undoubtedly a bandit (albeit one whose motives are above reproach), and he constantly smokes and drinks tequila. He is also far less proper in his advances to women, whom he courts far more directly and aggressively than his predecessor.

The Good, the Bad, and the Ugly (1966) signaled the death knell of the white hat/black hat Western of the traditional John Wayne sort. Clint Eastwood is the Man With No Name (credited as Blondie) and fills the good-bad role. A bounty hunter with a sense of honor, he does the right thing, such as giving a dying Confederate soldier a puff of his cigar, and he displays genuine regret for having to let the character Shorty die.

Moreover, banditry and legitimacy are in the eyes of the beholder. Take the intercultural case of Francisco "Pancho" Villa. The revolutionary (or was he a bandit?) touched the American consciousness beginning in 1910, first as a hero of Mexico's revolutionary enterprise, and again in 1915, when his persona was transformed in American public opinion into an offensive malefactor. On March 8, 1916, General Villa conducted the first and only invasion of the

Pancho Villa prayer card

United States by foreign military forces since the War of 1812. Leading 250 *dorados*, he entered the dusty little town of Columbus, New Mexico, with its 300 residents, thus propelling the town's entry into the firmament of myth, history, and film, "the stuff dreams are made of." The *dorados* of the "Centauro del Norte" later hit two small Texas towns on May 5, after the Pershing punitive expedition had already entered Mexico to fruitlessly search for the elusive Pancho Villa. He became very bad. *¡Ay bendito!*

One person's *bandido muy malo* is another's spiritual intercessor. North of the border, eventually a bandido, South of the Border, a *beato*, a spiritual intercessor. Pancho the man, the revolutionary, in turn the cross-cultural, transcultural, bicultural, and transgressive icon of mainstream U. S. culture and mainstream Mexican culture—and straddling the two, a third, Amerexican or Mexamerican culture—has launched a thousand works of art, polemic, vituperative, and even hagiographic. Some people pray to Pancho and publish their gratitude for his intercessions in newspapers. Prof. Jónsdóttir studies precisely this phenomenon of Pancho Villa as a popular religious hero.

Who is bad?

In the first Cisco Kid sound film, the character is far from good in any conventional sense. He has a certain Latin sense of honor since he refuses to steal money from individuals when he holds up a stagecoach and takes its strongbox. That's about it on the good side of the ledger. He steals cattle, kills other evildoers who are out to steal his ill-gotten money, has plenty of sex with Tonia, and fulfills the denouement of O. Henry's story "The Caballero's Way" by successfully conspiring to have her Anglo lover, Sergeant Dunn, mistake her for Cisco and kill her.

There are a couple of characters who come down on the bad in the title of the film, *Il buono, il brutto, il cattivo*, released in English as *The Good, the Bad, and the Ugly* (1966, director Sergio Leone). Lee Van Cleef is Angel Eyes, evil personified in the Anglo mode. Totally ruthless, he does whatever is necessary to achieve his ends. He also has his principles. When he's hired for a job, he always sees the job through. Eli Wallach plays Tuco, who is evil personified in the Tex/Mex mode. Impulsive and enraged, Tuco spins wildly throughout the film, stealing, lying, pretending to be Clint Eastwood's best friend, and then trying to kill him. Angel Eyes versus Tuco is, once more, lawful versus chaotic evil. Here are some consolidated examples besides the ones discussed, in the good-bad paradigm.

GOOD

- Duncan Renaldo in *The Cisco Kid Returns*
- Zorro as played by Douglas Fairbanks, Sr.
- Lady Robinhood (1925) as played by Evelyn Brent
- Anita Delgado, the Avenging Arrow, as played by Ruth Roland in a serial in 1921
- Don José as played by Chano Urueta in *The Wild Bunch* (1969, director Sam Peckinpah)
- Invariably, Emiliano Zapata, the man of impeccable morality
- Gen. Omar N. Bradley as played by Karl Malden in *Patton* (1970, director Franklin J. Schaffner)

GOOD-BAD

- The Cisco Kid films as played by Gilbert Roland as Cisco
- Pancho Villa as represented in a number of American films including *And Starring Pancho Villa as Himself* (2003, director Bruce Beresford, starring Antonio Banderas) and *Pancho Villa* (1972, director Eugenio Martín, starring Telly Savalas)
- The character Passin' Through as played by Douglas Fairbanks in *The Good Bad Man* (1916, director Allan Dwan)
- Blondie played by Clint Eastwood in *Il buono, il brutto, il cattivo*, released in English as *The Good, the Bad, and the Ugly* (1966, director Sergio Leone)
- General George S. Patton played by George C. Scott in *Patton* (1970, director Franklin J. Schaffner)
- Kris Kristofferson as Billy the Kid in *Pat Garrett and Billy the Kid* (1973, director Sam Peckinpah)
- James Coburn as Pat Garrett in *Pat Garrett and Billy the Kid* (1973, director Sam Peckinpah)

BAD

- The Cisco Kid as played by Warner Baxter in *In Old Arizona* (1929)
- General Mapache as played by Emilio "El Indio" Fernández in *The Wild Bunch*
- Gold Hat as played by Alfonso Bedoya in *Treasure of the Sierra Madre* (1948, director John Huston)
- Angel Eyes as played by Lee Van Cleef in *Il buono, il brutto, il cattivo*, released in English as *The Good, the Bad, and the Ugly* (1966, director Sergio Leone)
- Tuco as played by Eli Wallach in *Il buono, il brutto, il cattivo*, released in English as *The Good, the Bad, and the Ugly* (1966, director Sergio Leone)

BAD-GOOD: THE ROGUE'S REDEMPTION

s there a genuine bad-good, or is it merely an alternate word ordering of good-bad? I've been struggling with bad-good for a lifetime. Now, by means of this Bold Caballero and Noble Bandida project, and reading with inspiration the Gospel, I think I've got it! By George, I've got it! Hopefully.

Romances

Ruth Axtell Morren wrote *The Rogue's Redemption* (a mass market paperback by Steeple Hill, 2008). The Amazon product description reads:

> He was tall and dark with eyes as blue as cobalt. In a glittering London ballroom Miss Hester Leighton saw a man who interested her more than anyone she'd met since coming to town. A woman of deep faith, Hester knew she should not keep company with Major Gerrit Hawkes, a jaded, penniless soldier haunted by nightmares of war. But their connection would not be denied.
>
> Hester was the only woman who'd ever made Gerrit feel truly worthy of love, and he would not lose her. Separated from her by her father—and an ocean—Gerrit must decide whether he will risk his life and his soul to earn a home in Hester's arms forever.

What greater mission than that of the woman who leads the rogue to true love?

Picaresque Conversion Narratives

Daniel Defoe, after the success of his *Robinson Crusoe,* wrote the very popular *Moll Flanders* (1722). That's the abbreviated version. Here is the full title, what in the new millennium we might call an "executive summary":

> *The Fortunes and Misfortunes of the Famous Moll Flanders, Etc. Who was born in Newgate, and during a life of continu'd Variety for Threescore Years, besides her Childhood, was Twelve Year a Whore, five times a Wife (whereof once to her own brother), Twelve Year a Thief, Eight Years a Transported Felon in Virginia, at last grew Rich, liv'd Honest and died a Penitent. Written from her own memorandums.*

Defoe believed in hard work, devotion, and the providential award of grace. Moll's biography is a conversion narrative, but one devoted mostly to the sins and little to the salvation. Sounds like a technique most cinematographic! In the secure darkness and privacy of the cinema, you may experience sin vicariously with the confidence that she, you, and it will comfortably be made right once the light goes back on. Yet, there is a certain logic to it. Conversion from what?

When I was but an early twenty-something, my creative writing teacher was Grace Paley, a good soul, keen wit, generous and effective teacher, and a really great writer, may she rest in peace.

Some years after my mid-1960s studies with her at Columbia University, she wrote a gripping book of short stories with the title *Enormous Changes at the Last Minute* (1974), also a story in the collection. In Paley's writing, there is an undercurrent of good and evil in the little and larger disturbances of humankind, a glimmering of redemption, and a willingness to live up to the trials of life. *En español* we have a phrase, both psychologically descriptive and morally analytic, *vivir a la altura de las circunstancias*. What calamity, calumny, or callousness is required to provide us the opportunity to effect enormous changes at the last minute, or to rise to the exigencies of the occasion? Jorge Guillén's first book, *Cántico*, is a Franciscan-compatible canticle that with optimism and serenity exalts the perfection of creation and the poet's joy of existence. At the other pole, his book of poetry, *Clamor*, tempered by his experience of the Spanish Civil War, has a section with the subtitle *A la altura de las circunstancias*. It is not about the perfection of creation, but about the resources we have, even though we may not be entirely aware of them, that can be summoned forth at the very last desperate minute.

The characters played in *The Wild Bunch* by William Holden and Ernest Borgnine, respectively Pike Bishop and Dutch Engstrom, are very bad hombres. But in a final paroxysm of righteous fury, they cleanse and redeem themselves by aiding the villagers, killing Mapache, and routing the army scum who are in the service of Mexican national traitor General Victoriano Huerta. This makes them bad-good.

Hell's Heroes is the first example of the long-running cycle of *Three God-fathers* films. First, four bandits rob a bank and commit mayhem. The Mexican is shot down before they even escape town. The three remaining bandits go into the desert and encounter a woman with a newborn baby. The mother, who must rely on the kindness of strangers, entrusts the babe in the desert to them before she dies. Three bad hombres take the sacred trust and the promise of another soul's well-being and become wise and spiritual beyond their wildest imaginings. Like relay racers they rise to the exigencies of the situation. First the one and then the second sacrifices himself to fulfill their assignment. Finally, the third, dehydrated and spent, discerns that he must drink alkaline water, which will kill him but will get the baby out of the desert and into town. The last of the three desperadoes, three wise bandits at the peak of their personal eclipses, accomplishes this at superhuman cost, barely making it, babe in arms, and dying at the portal of the little town church on Christmas Eve. The parishioners, all inside for midnight Mass, are singing "O Holy Night." The parishioners all bear witness to this rising to *las alturas de las circunstancias,* as their singing of "O Holy Night" is miraculously fulfilled by this desperado's sacrifice. The passage of John the apostle, the evangelist, and the theologian quoting the very words of Christ Jesus is on the mark: "Greater love has no one than this, than to lay down one's life for his friends" (John 15:13, New King James version).

All of this is happening in Italy with musical accompaniment of the most cherubic kind. When we 500 to 600 archivisti, specialisti, and cognoscenti saw this silent film at Le Giornate del Cinema Muto, suddenly and without forewarning an entire chorus of local singers appeared from the top, the highest balcony of the Teatro Verdi, which is normally closed. As the silent movie came to its conclusion, they sang "O Holy Night" live, a cappella. For all of us in attendance, it was a supreme, spiritual moment.

Bad-good is a concept profoundly different in the way that it plays out from uncontested chivalric good. Yet both draw from a common inspiration. Anchored in Christian theology and practice are two paths to goodness: either through the volte-face by rising to the occasion and becoming good at the very last moment, or through a lifetime of admirable deeds performed by the good, unflagging caballero, who is the product of formation, training, and a long apprenticehood. The chevalier is good by virtue of his dependability, which is often put on trial—trial by fire, like that of the archetypal chevalier, St. George, in his struggle with the dragon. The bandit, rogue, cutthroat, and the like is bad, malo, malvagità, but not forever bad. What is on trial in this case? The ability to rise out of one's selfishness and be graced. Desperados of the world, renounce yourselves and be redeemed; you have nothing to lose but the chains of your past deeds and your self-centeredness. The ability of the human spirit to overcome all of the *basura,* the obstacles of the world, a life of misdeeds and lost chances, and find its true calling and its true substance at the very last minute is fundamental to Christian faith, hope, and love. The three profoundly wise bandits played by Charles Bickford and others in *Hell's Heroes* are made of this right stuff.

BAD-GOOD

- Characters played by Charles Bickford, Raymond Hatton, Fred Kohler, and Joe de la Cruz in *Hell's Heroes* (1930, director William Wyler)
- Characters played by William Holden, Ernest Borgnine, and others in *The Wild Bunch*

There is an additional profound question to explore. Here is the matrix.

> Good and no Evil;
> Good and Evil Combined (simultaneously, alternately)
> Evil and then Good
> Evil and no Good

Which moral category is to be the most cherished? The question is clearly answered in the Christian canon. Several events during the life of Jesus provide testimony of the special love for repentant sinners.

> For the Son of Man has come to save that which was lost. What do you think? If a man has a hundred sheep, and one of them goes astray, does he not leave the ninety-nine and go to the mountains and seek the one that is straying? And if he should find it, assuredly, I say to you, he rejoices more over that sheep than over the ninety-nine that did not go astray. (Matthew 18: 10-13)
>
> I say to you that likewise there will be more joy in heaven over one sinner who repents than over ninety-nine just persons who need no repentance. (Luke 15: 7)
>
> Then one of the criminals who were hanged blasphemed Him, saying, "If You are the Christ, save Yourself and us." But the other, answering, rebuked him, saying, "Do you not even fear God, seeing you are under the same condemnation? And we indeed justly, for we receive the due reward of our deeds; but this Man has done nothing wrong." Then he said to Jesus, "Lord, remember me when You come into Your kingdom." And Jesus said to him, "Assuredly, I say to you, today you will be with Me in Paradise." (Matthew 23: 39-43)

In a discussion that I had with Father Deacon Michael J. Sullivan of the St. Thomas the Apostle Byzantine Catholic Church, Sullivan referred to the following explanatory passage from C. S. Lewis, *The Great Divorce* (San Francisco: Harper, 2001, p. 69) originally published in 1946. This text explains a lifetime of good and bad human acts in relationship to a key Christian concept that God lives outside of time and space in an eternal present.

> . . . ye cannot in your present state understand eternity . . . But ye can get some likeness of it if ye say that both good and evil, when they are full grown, become retrospective. . . . all their earthly past will have been Heaven to those who are saved. Not only the twilight in [Hell], but all their life on Earth too, will then be seen by the damned to have been Hell. That is what mortals misunderstand. They say of some temporal suffering, "No future bliss can make up for it," not knowing that Heaven, once attained, will work backwards and turn even that agony into a glory. And of some sinful pleasure they say "Let me have but *this* and I'll take the consequences": little dreaming how damnation will spread back and back into their past and contaminate the pleasure of the sin. Both processes begin even before death. The good man's past begins to change so that his forgiven sins and remembered sorrows take on the quality of Heaven: the bad man's past already conforms to his badness and is filled only with dreariness. And that is why, at the end of all things, when the sun rises here [in Heaven] and the twilight returns to blackness down there [in Hell], the Blessed will say "We never lived anywhere except in Heaven," and the Lost, "We were always in Hell." And both will speak truly.

C. S. Lewis explains that from the vantage point of the eternal divine, the triumph of good by an individual retrospectively, ultimately transforms the bad into good. Conversely, when evil overcomes the human spirit, in the end it contaminates all past experiences.

We have described the Bold Caballeros Noble Bandidas project in some detail both sequentially and in its scope. We have executed one full conceptual revolution. We started with the left brain-right brain. We discussed *algo,* substance based on the enduring chivalry of a nobleman abreast a horse. We've completed the full revolution or medieval wheel of fortune with the right brain-left brain phenomenon of redemption at the last genuine moment of free will.

Movies have the uncanny ability to permit us to watch things in darkness and security that would make us uncomfortable in the public light. It may be that movies about bad-good heroes and their deeds are profoundly counterintuitive. Who in the new millennium worries about carnage and extreme sex? Kids see worse in their video games. Here the revelation may be that we can experience without embarrassment or cynicism the "enormous changes at the last minute." To travel with bandits and malefactors of canonical status who learn in their climax that their raison d'être is to be eternally graced by the heroic deeds they barely knew they had within them in order to fulfill their providential assignment.

PART ONE

GOOD, BAD, GOOD-BAD HEROES AND VILLAINS ACROSS HISPANIC CULTURE

Of Gay Caballeros and Other Noble Heroes

David William Foster

ARIZONA STATE UNIVERSITY

The Cisco Kid was a friend of mine.

A song by War on their 1972 album, *The World Is a Ghetto*

[S]ome of the most interesting deployments of "queer/queerness" are related to the word's ability to describe those complex circumstances in texts, spectators, and production that resist easy categorization, but that definitively escape or defy the heteronormative.

Doty, *Flaming Classics* 7

INTRODUCTION

In 1889, less than ten years before the U.S. takeover of Cuba, José Martí found it necessary to answer, in the pages of the March 25, 1889, *Saturday Evening Post,* a column in the March 6, 1889, issue of the *Manufacturer of Philadelphia*, apparently signed by several prominent Republicans regarding the character of the Cuban people (Bejel 11). Although there are a number of, as Martí characterizes them, injurious criticisms of the Cubans, none is more stinging than the notion that the Cubans are "effeminate." Martí defends his fellow countrymen against this charge by citing their resistance in the face of the hostile government of Spain and their efforts to gain independence, precisely part of the spectrum of reasons that motivated the American invasion in 1898.

This exchange, which is characterized in detail by Bejel (10-27), was related directly both to the growing debate in the United States at the time over the value of Cuba—the *Manufacturer* column is entitled "Do We Want Cuba?"—and, after 1898, the matter of whether Cuba should become a permanent part of the United States. While Pérez, in *The War of 1898,* avoids dealing with what was clearly, to Martí (and to the inquiring Republicans), unquestionably a pressing matter, it is symptomatic of this sort of debate that nowhere is the matter of "effeminacy" usefully defined. The fact of the apposition of the word to the Cubans and, throughout the history of U.S./Latin American relations, to "Latins" in general, makes it even more pressing to inquire into its semantic nonspecificity.[1]

Moreover, the attribution of effeminacy to the Latin man works in tandem with the inverse proposition that he is oversexed, a macho with dangerous levels of testosterone poisoning and, therefore, always to be feared for his potential violence and as a potential rapist.

One assumes that the term "effeminacy" is being used in the sense of the definitions provided by a classic source like the second edition of *Webster's New*

23

International Dictionary: "Womanish quality unbecoming a man, such as softness, delicacy, or weakness" (1956 edition; orig. 1909). One could also do a minute tracking of its use over the centuries in the English language in the *Oxford English Dictionary*. However, none of the prevalent uses of the terms in the nineteenth century and most of the twentieth century is useful in sorting out exactly what is supposedly covered by the term and precisely why there is allegedly a problem with effeminacy. That is, how does the word "effeminate" function as a word to describe not that which can be expressed via a chain of synonyms with a common core of semantic meaning, but as a code word used to evoke mostly that which is not convenient to state clearly, both for presumably conscious reasons of decorum and likely unconscious reasons of semantic incoherence?

Thus, initially it becomes imperative to attempt to factor out some of the contradictory meanings of the term. Certainly the matter cannot simply be its function as a descriptor of a man who, for some reason or another and to one degree or another, adopts the tertiary sex characteristics of those social subjects accepted, in an unanalyzed fashion, to be women. Such tertiary sex characteristics refer to features of voice, physical bearing, dress, and language (some features of grammar, but mostly the use of lexical items and, definitely, the inappropriate use of pronouns and predication). These major features constitute a cluster of visible traces that allow for the observer—specifically, the observer with a vested interest in the semiotics of the body, such as the agents of nineteenth-century public hygiene who came to work in tandem with the guardians of religious morality—to identify a specific social subject as marked by effeminacy.

Yet, once again, all of this begs the question as to why such an operation of identification has social meaning: why, in effect, does it matter? Martí's response provides us with one possible clue: that such an attribution is injurious to Cuban men because it contradicts the manifest virility of those who have so valiantly resisted a hostile Spanish government. And it is, indeed, this virility that will enable Cuban men, once free of the Spanish yoke, to construct the great Cuban nation. It is no accident that the question of virility = courage; effeminacy = non-courage will reemerge almost a hundred years later in the context of the Castro Revolution and the need to count on virile men (and therefore, with no questions asked, either to "virilize" the effeminate men or to expunge them completely from civil society; this history is covered by Lumsden).

If virility in this case is a synonym of courage and if by effeminacy one understands the subtraction up to the extent of total absence of courage, what is at issue is both a particular model of manliness and the threat to that manliness of any encroachment from the antithesis of manliness, which is womanliness. What becomes at issue, at least in a first instance, is the privative nature of courage (and related overlapping and intersecting virtues of patriotism, stoicism, fortitude, responsibility, bravery, and so on) and the implication that such virtues are totally—or, at least, significantly—lacking in women, a correlative of other characteristics of women that can be neatly summarized in the assertion that she is the "daughter of Eve," who one must always bear in mind was the cause of the man's fall from grace.

In terms of the stark sexism one can attribute to the unreflective voice of, in this case, late nineteenth-century masculinist discourse, a man is virile to the extent that in each and every detail of his life he refutes what is paradigmatically established as womanly because that is the terrain he has wrested from Eve's original sin. Moreover, since the effort to overcome Adam's weakness in giving in to Eve's temptation, the struggle for manliness is unstinting, unrelenting, and irreducible. And herein lies an important point to be made about the virility at issue in Martí's protestations: it is an ongoing project (in this case, one that parallels the ongoing project to free Cuba from the Spaniards), while effeminacy is static and, indeed, regressive in nature.[2]

In these formulations, which swirl around the presumed correlation between manners of being in the world (such as those of men who wear flashy and/or colorful clothing), the ability of men to conduct energetically the business of state and society (such as the struggle for independence and, subsequently, nation building) appears to be fundamentally at issue. The matter of sexuality, understood as an erotic program, is never mentioned. Yet it is always and ever the shadow that haunts the primary attribution of effeminacy. This is so because, as Freud was theorizing at about the same time Martí was constrained to defend his countrymen against charges of effeminacy, sexuality (Freud uses the word "Eros") in anything other than a strictly reproductive fashion (what went on to be called the heteronormative imperative or, simply, heterosexism) is antithetical to the properly understood attributes of civilization.[3] Since sex(uality) is a threat to civilization, more so is it when it begins to blur the parameters of meaning in which civilization is grounded.

It is at this point that we must make the transition from understanding virility as a synonym of, redundantly, manly courage, to understanding virility as signaling appropriate sexual role playing. While there is nothing inherent or inevitable in effeminate men shunning the sexual company of women (if this were so, the conventional image of the court of Louis XIV would have been no better than a Carmelite nunnery to Madame Pompadour and associates), the semiotic practice via which effeminacy is identified always brings with it the implication of homosexuality (or of sodomy, as was the prevalent term as one of practice, before the late nineteenth-century emergence of the term "homosexuality" as an identity, a way of being in the world, as Foucault famously perceived). Although "sodomy" is historically never defined or—at best it is underdefined—as the sin that "dare not speak its name" (Jordan), homosexuality becomes a much-touted word in the late nineteenth and early twentieth centuries, even when its spoken articulation is often accompanied by special inflections. Homosexuality, as it emerges–as it is invented (Katz)—in the company of the modern organization of society and its social subjects, is, no more than effeminacy, not free of contradiction, even when it purports to be part of the vocabulary of a scientific psychiatric discourse. The term has at least the following prevalent meanings:

1. The conduct of some social subjects—for a variety of reasons that are a mixture of willfulness and the "mistakes of nature"—such that they assume, to one degree

or another, the traits of the biological sex other than the one to which they were assigned at birth (such assignment is not, itself, unproblematical, as though the biological binary were consistently manifest in unquestionable ways). Such conduct might today be more commonly known as transexuality, with the assumption that if X, assigned at birth the gender of male, wishes to be publically identified as a woman, when he desires sex with a man, X is behaving in a heterosexual way.

2. Nevertheless, the prevailing proposition, prior to the emergence of the proposition of transexuality (which is customarily understood to be a matter of transgendering, should full gender reassignment surgery take place), is that a man who conducts himself as a woman is doing so in order to attract another man as a sexual partner. Such a position accepts unquestioningly a) that such conduct is always driven by the attempt to procure a sexual partner, and b) that such a social subject will never desire a woman as a sexual partner. The important point to be made here, although it often remains more implicit than articulated in the depictions by popular discourse and cultural production, is that sexual desire of a nonheterosexual nature is always at issue. That is, such a presumption accepts as an unanalyzed given that the conduct at issue can never be an end in itself and that its covert agenda—covert because of the dangers customarily associated with it being announced unequivocally—is sexual fulfillment. If cross-dressing/transvestism may provoke a humorous reaction in the spectator, as is often the case of some of the cultural production that I will be examining below, one can expect it to be accompanied by the dark shadows of illegal and sinful lust. This circumstance explains why cross-dressing/transvestism in many societies has been treated as a punishable crime: gender confusion cannot but help to lead to illegal acts and the heinous sin of sodomy.

3. The concomitant response to propositions of homosexuality is homophobia. Homo-phobia is usually understood to mean an irrational response, and accompanying violence, in the face of the signs of homosexuality. Historically, the violence of homophobia has been excused—rarely condemned and infrequently prosecuted—because it is presumed to be the consequence of a reaction to the presence of homosexuality that is irrational: the witnesses to homosexuality cannot control themselves and are, therefore, blameless in the face of what is, after all, culpable provocation induced by those who would display the signs of homosexuality.

4. The matter of the signs of homosexuality is of crucial importance here, since homophobia is something like a street-level semiotic science. The homophobic eye scans the body of the other in the search for a sign, any sign, that would betray deviance from the heterosexist norm: such a sign is the manifest trace of an occult desire that must necessarily lead to illegal and sinful acts. That is, there is an inflexible semiotic chain that connects visible signs with inevitable behavior. Neither the validity of the sign, the chain of narrative deduction, nor the nature of the behavior can ever be questioned: homophobia cannot, historically, be called on justify itself as a semiotic operation and neither can the logic of its implacable interpretive process. Even when homophobia remains, in a given social or narrative universe, unpracticed, there is, for the bystander, the

constant frisson of the possibility that it will, to use an appropriate metaphor under the circumstances, kick in, with grimly foreseen consequences.

We have learned that issues of gender cannot be divorced from those of class and race/ethnicity, that there is a fundamental triangulation between the three categories (assuming that race and ethnicity are really only one category). In the case of the Anglo audience of a cultural production featuring Latinos, the ground zero assumption is the class inferiority of the latter. In terms of gender, the ground zero assumption is that Latinos cannot be counted on to adhere to the decent assumptions of heteronormativity. Such an assumption means that the oversexed macho rapist and the simpering effeminate individual are, in reality, two sides of the same coin: neither adheres to a decent standard of heterosexual conduct, either toward women or toward other men. Finally, even in those circumstances in which the Latino does, in fact, occupy a superior social position, such as in the case of the don, the caballero of the landed aristocracy, he will be seen as indolent as the consequence of his wealth acquired by inheritance rather than by hard work (a virtue prized exponentially by the hardscrabble Western settler), and indolence is, in accordance with a variant of the homophobic semiotic science, a correlate of social indecency. Thus the don, infrequent evidence to the contrary not withstanding, is also seen as indecent, prone to either rampant machismo or unbridled effeminacy. Indeed, the sumptuary practices of the real or feigned aristocracy of the don, as against the sartorial sobriety of the Boston gentleman (the Anglo standard throughout much of the nineteenth century) become inevitably interpreted as a manifestation of gender deviance.

The same sort of inevitable interpretation accompanies physical attributes quite separate from practices of dress and other refinements. Homophobia works off a series of axioms, one of which is that the "pretty" male face, which may or may not be accompanied by a body described as "delicate," is a sign of gender deviance.[4] Prettiness works in tandem with garrulousness, volubility, excessive smiling, affability, and even courtliness as signs to be heeded by the scopic operations of homophobia. Since part of the anti-Latino prejudice is that Latinos are handsome and, indeed, pretty in a menacing way, underscores the fact that this cluster of features does not involve Latinos as they may see themselves, but the way in which they function in the Anglo social imagination as recorded by Hollywood and correlative forms of cultural production.

All of the foregoing is admittedly an exercise in overgeneralization, and one cannot assume that it is supported by unimpeachable sociological evidence. But the point is that we are not talking sociology here, but rather about the practices of the cultural imagination such as we will find them evinced in the record of cultural production: our record here will be a broad representative sampling of Hollywood filmmaking of the past century.

There is a final point to be made here with respect to the cultural production at issue and the theoretical principles on which we might ground an understanding of how that production constructs meaning for its audience. I am referring to the emergence of an ironic stance against the complex of effeminacy and the emergence, at least in the final decades of the twentieth century, of queer theory.

Queer theory is a critical deconstruction of the assumptions of heteronormativity and compulsory heterosexuality and an inquiry into the foundations of any and all sexual ideologies. As such, queer does not equal gay, to the extent that the latter represents a new form of normativity (the legitimacy of same-sex desire), whereas queer theory is all about questioning normativities, even gay ones.[5] As queer theory emerges and as it infiltrates the cultural imagination such that formerly prevailing concepts of homosexuality (and the twin practice of homophobia) are challenged, revised, or annulled, there arises the installation of various ironic stances with regard to heteronormativity. Such stances may not categorically escape the process of homophobia: irony may function as another form of homophobic ridicule. But irony may also echo, as a way of reacting to a social formulation, the deconstructive inquiry of queer theory, such that what is ridiculed are the notions of gender stability, privileged virility, and decent heterosexuality that provided effeminacy and the whole range of social meanings it enacted with the shroud of social unacceptability, accompanied, in the case of the record of cultural production at issue here, by racial and ethnic condemnation.

O. HENRY ORIGINS

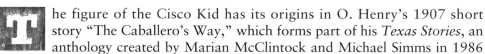he figure of the Cisco Kid has its origins in O. Henry's 1907 short story "The Caballero's Way," which forms part of his *Texas Stories*, an anthology created by Marian McClintock and Michael Simms in 1986 from texts included in O. Henry's *Complete Works*; the story originally appeared in O. Henry's *The Heart of the West* (1907). In the original text, Tonia Pérez is part of a love triangle that includes two men, the Cisco Kid and Lieutenant Sandridge, who both desire her attentions. Sandridge has been sent to investigate the charges against the Cisco Kid regarding his marauding and murderous ways, but decides rather to go after Tonia when he comes upon her in his search for the Kid. Since it is not in his character to share his women with others and much less to be duped by them, the Cisco Kid maneuvers Sandridge, through a ruse of mistaken identity, into killing Tonia: thus, the Kid escapes, avenges himself of an unfaithful lover, and leaves her new lover and his rival behind to suffer the heart-wrenching consequences of having killed the beautiful Tonia by mistake.

In O. Henry's story, the Cisco Kid appears to be Anglo (the narrator never makes it clear, despite his name[6]) and Sandridge is unquestionably Anglo; part of the interest of the story recounts the seductive allure for both of them of the Mexican feminine other ("with her Madonna face and Carmen beauty and hummingbird soul" [64]), who is nevertheless—and in terms of the Victorian moral code of the day—portrayed as fickle and unfaithful as, it is implied, only a woman of color can be. Additionally, part of the rivalry between the two men, who never meet, is the fact that, while the Cisco Kid is described as small and dark, "with black straight hair and a cold marble face that chilled the [desert] noonday" (65), Sandridge is nothing less than a "Viking" of a man (64).

Thus, in terms of the rivalry of options, an Anglo who appears to look Mexican, or who may even be a Mexican, is upstaged by a magnificent specimen of blond Anglo beauty. "The Caballero's Way" accords little space to the Cisco Kid, and one assumes that the reference of the title is to Sandridge, even if it is the "caballero" who is in the end outwitted by the vile bandit he attempts to do battle with. O. Henry, in the end, appears more interested in the pathos of the seductive Mexican woman who distracts the Anglo military man from his duty, only for him to be left emotionally destitute and shamed in non-fulfillment of his duty. That is, to emphasize the point, "The Caballero's Way" turns on the inherent treachery of Mexican culture, with the bandit as much its agent as is Tonia, who as a Mexican woman is, consequently, doubly to be mistrusted.

O. Henry's story was originally made into a film in 1914 by Webster Cullison, with Anglo actors William R. Dunn and Jack W. Johnston as the Cisco Kid and Sandridge, respectively. One will note immediately that the Cisco Kid has here moved into the position of first billing. Moreover, Tonia is played by Anglo actress Edna Payne (and she has acquired a father, played by Hal Wilson). Thus, in keeping with an entrenched Hollywood tradition that has had a long life, people of color (Mexicans, Native Americans, blacks, Asians) are played by Anglos; this practice was true even when the former were as much the evil and perfidious enemies of the latter as their benefactors.

THE CISCO PARADIGM

 n 1928 Irving Cummings made *In Old Arizona*, the first major sound Western.[7] O. Henry's story is moved to Arizona and the Cisco Kid, unlike O. Henry's original, is a charismatic and even Robin Hood-like bandit eluding the U.S. army's Sergeant Mickey Dunn, who, with the help of the Kid's lover Tonia, sets out to ambush the Kid and remove him from the scene both as a bandit and as a rival. The first version of *The Cisco Kid*, with the Kid now firmly in the title role and now unquestionably the main character of what became an extensive series of films released in the 1930s and 1940s,[8] was directed in 1931, also by Irving Cummings, with Warner Baxter as the Kid and Edmund Lowe as his rival, once again Sergeant Dunn. Tonia has, however, become Carmencita, played by the Spanish actress Conchita Montenegro. I underscore these shifts in the names and in the plot details, particularly the dynamics between the three characters, because of the Hollywood insistence on the comic, on foregrounding the treachery of Mexicans, and—despite O. Henry's original model—ensuring that evil never triumphs.

Warner Baxter as the Kid

The first major—and, therefore, pacesetting—cinematographic embodiment of the Cisco Kid was actually Irving Cummings's aforementioned *In Old Arizona* (1928), a film for which Warner Baxter in the title role won the 1929 Oscar for the best male lead.[9] No Hispanics play significant roles in the film, and Baxter's Tonia is played by the perennial second-rate female star Dorothy Burgess, although there are plenty of "Mexicans" in the background, including Tonia's Celestinesque cook,[10] who is played (but uncredited) by Soledad Jiménez, who was of Spanish origin. Tom Barry's script follows O. Henry's short story very faithfully. But there are three major innovations: 1) The story is set in Arizona (probably the Tucson area) rather than in Texas, although it was filmed in Utah; 2) The Cisco Kid claims to be originally from Portugal, the son of a Portuguese mother and a father (ethnicity unspecified, but one assumes Hispanic, because we are given to understand he speaks Spanish) from San Luis Obispo, and Cisco's dream is to return to Portugal with Tonia, although he recognizes this is something of a fantasy, as he has not lived there since he was a child; and 3) Barry supplements O. Henry's story with a fleshing out of the figure of the Cisco Kid, who never appears directly in the original literary text.

The latter is a significant innovation because it allows the film to work off a double circumstance of "misrecognition." Misrecognition is Émile Durkheim's theoretical concept to account for the way in which, in the field of systems of meaning, we miss something important or mistake someone else's meaning. In this sense, it is the attempt to ground conceptually the ways in which we "just don't get it." In the field of cultural semiotics, thus, we often fail to pick up on markers that so-called native speakers of the language or (if I may extend the metaphor of being a native) the culture will get intuitively; and it may mean also attributing meaning in an incorrect way, one that does not jibe with the presuppositions of those who belong naturally and customarily to particular circumstances. Not getting it right and getting it wrong—and the area of possibilities in between can be frustrating, embarrassing, confusing, and downright dangerous: in Cummings's film it becomes lethal.

One will recall from O. Henry's story that the army officer sent to hunt him down and the Cisco Kid never meet. Rather, they are bound together by the love of the same woman, who attempts to cheat on the Cisco Kid with the army officer, and is in turn, in a situation of supposed cross-dressing, killed by the Kid, who is supposed to believe he is really killing the disguised officer. The Kid rides away, avenged of both the woman's betrayal and, in depriving him of the object of his affections, the perfidy of the army officer in attempting to steal his woman from him.

In Cummings's film, there is a long central sequence in which, having robbed the stagecoach, the Cisco Kid goes to the town barbershop, presided over by the Figaro-like Garibaldi, to get spruced up before going to see Tonia. There he learns that part of the money he has stolen was being sent through Wells Fargo by the barber to his family back in Sicily. The Kid promises to make good on the money if Garibaldi will prepare him a "bath with nice sweet soap, with nice new towels" in order for him to be presentable for his upcoming tryst with the saucy Tonia. As the barber gladly acquiesces to this demand and goes to prepare the bath off screen, Sergeant Dunn, who has been ordered to hunt the Kid down with no questions asked, arrives to get spruced up himself. There ensues an amiable exchange between the two men, who become friends as they banter with each other, one the self-styled tough army man from the bowery, the other the foppish Kid; Dunn even calls the Kid a "Lord Fauntleroy," a euphemism of the era for a delicate and effeminate man. One axis of this banter involves the

Kid trying to convince the Sergeant to treat himself to the same sweet-smelling perfume with which the Kid douses himself. It is immaterial if the late-1920s audience saw anything queer in this exchange. Rather, the point is that the army sergeant is so mesmerized by the charm of the Kid that it never occurs to him until after the Kid has left to find out who he is. He is dumbfounded to learn that he has been discussing aftershave lotions with the man he has been sent to kill.

This scene of misrecognition establishes the doltishness of Dunn the Anglo army man and, in a parallel fashion, the Cisco Kid's superior cunning, whom some of his adversaries have called "smart and brave." The fact that Cisco uses man-on-man charms to outwit Dunn is less a nod toward the queer (although Barry and Cummings may well have meant it to be) than it is a confirmation of the Kid's survival smarts. This will play out in the correlative scene of misrecognition in which Tonia sends a missive via Elena that will allow Dunn to entrap the Kid so that she and the former can run away together to New York. Cisco intercepts the message and rewrites it in such a way that Dunn will mistake Tonia for his cross-dressed rival and shoot him; Dunn, of course, shoots and kills Tonia instead. The Kid takes this in stride and rides off into the night, his superior cunning, non-Anglo if not specifically marked as Hispanic, prevailing against the dumb Anglo. While Tonia is something of a slut, playing both sides of the cultural divide, the Kid, whose love and loyalty are sterling, must, however, do what is necessary in order to survive, and so closes the film with something of a prayer for a Tonia who is now "settled down."

There is much that is campy about *In Old Arizona*, which allows the spectator, especially the contemporary one, to invest in the plot-productive nature of misrecognition, especially as it is built on man-to-man bantering: same-sex bantering is a recognized form of queer speech,[11] quite different from the manly "shooting the breeze" or "shooting the bull," in which we see Dunn engaged elsewhere with his army buddies. And then there is the matter of cross-dressing. One very campy aspect of the film is the fact that Spanish is supposed to be spoken at crucial moments. When actual Spanish is spoken by Elena and her friends, it is interestingly left untranslated, although significant content is often present; the DVD version has English subtitles, but not even here is the Spanish translated, as though, if you don't know Spanish, it's too bad. Cisco and Tonia are supposed to be speaking Spanish (Baxter makes some feeble attempts with an atrocious pronunciation), but mostly they speak in pseudo-accented English. All of this provides another level of misrecognition in the film, but in terms of the audience and not in the universe of the narrative. One can, however, view this Spanish-language privilege, which I repeat involves Elena and company, as related to the Hispanic moral superiority and cunning the Cisco Kid embodies.[12]

Thus there is much that is slapstick about *In Old Arizona*, which also very much exemplifies the singing-cowboy genre of Westerns, as a handful of traditional songs get sung, less as integral parts of the film than as fillers to achieve the hour-and-a-half extension O. Henry's story is apparently required to meet. Set around 1898 (mention is made of sending the army to Cuba), the overall effect of *In Old Arizona* is that of a picture postcard, surely important in the postwar period for the opening up of Arizona to white settlers who would come in en masse less than twenty years later after the next world war. Yet Cummings's film adheres to O. Henry's drolly ironic advancement of the Cisco Kid's bold stature as a bandit whose enemies are the white settlers and their army. One final note: Baxter, like many Western heroes of the old black-and-white era, is heavily made up, down to very precise bold lip-liner. This is a consequence, to be sure, of the technical questions of the limits of filmmaking at the time, but when Cisco starts splashing around Garibaldi's aftershave and wallowing in the sweet soap of his bath, it does suggest what are likely meanings of unintended thematic consequences.

ENTER THE GAY CAVALIER

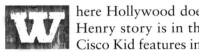here Hollywood does develop a much more original take on the O. Henry story is in the 1946 *The Gay Cavalier*, which is one of six Cisco Kid features in which Gilbert Roland (who was born in Juárez, Chihuahua, in 1905–the first authentic Mexican to play the Cisco Kid[13]) plays the Kid in a decidedly over-the-top, affected way. While it is clear that "gay" here is not meant to have a homosexual connotation (hardly possible for a 1946 Hollywood hero, even if played in a comic mode[14]), Roland's Cisco is very much the amorous subject with a fully developed picaresque, but nonetheless benevolent, character quite in jarring contrast to the sober Anglo men with whom he interacts. This ebullient, irrepressible Mexican bandit even recites poetry, which is presumably part of the quirkiness of his being Mexican rather than Anglo. The VCI Entertainment 2001 release of the film makes use of the phrase "This Monograph production represented Gilbert Roland's first outing as the Cisco Kid." One could well accept "outing" here in the sense of "foray," and "outing" is also used in the user comment posted on the Internet Movie Data Base listing for the film (http://www.imdb.com/title/tt0038552/). And yet, and yet. . . .[15]

There are two "gay" dimensions of Roland's characterization of the Cisco Kid that merit some degree of inquiry: Cisco's condition as an outsider who prefers the homosocial company of other men, and the degree to which, despite not being a player in it, he is an enabler of heterosexual romance.

The plot of William Nigh's unusually short film (a bare sixty-five minutes) is very straightforward. In order to save the ancestral hacienda of her father, don Felipe, from foreclosure, Angela agrees to marry the Anglo Mr. Lawton, spurning Juan, the man she really loves. But Lawton, in order to have the wealth that will enable him to marry the gorgeous Spanish beauty, robs a caravan carrying a bounty of silver destined for the building of a mission. The Cisco Kid is accused of the robbery and the accompanying slaughter of the caravan's guards. When he learns of this accusation, Cisco goes to Angela's father's hacienda to confront Lawton, while at the same time recovering the silver and turning it over to the friar in charge of the mission.

In his pursuit of Lawton, which involves bringing Angela and Juan back together (although the matter of Don Felipe's financial solvency is left unresolved),

Cisco plays up to a number of women, ranging from being gallant to a number of humble women and forthrightly romantic with, first, a fisherman's lonely wife and with Pepita, Angela's older sister. However, they are only passing fancies for him and, while he rewards the latter two with impressive silver necklaces, in the end he always rides off with his Robin Hood-like band of merry men to continue to steal from the poor and enforce simple social justice across the land.

The land in this case is old California in 1850 and, with the exception of Lawton and his men, the money-coach riders, and don Felipe's creditors, the world of the film is Hispanic, and a certain amount of high-class Spanish is spoken, although the dialogue is mostly in English, which is stilted but well pronounced by the upper class and simply mangled, in the best fashion of Hollywood stereotypes, by the peasants and servants. This is apparent in the juxtaposition between Cisco and his Sancho Panza-like sidekick, Baby[16]: Cisco speaks perfect English and perfect Spanish, while Baby speaks ridiculously pronounced English but sings in perfect Spanish.[17] Yet in terms of the overall universe of the film, it is remarkably sympathetic (stereotypes aside) to the Hispanic world it represents and, indeed, the villain of the film, Mr. Lawton, is defeated in his double assault on that world, in the form of the deceitful seduction of Angela and the robbery of the silver destined for the Catholic mission.

What is noteworthy is the way in which, despite the fleeting expression of a deep passionate interest in certain women, Cisco's commitment is to the male bonding of his band of horsemen, and we see them galloping across the landscape singing a merry song that celebrates their loyalty to each other: "Ride, amigos, ride." This song is sung as the band sets out to recover the purloined silver and as the finale of the film. Sedgwick's principle of homosociality is very much present here in the way in which the patriarchal society depends on a strong reciprocal male bonding in which women are the facilitators—sometimes in a positive fashion, sometimes in a negative fashion—of that bonding. Such bonding, while deeply emotional with often compassionate commitments between men, is typically not homosexual: indeed, homosexual passion is viewed as a disruptive threat to the integrity of a fully functioning homosocial bond.[18] To this extent, *The Gay Cavalier* does not represent a "gay" Cisco Kid in the prevalent homosexual sense of the word: his pitch-perfect romancing of women guarantees his heterosexuality (or, at least, his smooth performance of heterosexuality), but his commitment to the victory of freedom and justice (lovely American shibboleths in the old California recently acquired by the United States from Mexico) obliges him to turn away from the women who are so willing to fall at his feet, in order to remain loyal to his men.

And yet, there are two important suggestions of a disruption of Cisco's heterosexuality, at least as might concern the sober Anglo culture that backdrops the film, both in terms of what will be the history of California in the years following 1850 (as represented, perhaps, by the three Anglo bill collectors who will, one is certain, revisit Don Felipe to call in their loans) and what is present in terms of the majoritarian audience of the film as a Hollywood product. One is the point I have already alluded to: Cisco's ebullient and even extravagant manner of being in the world. Since the film is in black and white, there is no knowing (and there is never an independent mention of it in the film) whether his dress is in any way "deviant," although Cisco is manifestly more elegant and finely turned out than either Mr. Lawton or Don Felipe. Moreover, his horse is decked out in expensive silver gear that is an obvious concession to flashiness that contradicts his Robin Hood-like conduct on behalf of the poor. Even if Cisco is not gay in the now prevalent sexual sense of the term, in terms of the semiotic interpretive chain that I have mentioned as part of the conceptual grounding of this study, he deviates from an accepted norm of masculinity such as we see enacted by both the Anglo Mr. Lawton and the Hispanic Don Felipe. And in the sword-fight scene in which Cisco vanquishes Mr. Lawton, there is an element of foppishness in Cisco's bearing that is affirmed by the grandiloquent gesture of burying the point of his winning sword in the ceiling of Don Felipe's drawing room.

Even more telling is the relationship between Cisco and his Sancho Panza-like sidekick, Baby, a name that plays off the second element of the Cisco Kid's name and refers to the former's roly-poly appearance and childlike manner (one will recall that the Mexican, or any person of color, as childlike was already a venerable Hollywood stereotype). Cisco savors his moments of leisure made pleasant by Baby's serenading with romantic Spanish lyrics. This is most definitely not one of the tasks assigned to Sancho Panza or to any of the other many sidekicks of the Cisco Kid's numerous Hollywood incarnations.[19]

The second way in which Nigh's interpretation of the Cisco Kid is of gay interest is the way in which the dashing hero is an enabler of heterosexual romance rather than a full and sustained participant in it. While Cisco romances several women and is gallant with all who cross his path, these in the end are all fleeting encounters, given whatever the pulls of his band of followers may be. Cisco does not follow through, so to speak, on any of his constant amorous opportunities, much to the visible chagrin of the fisherman's wife and Pepita, who might legitimately see the silver necklaces as minor trinkets in comparison with the presumed manly attributes of his body: the necklace is a paltry substitute for the physical charms that must correlate directly with his rhetorical ones. Contemporary viewers, educated outside the framework of the hermetic heterosexist world of the 1940s, may well want to see the excessiveness of the latter charms as a substitute for the inability to wield the always withheld physical ones: a quick kiss appears to be the best the Kid can muster.

But Cisco's disruption of the romantic narrative as far as his own life is concerned (contemporary viewers will also indulge themselves in imagining what comes after Baby's romantic singing) is pronouncedly countered by his enabling the romance of others. Angela's Juan is almost limp-wristed alongside the other men in the film, but he proves his masculinity by aiding Cisco in recovering the stolen silver, and Cisco rewards Juan by bringing him and Angela back together. One is not sure of how much of a happy ending this will be, since don Felipe is still threatened with destitution, but having fulfilled a significant quota of good deeds, the Cisco Kid rides off with his band of men, their merry voices raised in their song of triumphant solidarity.

In balance then, *The Gay Cavalier* is of interest to this essay not because "gay" is used here as a euphemism for the homoerotic, but rather because of fissures in the texture of Hollywood's understanding of compulsory heterosexism represented by Cisco and his relations, on the one hand with women, and on the other with Baby and his fellow horsemen. Those fissures—queer fissures, then— are reinforced most remarkably by the fact that they are attributes of a world of Hispanic values and demeanor that triumph over the machinations of an evil Anglo villain: this is precisely the sort of plot dynamic Peter Medak will play up in *Zorro, the Gay Blade*, in which the Latino character can be manifestly gay and at the same time triumph against villainy. Harvey Fierstein asserted, in his interview in *The Celluloid Closet*, the 1995 documentary on lesbians and gays in Hollywood film directed by Rib Epstein and Jeffrey Friedman (and based on Victor Russo's book of the same name[20]), a commitment to "visibility at any cost." The sort of tightly controlled "maybe yes/maybe no" gay subtext of *The Gay Cavalier* is undoubtedly the sort of representation Fierstein had in mind, as surely also did Susie Bright, who expresses the gratitude of pre-liberation movement viewers as grateful for any crumb of representation.

ENTER THE GAY ZORRO

eter Medak's 1981 film is built around the venerable motif of paired siblings (frequently identical twins), in which the supposed similarities and differences between them, no matter the proximity or the distance between them in their rearing (separation at birth is a frequent plot feature), is crucial to the plot evolution. Paradigmatic examples are Antipholus and Ephesus in Shakespeare's *The Comedy of Errors* (in addition to other Shakespeare plays) and the sisters Justine and Juliette in several of the Marquis de Sade's texts; one might even refer to Chava Flores's droll ballad about the juxtaposition in fate between the good sister (Marthita [*sic*; not the expected Martita]) and the naughty one (Matilde): "Marthita la piadosa." Other famous examples, in film, are Betty Davis's good sister/evil sister (they are twins) portrayal in *Dead Ringer* (Paul Henreid, 1964) and Jeremy Irons as identical twins in David Cronenberg's *Dead Ringers* (1988). Certainly, the proposition that one sibling/twin is good while the other is evil captures very well the moral binarism that drives so much of Judeo-Christian belief, which, indeed, takes the motif as far back as Cain and Abel.

Medak's film could well have recycled the good and evil disjunction, based this time on the contrast between a straight brother ("good" in conformance with the heteronormative imperative) and a gay brother ("bad" as a consequence of noncompliance with the same); what constitutes that noncompliance would admit of various possibilities. In *Zorro, the Gay Blade*, however, George Hamilton's dual role as both brothers not only disrupts the hoary moral binary but in effect reinscribes it, such that the putatively deviant brother is, in fact, the agent of social salvation, which is certainly the primary characterization of the noble caballero. In order to comply with this role, he is ingeniously clever, according him a level of intelligence that allows his gay agency to triumph in a way that would be inadmissible in heteronormative farce, where gay equals evil: that over which good (confirmed by gender conformity) will prevail. Indeed, released in 1981, Medak's film could well have reiterated standard homophobic paradigms, even if in "only" a comedic mode, but this he decides not to do, and one standard guide to queer filmmaking, *Images in the Dark*, takes note of how *Zorro, the Gay Blade* is notable because of its favorable image of gayness (Murray 501).

Medak sets up his interpretation of the juxtaposition of twins in the following way. Don Diego Vega learns that his father, an alcalde in old California, has been killed in a riding accident and replaced in his position by the latter's good friend, Don Esteban. However, in a variation of the good and evil brothers—although here childhood friends—Esteban is as greedy and abusive an administrator as the elderly Vega was a generous and benevolent one. Moreover, the younger Vega learns that his father was in secret the legendary hero El Zorro. Diego decides to assume this role and his father's commitment to an agency of social virtue. Thus it becomes the younger Zorro's task, in all of his noble splendor (and despite his normal pastime as a charming womanizer), to defeat Esteban and restore tranquility to the life of the peasants. Unfortunately, after having first prevailed against Esteban in one of the latter's acts of dastardliness, Diego breaks his foot. In order not to disrupt the momentum of the challenge to Esteban, he turns to his twin brother to replace him in his noble undertaking, which is colored by the tribute to the father and the heroic legend of the figure of El Zorro. Appealing to his brother Ramon[21] on such lofty grounds compels the latter to accept. However, there is a minor inconvenience. While Diego fulfills in aces the paradigm of imposing masculinity, that of a man among men, Ramon has pursued other models. He joined the British navy and adopted the name of Bunny Wigglesworth: the allusion to the inherent faggotry of navies (the most notorious being that of queer pirate companies, with the added slander of Spain's archenemy, the British) is transparent here. Thus, although Ramon agrees to continue the family tradition of donning the Zorro costume and to fight valiantly—and, in the end, triumphantly—against malefactors, he can only execute this investiture on his own terms, which is as ever and always the flamboyant Bunny Wigglesworth (both names, to be sure, constitute sexual innuendos).

The convoluted details of how this third incarnation of El Zorro wins out against the malefactor Esteban in the end becomes a bit tiresome in the film, but it does provide for some outrageous moments of high camp and the confusion one might expect in the transition from Diego's traditional enactment of the Zorro type to Ramon's queer one. What is important, however, is the way in which queer camp prevails, as Ramon, dressed as Zorro in glorious faggy yellow, saves his brother, who favored conventional black outfits, from the firing squad; Esteban is subsequently overthrown, having been totally humiliated and discredited by Ramon's embodiment of El Zorro. In the process, gay is shown to be good: morally powerful and an effective agency. In terms of the visual language of film, the juxtaposition between the ancient black of masculine sober manliness and the yellow of Ramon's flamboyant queerness is an objective correlative of the paradigmatic shift between two ways of enacting masculinity. In one version, it is the business of male supremacy as usual, with a play between the good and evil of different versions of that supremacy (the virtual twins, former alcalde and Esteban). In Medak's revision of the Zorro story, the interplay is grounded on different versions of the agent of good, the straight and the queer. While straight agency is effective, it is circumscribed by chance when Diego breaks his foot in an initial skirmish with Esteban. Good can only prevail when the narrative of the defeat of evil is carried through and fulfilled by the queer agent, Ramon/Bunny. In the end, queer is validated as an enhanced enactment of the noble caballero, as yellow becomes the new style of El Zorro.

It is worth considering Hamilton's portrayal of the gay Zorro. And it is also worth pausing to note the way in which the subtitle of the movie, the "gay blade" plays, on the one hand, with the time-worn phallic imagery of El Zorro's sword (once straight, now queer), while on the other hand it plays on the meaning of "blade" as a dashing young man and, by implication, someone sexually attractive, whether in a heterosexual or a homosexual manner. Despite the phallic allusion, there is, nevertheless, no allusion in the film to active sexuality on the part of Ramon/Bunny/Zorro 3. True, Diego/Zorro 2 is accorded a love object in the film who has a role in the plot development, particularly as regards the hidden vs. true identity of Diego as the heir to his father's heroic figure. As is common in American popular culture's representations of the queer, Ramon/Bunny/Zorro 3 can only be portrayed as queer via displayed features of dress and behavior, but never through sexual agency.

Such dress and demeanor are inscribed as effeminate and "gay" (yellow and flamboyant), but how it is expressed remains vague. Should spectators wish to entertain themselves as to the particulars of such a person's sexual proclivities, the assumption must be that any object of affection is another man, and it is presumed that such affection would involve the unacceptable seduction of a man (self-) identified as straight (although, as in the Leopold and Loew paradigm [see Alfred Hitchcock's *The Rope*; 1948], the object of affection could be another gay man). However, the Hollywood convention is resolutely to deny sexual orientation, especially when the genre of comedy is involved, as is the case here. In such a formulation, there can be no consideration of the errors or ambiguities of such stereotypical representation, and the denomination "gay blade" must be accepted as an unanalyzed given. The very fact that it is the gay that proves to be more efficacious than the straight in redefining the beneficent social agency of the noble caballero in his legendary version as El Zorro is a sufficient accomplishment of Medak's film.[22]

CHICANO PARODY

In 1994 Luis Valdez directed a made-for-TV movie in which Jimmy Smits plays the Cisco Kid and Cheech Marín plays his sidekick, Pancho. In the context of the French occupation of Mexico, the film (which specifically announces the year 1867, the concluding year of the intervention that began in 1864), the two heroes portray anti-gringo Mexican revolutionaries struggling against both Texas gunrunners and the French army. In this version,

Cisco, who states that he was born in California, "which used to be Mexican," escapes from jail with Pancho, who is disguised as a monk. While Cisco is in cahoots with the gunrunners, his newfound relationship with Pancho and his people convince him to aid in the expulsion of the French. After dealing with the gunrunners, he pledges himself to Benito Juárez (played in cameo fashion by Luis Valdez himself), and he and Pancho set off to wrap things up with the French.

This film is pretty much a silly spoof on the many versions of the Cisco Kid story, although it is innovative in transporting the Kid back to the Mexico of his ancestors and allowing him to commit himself to Mexican social history. Many of the laugh lines in the film are parodies of former versions, such as when the two ride off to deal with the French army in the final scene of the film, reprising the campy exchange between the two (based, as has been noted by the fact that Cisco and Pancho are both familiar forms of Francisco), "Eh, Cisco!/Eh, Pancho!"

However, there is nothing that can be read as a direct gay reference in the film and little that lends itself to innuendo. True, the two men ride off into the sunset arm in arm (and in arms), so to speak, leaving behind their amorous interests. In the case of Pancho, it is his wife and six-and-a-half children (when he seeks her out after the prison break, he discovers she is pregnant), while in Cisco's case it is the lusciously French Dominique who, after being held hostage by the gunrunners, is to return to France, alas, without her savior. Although Cisco is chivalrously consoling, it is evident he is anxious to hit the road with Pancho, and thus an austere womanly homosociality is once again established as the lot of the Cisco Kid. The only real innuendo in the film is after the two men have escaped from prison and are still chained together. They ride face to face on a horse—Cisco facing forward. As the viewer contemplates what looks like a Kama Sutra tableau, Cisco says to Pancho that there are many women who would like to be in such a position with him: the safe reading refers to having him chained to the other; the innuendo reading would reference the sexual athletics.

There is no reason to fault Valdez for not combining camp with parody in his version of the Cisco Kid's story, although it is legitimate to speculate that the "missed" opportunity has as much to do with the fact that this is a made-for-television movie pitched, it is assumed, for a general audience, especially since it is the first explicitly Chicano interpretation of O. Henry's bandit. It is not surprising that it is an unmitigatedly heroic version uncomplicated by the controversies any level of queer reading would involve. And too, both Cheech Marín, who plays Pancho, and Jimmy Smits, who plays the Kid, have, to the best of my knowledge, refrained from deviating in their roles from hypermasculine representations. Marín mostly enacts a freewheeling lechery, while Smits is usually a statuesque stud, for which he may appeal to gay moviegoers (who undoubtedly appreciated his moment of fleeting posterior nudity in Luis Puenzo's 1989 *The Old Gringo*), but which he has not lent to any homoerotic representation. One might well view Valdez's entire film as more camp than parody and mine the general over-the-top nature of the entire proceedings, but the results are likely to be significantly less than Gilbert Roland's much more suggestive queering, unconscious or otherwise, of heterosexual masculinity.

CONCLUSIONS

The International Movie Data Base (imdb.com) lists twenty-seven films made featuring the character of the Cisco Kid (excluding the 156 thirty-minute episodes of the 1950-56 TV series), while sixty-four are listed for Zorro. However, the figure of Zorro is played pretty much "straight" in this extensive filmography, although perhaps someone with an unblinking queer eye might be able to tease traces of pertinent elements out of those titles that are still available for viewing (Noriega recognizes the importance of the TV series as the "first popular syndicated program and one of the first *filmed* programs on television" [218, n18]. It is, rather, the Cisco Kid films—perhaps because of their origins in the story written with O. Henry's signature irony—that the character has been opened up more by successive versions to a dwelling on Cisco's particular manner of being Hispanic that is meant, time and again, to stand in contrast to Anglo culture. Moreover, the creation of a sidekick for the Kid, which does not happen with the intransigently solitary Zorro, allows for a privileged relationship between them that may contain, among other elements, a dimension of homosocial veering toward (albeit unacknowledged) homoerotic bonding.

But really what is at issue here is, in all of these cultural products, a process of differentiation of the Hispanic subjects such that they will stand in sufficient contrast to their Anglo ones. This is done through playing off stereotypes, ones that Hollywood helped to create, but also ones that have circulated throughout American Anglo culture in the centuries of contact with Latin America. It is this process of differentiation where the stereotype of ebullience, tinged with delicate sensitivity and even nontraditional or unconventional exceptions to sober manliness, has carried a heavy burden of contrast. Although few of the gay caballeros are really gay (except in George Hamilton's parody), the exceptions to the stringent norms of the heteronormative imperative as regards not just sexual desire but the very way in which one is a man in the world do evoke the conceptual category of the queer, in the way in which that category examines both challenges to the heteronormative imperative and the complex range of failures to abide by it. What is, then, at issue is the Hispanic caballero who moves through an Anglo world (or, in one case, a Mexican world taken over by the French)—both in terms of the universe of a particular film or the presumed hegemonic world of the spectator at different times in American sociocultural history—in such a way as to be a deviant within that world.

Yet the deviant nature of the gay caballero becomes his virtue, rather than the locus of his demise, as would be the case in a film dealing with the alleged "horror" or "tragedy" of homosexuality. As much as the gay caballero introduces forms of turbulence all over the place because he is Hispanic, because he is a dandy/fop/preening firebird, because he disrupts the Anglo privilege of superior non-Hispanic cultural primacy, because he may not play by the rules of his self-satisfied adversary, it is the gay caballero who triumphs in the end against evil and injustice. This he does through the advantage of what is perceived to be his deviant behavior, throwing his adversary off guard, and he does so through his cunning, outwitting those with superior symbolic and real power. In this sense, one might say that the gay caballero always prevails in the game of survival because of the ways in which he is queer as regards the hegemonic standards of manly conduct. Therefore, by the same token, those standards, as much as they are hegemonic and a part of a power dynamic turned against the Hispanic social subject, must surrender their efficacy to the Hispanic other.[23] This is the note of triumph that underlies the "Eh, Cisco! /Eh, Pancho!" exchange that is one of the trademarks of these films.[24] Maybe even José Martí would have been pleased with such vindications of the Hispanic male.

NOTES

[1] Rather than document each one of the points made in subsequent pages about Latin American masculinities and their intersection with the queer, I refer the reader to the literature survey by David William Foster, "Homoculturas latinoamericanas a partir de 1980," which appeared in a special issue of the *Revista iberoamericana* devoted to Latin American lesbigay/queer culture. See also David William Foster, *Producción cultural e identidades homoeróticas; teoría y aplicaciones*. I have drawn heavily on the research on film and popular culture and intersections with the queer of Alexander Doty, Richard Dryer, Chris Holmlund, and Vito Russo, although none of them makes reference to the texts discussed in this essay.

[2] The opposite formulation, women who assume masculine traits, is not at issue in this debate, although it is important to note that Latin America has its history of heroically masculinized women such as the case of Catalina de Erauso, "la monja alférez" (1585?-1650). Behind historical figures like Catalina de Erauso stand mythological figures such as the female warriors known as the Amazons.

[3] Allow me to provide an Arizona-based example of the reproductive imperative. In Clarence Buddington Kelland's famous 1938 novel *Arizona*, the central character, Phoebe Titus, asks her husband if he is happy that she is going to have his baby. He replies that "A man hain't a man till he's had a baby" (238). It is important to note that this exchange takes place in the overall context of the attempt to secure Arizona for the United States, and the baby that is eventually birthed is the first white child to be born in Tucson (ca. 1870); the birth of white babies will Americanize Arizona in the face of the still-at-that-time overwhelming Native American and Mexican presence.

[4] The Mexican belief that a man must be "feo, fuerte y formal" is to the point in this regard.

[5] I am fully aware of how my language throughout here is insistently male-oriented. This is so first and foremost because women's history is not simply a parallel version of men's history—that is, it is insufficient simply to modify everything with the gender-balanced "s/he." Women's history—including lesbianism—must be written with different assumptions and principles in mind. It is for this reason that I would always wish to avoid the implication that the effeminate man, the cross-dressing/transvestite man, or the so-called homosexual has anything to do with women's history properly understood: that is, they are not surrogate women, but rather men uncomfortable—or perceived to be uncomfortable—for whatever reason with their male gender assignment. However, in this case my focus is a consequence of the simple fact that this essay is an investigation into a certain category of male figures, those that can be subsumed under the heading "gay caballero."

[6] One is tempted to see Billy the Kid as the model for O. Henry's Cisco.

[7] Although I can find little information about it, there appears to be a 1909 film with the same title, produced by the Selig company and in which the U.S. army routs the Mexi-

can bandits. Abel mentions the film under the heading "The Western as White Supremacist Entertainment" (81).

[8] After being a radio series in the early 1940s, *The Cisco Kid* also became a well received TV series that ran from 1950 to 1956, with Eddie Davis and others directing 156 episodes. The Kid, who was unambiguously Mexican but possessed of good English, was accompanied by an English-mangling Mexican sidekick named Pancho, and their adventures were in the tradition of the Lone Ranger and Tonto (Cisco and Pancho are, of course, both affective variants of the name Francisco). Of particular interest for this essay is the fact that each episode concluded with the two men confirming the bond between them by the Kid exclaiming, "Oh, Pancho!" while Pancho replied, "Oh, Cisco!" What more than this sort of campiness could one ask for from a 1950s family-oriented series? Pancho was played by Leo Carrillo (born in Los Angeles), while Duncan Renaldo played Cisco. The team also made a dozen semi-feature-length films (i.e., of the order of seventy minutes in length). What is of interest is that Renaldo's origins are shrouded in some doubt as to whether he was actually Spanish, as he claimed to be. In any event, what is significant about the TV series is the class difference between Cisco and Pancho (paralleling the racial difference between the Lone Ranger and Tonto, about whom popular culture, as in the case of other dynamic duos such as Batman and Robin, has assigned a latent if not fully fulfilled gay relationship), driven by the "non-Mexican" air of Renaldo's Cisco. In the midst of the ambiguity over the ethnic nature of Renaldo's Cisco is the fact, which bears underscoring here, that "Cisco" is a diminutive form of "Francisco," thus confirming a Spanish-language connection for his character. Boddy comments on how the whole series was made on the cheap, "not inexpensive, but cheap" (122). Finally, Horowitz points out (253-54) how Renaldo went out of his way to make his Cisco Kid a benevolent figure that would be more acceptable to Mexican audiences who, it would appear, were offended by the "mincing" manner of César Romero's embodiment of the Kid (Horowitz 255), which threatened to "queer" U.S. Mexican relations (Horowitz 253). García Riera's essay, as one might expect, alludes repeatedly to negative stereotypes of the Cisco Kid and related Hollywood "gay Latin bandits" of presumed Mexican origin; of particular interest is the question of broken English and a Hispanic accent.

[9] Baxter made two other Cisco Kid films: *The Cisco Kid* (1931) and *Return of the Cisco Kid* (1939). He also made an appearance as the Cisco Kid in a promotional film entitled *The Slippery Pearls* (1931).

[10] The reference here is to the so-called Spanish bawd, the main character of Fernando de Roja's drama *La Celestina* (1502; originally published in 1499 under the title of *Tragico-media de Calixto y Melibea*). The Celestina is a madame/procuress/go-between/all-around purveyor of sexual trysts, who is seen as the enabler of all that is sinful and illicit. She is a figure both Rabelaisian and profoundly cynical. Elena, as Tonia's cook is called, is perhaps more of a complicitous duenna, although her cooperation with Tonia, like the Celestina's with Melibea in Rojas's drama, brings about Tonia's death.

[11] The exact phrase "gay banter" provides almost 6,000 hits on Google; gay banter is also known as gayspeak, which produces over 6,000 hits (see Hayes's pioneering work on gayspeak). Statistics based on an Internet search conducted in September 2007.

[12] A note concerning the Spanish language in the universe of these films is necessary here. In terms of cultural capital, English and German are often contrasted with French along an axis of manly vs. effeminate (Livia 7: "French has traditionally been considered, in the English folk-linguistic view, soft, feminine, even effeminate"), a circumstance evident in the preference of French as a foreign language of choice among many gay men. Spanish occupies a third position, so to speak, in that it is considered manly when attached to the macho mystique, but effeminate when attached to presumed Hispanic ebullience and expressiveness; this is even more the case when much is made of the so-called Castilian lisp, even when the sound involved, phonetically [ ], exists in English, where it is never considered a lisp.

[13] This makes Roland a rather long-in-the-tooth Cisco Kid, who is described in O. Henry's original story as being twenty-five; in 1946, when Rolando made *The Gay Cavalier*, he would have been just over forty. Nevertheless, this more mature presence is appropriate to his well-formed heroic presence, as opposed to O. Henry's callow bandit, destined to die young. The other five Roland embodiments of the Cisco Kid are *South of Monterey* (1946), *Beauty and the Bandit* (1946), *Riding the California Trail* (1947), *Robin Hood of Monterey* (1947), and *King of the Bandits* (1947). Roland also made *The Mark of Zorro* (1974), having played in a number of spaghetti Westerns in the 1960s.

[14] By the same token, the nine entries under "gay" in Keller's registry can safely be assumed not to evoke the synonym of homosexuality. García Riera, in his essay on the gay Latin bandit, makes it clear that his examples are not homoerotic in nature (146).

[15] Although Roland is never openly (or, apparently, otherwise) identified as gay, he gets mentioned repeatedly by César Romero in his interview with Boze Hadleigh on gay Hollywood. In 1940 Otto Brower directed Romero in *The Gay Caballero*. This is probably the shortest of the Cisco Kid films (fifty-eight minutes) and is excruciatingly bad, beginning with Romero's permanent toothy grin and macaronic English (although his Spanish is authentic). The plot contains several incoherencies, but is notable for the main adversary of the Kid being a woman, the large landowner Ms. Brewster. Romero's dress is appropriately flashy, and he probably wears the tightest pants of any of the incarnations of the Kid. Romero made two other Cisco Kid films during the same period: *The Cisco Kid and the Lady* (1939), *Viva Cisco Kid* (1940), *Lucky Cisco Kid* (1940), and *Romance of the Rio Grande* (1941). What is, however, notable is that the protagonist is played by a Latino male (Romero's mother was Cuban) and Romero was as much of an open gay as was possible in the Hollywood of the day. One doubts if this makes the Cisco Kid any more specifically gay as far as the internal meaning of the film is concerned, but it does undoubtedly add a layer of ironic viewing to those audience members for whom Romero's personal sexual life might be important. As I have already noted above, James Horowitz, in his highly personal account of the Western, is quite pointed in addressing the queer dimension of Romero's embodiment of the Cisco Kid (253).

[16] It is obvious that the script draws not only on O. Henry's story (barely), but on both the Robin Hood legend and *Don Quijote*, although Cisco is hardly the tragic Alonso Quijano.

[17] Referring more specifically to the Gordito character of the TV series, Berg lumps the Kid's sidekick under the heading of "The Male Buffoon." Berg has little else to say about the Cisco Kid films.

[18] This is so to the degree that homosexual passion is viewed as a reduplication of heterosexual passion, which necessarily involves a hierarchy between its participants (the so-called active/passive binary is only one example of such a hierarchy, which, at its heterosexist best, is co-extensive with a male/female binary and the subjugation of the woman to the man) that contradicts the collegiality of the homosocial buddy system, even if the latter does often involve a degree of hierarchy, although for reasons other than the expression of sexual passion. Clearly, any relationship of passion (homosexual or heterosexual) that eschews a hierarchical binary is a different matter. The point, however, is that patriarchal heterosexuality, and its homosexual reduplication, is grounded on hierarchical binaries. It is notable that the film in question, as well as the other Cisco Kid productions of the 1930s to1950s, coincides with the buddy system still so very much in place at that time and in abundant evidence in the war films of the period.

[19] The homoerotic dimension of "the lives of the cowboys" has only recently begun to be explored in a systematic scholarly way; Packard's monograph is fundamental.

[20] In his book, Russo characterizes the treatment of Medak's Zorro as a sissy as "generally humorous" and far from offensive (266).

[21] I adopt here and in subsequent analyses the spelling of names as used in printed material in English on the films.

[22] A delightful gay parody of the caballero theme is to be found in Richard Lester's film *The Ritz* (1976), based on Terrence McNally's play of the same name. In the context of disguise and mistaken identities in a gay bathhouse (and bearing in mind that gay culture is all about laying bare mistaken and disguised sexual identities), three patrons attempt to sidetrack a Mafia hit by disguising themselves for a talent night show as the Andrews Sisters, in a reprise as "The Three Gay Caballeros" of the title song of Walt Disney's famous 1944 Donald Duck hit *The Three Caballeros*, whose lyrics actually introduce the adjective "gay," but, to be sure, not with the sense in which *The Ritz* performers use it: "We're three caballeros / Three gay caballeros / They say we are birds of a feather." Disney's film is, in turn, parodied by John Landis's 1986 ¡*Three Amigos!* (note the linguistically queer use of the inaugural exclamation point), starring Chevy Chase, Steve Martin, and Martin Short as the three insouciant caballeros; Patrice Martínez plays Carmen. One supposes that the use of three buddies in place of the Cisco Kid-Pancho (etc.) duo ups the ante on the implausibility of any real homoerotic bond between them. However, they do enact an outrageously effeminate dance routine to the tune of "My Little Buttercup." Mostly a gag-driven film, ¡*Three Amigos!* may well be the ultimate camp version of O. Henry's original story, particularly in the way in which very little of the latter remains. There is no discernible pertinence to the topic of this essay of the 2003 TV movie *The Three Amigos*.

[23] Nash Candelaria's clever story "The Day the Cisco Kid Shot John Wayne," which involves the Hispanic narrator's prevailing as a child against Anglo culture, demonstrates very eloquently why young Hispanics felt an empowering identity with Cisco's and Pancho's shrewd methods of survival and ability to prevail over Anglo injustice and stupidity.

[24] It is worth noting that many of these films are included in Garcia Riera's six-volume registry of thousands of American films, as of 1990, that deal in some way with Mexico. The image of the Cisco Kid is specifically discussed in capítulo IV of the first volume.

WORKS CITED

Abel, Richard. "'Our Country'/Whose Country? The 'Americanisation' Project of Early Westerns." *Back in the Saddle Again; New Essays on the Western*. Ed. Edward Buscombe and Roberta E. Pearson. London: BFI Publishing, 1998. 77-95. Print.

Bejel, Emilio. *Gay Cuban Nation*. Chicago: U of Illinois P, 2001. Print.

Berg, Charles Ramírez. *Latino Images in Film; Stereotypes, Subversion, Resistance*. Austin: U of Texas P, 2002. Print.

Berlinerblau, Jacques. "Durkheim's Theory of Misrecognition; In Praise of Arrogant Social Theory." *Teaching Durkheim*. Ed. Terry F. Godlove, Jr. Oxford: Oxford UP, 2004. 213-33. Print.

Boddy, William. "'Six Million Viewers Can't Be Wrong': The Rise and Fall of the Television Western." *Back in the Saddle Again; New Essays on the Western*. Ed. Edward Buscombe and Roberta E. Pearson. London: BFI Publishing, 1998. 119-40. Print.

Candelaria, Nash. "The Day the Cisco Kid Shot John Wayne." *Growing Up Ethnic in America; Contemporary Fiction about Learning to Be American*. Ed. Maria Mazziotti Gillan and Jennifer Gillan. New York: Penguin Books, 1999. 45-63.

Taken from his collection *The Day the Cisco Kid Shot John Wayne*. Tempe: Bilingual P/Editorial Bilingüe, 1988. Print.

Doty, Alexander. *Flaming Classics; Queering the Film Canon*. New York: Routledge, 2000. Print.

Doty, Alexander. *Making Things Perfectly Queer; Interpreting Mass Culture*. Minneapolis: U of Minnesota P, 1993. Print.

Dyer, Richard. *Studies on Lesbian and Gay Film*. London: Routledge, 1990. Print.

Foster, David William. "Homoculturas latinoamericanas a partir de 1980." *Revista Ibero-americana* 225 (2008): 923-41. Print.

Foster, David William. *Producción cultural e identidades homoeróticas; teoría y aplicaciones*. San José, Costa Rica: Universidad de Costa Rica, 1999. Print.

Foucault, Michel. *The History of Homosexuality*. Vol. 1. Trans. from the French by Roberto Hurley. New York: Vintage P, 1980. Print.

García Riera, Emilio. *México visto por el cine extranjero*. México, D.F.: Ediciones Era; Guadalajara: Universidad de Guadalajara, Centro de Investigaciones y Enseñanzas Cinematográficas, 1990. Print.

Hadleigh, Boze. *Hollywood Gays*. New York: Barricade Books, 1996. Print.

Hayes, Joseph J. "Gayspeak." *The Language and Sexuality Reader*. Ed. Deborah Cameron and Don Kulick. New York: Routledge, 2006. 68-77. See James Darsey's "Response." 78-85. Henry, O. *Heart of the West*. Garden City, N.Y.: Doubleday, Page, 1920. Print.

Henry, O. "The Caballero's Way." *O. Henry's Texas Stories*. Ed. Marian McClintock and Michael Simms. Dallas: Still Point P, 1986. 63-75. Print.

Holmlund, Chris. *Impossible Bodies; Femininity and Masculinity at the Movies*. New York: Routledge, 2002. Print.

Horowitz, James. *They Went Thataway*. New York: E. P. Dutton, 1976. Print.

Jordan, Mark D. *The Invention of Sodomy in Christian Theology*. Chicago: U of Chicago P, 1997. Print.

Katz, Jonathan Ned. *The Invention of Heterosexuality*. New York: Dutton, 1995. Print.

Keller, Gary D. *A Biographical Handbook of Hispanics and United States Film*. Tempe: Bilingual Press/Editorial Bilingüe, 1997. Print.

Livia, Anna. *Pronoun Envy; Literary Uses of Linguistic Gender*. Oxford: Oxford UP, 2001. Print.

Lumsden, Ian. *Machos, Maricones, and Gays; Cuba and Homosexuality*. Philadelphia: Temple UP, 1996. Print.

Martí, José. "On the Character of the Cuban People." *New York Evening Post*, 25 Mar. 1889. Web.

Murray, Raymond. *Images in the Dark; An Encyclopedia of Gay and Lesbian Film and Video*. rev. and updated. New York: Plume, 1996. Print.

Nevins, Francis M. *The Films of the Cisco Kid*. Waynesville, NC: The World of Yesterday, 1998. Print.

Nevins, Francis M., and Gary D. Keller. *The Cisco Kid: American Hero, Hispanic Roots*. Tempe: Bilingual Press, 2008. A revised and illustrated edition of the foregoing entry. Print.

Noriega, Chon A. *Shot in America; Television, the State, and the Rise of Chicano Cinema*. Minneapolis: U of Minneapolis P, 2000. Print.

Packard, Chris. *Queer Cowboys and Other Erotic Male Friendships in Nineteenth-century American Literature*. New York: Palgrave Macmillan, 2006. Print.

Pérez, Louis A. *The War of 1898: The United States and Cuba in History and Historiography*. Chapel Hill, N.C.: U of North Carolina P, 1998. Print.

Russo, Vito. *The Celluloid Closet; Homosexuality in the Movies*. rev. ed. New York: Harper & Row, 1987. Print.

Sedgwick, Eve Kosofsky. *Between Men: English Literature and Male Homosocial Desire*. New York: Columbia UP, 1985. Print.

Zapata Westerns
THE SHORT LIFE OF A SUBGENRE (1966-1972)*

Carlo Gaberscek
UDINE, ITALY

ver six hundred European Westerns were made from the early 1960s to the late 1970s. Most of the so-called spaghetti Westerns deal with the Mexican border in the American Southwest (Texas, New Mexico, and Arizona). Some of them are set in Mexico. Usually they are adventure films in which Mexico simply provides exotic color, a series of spectacular backdrops, or colorful exteriors. A group of Italian Westerns deals with overtly political themes. They form a subgenre and are called Zapata Westerns, as they take place during the Mexican Revolution of 1910.

A Bullet for the General (1966), directed by Damiano Damiani, is the first of them. It tells the story of El Chuncho (Gian Maria Volonté), a Mexican gun-runner, an uncouth "bandido" more concerned with the acquisition of money and women than any revolutionary commitment, and a young Anglo, Bill Tate (Lou Castel). Following a train robbery, Tate teams up with El Chuncho's gun-runners as they steal armaments for General Elías, a leader of the revolutionary army (Jaime Fernández). Tate, apparently naïve, who is christened "El Niño" by El Chuncho, is actually a hired killer for the Mexican government. He uses El Chuncho to reach Elías's camp and murder him. Adaptation and dialogue of *A Bullet for the General* were written by Franco Solinas, an important figure in the Italian political cinema of the 1960s. He was a Marxist writer who wrote or collaborated on several political films. His best known scripts are for *Salvatore Giuliano* (1962), directed by Francesco Rosi, about a notorious Sicilian bandit; *The Battle of Algiers* (1966) by Gillo Pontecorvo, a faithful depiction of revolution and terrorism; and *Burn!* (Italian title *Queimada*, 1969), a political drama directed by Gillo Pontecorvo and starring Marlon Brando.

A Bullet for the General presents, for the first time, the two leading key characters of the Zapata Westerns: a Yankee or European outsider who is a laconic, cool, cynical opportunist and a Mexican, a rough, instinctive, energetic, flamboyant, noisy, talkative revolutionary peasant-bandit who gradually becomes aware of the importance of the value of ideals and becomes a "hero," a symbol of the freedom fighting of his people. The Anglo usually offers the Mexican technical assistance (guns, explosives, expertise) in hopes of finding gold or being led to his "hit." Due to Solinas's contribution, a political slant is put on

*Additional visual material for this article may be seen at http://noblebandits.asu.edu/Topics/GoodBandits2009.html

the relationship between the gringo outsider and the Mexican "primitive rebel." The political resonance given to the confrontation between them is related to the concerns of Third World (specifically Latin American) politics. In Damiano Damiani's film the Mexican characters represent the polarities of Mexican culture: oppressed, illiterate peons, gunrunners, rich landowners, vicious army officers, and government troops as the villains. *A Bullet for the General* takes place between 1915 and 1916, during Venustiano Carranza's government. "Carrancistas" (as Carranza's followers were called) execute many of Francisco "Pancho" Villa's supporters, and Damiani's film opens with graffiti reading "Viva Carranza el Pacificador." The pre-title sequence establishes a realistic approach. Four Mexican civilians are lined up to be shot. A group of peasant women and children look on, crying and shouting. One of the condemned men yells "Tierra y libertad!" as the firing squad shoots, while a voiceover sets the scene: "From 1910 to 1920, Mexico was torn by internal strife. During the entire decade, the vast territory was devastated by bands of marauding bandits. Scenes of this kind were commonplace, as the various factions tried to dominate the others and bring order out of the chaos."

A Bullet for the General deploys an eclectic international cast. Italian actor Gian Maria Volonté portrays El Chuncho, whose great histrionic acting makes this movie unforgettable. He became a star due to the first two Sergio Leone "Dollars" films, *A Fistful of Dollars*" (1964, in which he plays Ramón Rojo) and *For a Few Dollars More* (1965, as the vicious bandit El Indio). Colombian actor Lou Castel (real name Ulv Quarzell) is cast in the role of Bill Tate/El Niño. Castel burst onto the international scene in *Fist in the Pocket* (1965), an Italian movie about a dysfunctional family directed by Marco Bellocchio. The German actor Klaus Kinski portrays El Santo, the delirious and bloodthirsty El Chuncho's half-brother, an ardent revolutionary, dressed in a monk's robe strung with bandoleers. Jamaican-born Martine Beswick is Adelita (like the heroine of a famous Mexican folk ballad), who rides with El Chuncho. Other actors in *A Bullet for the General* include Aldo Sambrell as the officer in charge of an armaments train (this Spanish actor worked in dozens of Westerns) and the Mexican actor Jaime Fernández (younger brother of the famous director Emilio Fernández) who plays General Elías. His portrayal owes much to Marlon Brando's Emiliano Zapata in *Viva Zapata* (1952) by Elia Kazan. Jaime Fernández had played Zapata in *Lucio Vázquez* (1965) and later appeared in *Emiliano Zapata* (1970) and *The Death of Pancho Villa* (1973). The director Damiano Damiani himself briefly appears as a journalist at General Elías's camp.

A Bullet for the General was shot in the Almería and Guadix areas (in the province of Granada) in July and August 1966. Of the extensive production of the European Westerns the movies shot in Spain make up the majority. About four hundred Westerns were filmed in Spain, and about two hundred of these were shot in Almería. This province of eastern Andalucía bordering the Mediterranean Sea has become most associated with the European Westerns because of its stark, barren land, its landscape defined by dried-up gullies and riverbeds (called "ramblas"), the gray Miocene clay, and treeless plains rising into the hills and sierras. Western towns and Mexican villages were built there for the movies in Spain. The filmmakers also took actual Spanish architecture into consideration. They especially used the architectural structures of Almería country. Almería province basically was an agricultural area in the 1960s with typical blinding-white farmhouses ("cortijos"), whitewashed villages, and tiny towns scattered in a dry and sunny landscape. From the beginning of the making of Westerns in Spain, the filmmakers used those structures because their movies were usually set in Mexico or in the borderlands of the American Southwest, where there is a similar landscape and where a Spanish architectural inheritance prevailed in the nineteenth century. The European filmmakers since *The Savage Guns* (Spanish title *Tierra brutal*, whose story is set in Sonora, Mexico), an American-Spanish co-production, made in 1961 (which was the first Western filmed in Spain), used the old villages of Almería, like San Miguel de Cabo de Gata, Polopos, Puntal de Polopos, Los Albaricoques, and El Argamasón. When the plot required a big farm to represent a Mexican hacienda or a mansion of rich landowners the filmmakers used Finca El Romeral (it is Don Felipe's hacienda in *A Bullet for the General*) and Cortijo del Fraile, a beautiful example of nineteenth-century Andalucían architecture, which also has a historical and cultural importance, because in the summer of 1928 on that big farm events took place that gave Federico García Lorca inspiration for his folk drama *Bodas de sangre* (*Blood Wedding*), staged in Madrid in 1933. Cortijo del Fraile is the fort where, in Damiani's film, El Santo appears on the roof and grenades the government troops during a decoration ceremony, calling them "assassins of Mexico." As a lot of Westerns set in Mexico (including the so-called Zapata Westerns) were actually filmed in Spain, especially in Almería, the Spanish landscape, rural architecture and structures became a hallmark, a visual convention to represent Mexico on the screen. As Westerns and movies on the Mexican Revolution often require trains and railroads, the filmmakers used them in the Guadix and La Calahorra areas of Granada province (such as in *A Bullet for the General*) and in the Madrid area.

Damiano Damiani's film is authentic in its depictions of a band of guerrillas constantly on the move in an effort to stay ahead of government troops. The director staged some impressive scenes, including raids on a Mexican army fort and machine-gun shootouts. The set designer is Sergio Canevari, the art director from *Battle of Algiers*. Several scenes look like photos of the period, and Canevari's attention to detail attempts historical authenticity. The impressive score is composed by Luis Enrique Bacalov, under Ennio Morricone's supervision. The Italian title of Damiani's film is *Quien sabe?* The Spanish title is *Yo soy la revolución*. The English-language title, *A Bullet for the General*, made it clear what the film was about, tying up the main gunrunning plot with the assassination subplot. The film was very successful when it appeared in Italy in December 1966 (a week before *The Good, the Bad, and the Ugly* by Sergio Leone). In the United States *A Bullet for the General* was distributed by Joseph E. Levine's Avco Embassy. American critics noted that the director Damiano Damiani had made a rarity: a commercial art film. But opinions were divided. Some claimed the film wasn't incisive enough for a political film, or exciting enough for a Western. Damiani was indignant that *A Bullet for the General* looked like a Western, and many critics categorized it as one. In fact, the director has never considered it a true Western movie, since it is his opinion that a "real" frontier movie is limited to certain situations and locations typical of the United States. "If you go south of Rio Grande, well, that's no longer the West, that's Mexico . . . *A Bullet for the General* is a film about the Mexican Revolution, set during the Mexican Revolution, therefore, it's a political film . . ."

In 1966, *Seven for Pancho Villa* a.k.a. *The Vengeance of Pancho Villa* (*Los siete de Pancho Villa*), a Spanish production, directed by José María Elorrieta, was filmed in the Ciempozuelos and Seseña areas, south of Madrid. The story takes place in 1916 at the time of Venustiano Carranza's government. This little movie doesn't contain "political" elements. It is a "Mexican-Western," in which the usual treasure hunt theme becomes predominant (but in the second part of it), whereas the first part is focusing on General Pancho Villa who, wounded and pursued by "federales," is rescued and nursed by a small band of supporters. Together with a cause-friendly Anglo (English actor John Ericson), they resume the revolution. The depiction of Villa (played by Spanish character actor Ricardo

Ciempozuelos (south of Madrid), site of the filming of *Seven for Pancho Villa*

Palacios) is interesting because it was made without exaggerated or mythical components. Spanish Actor Gustavo Rojo plays Villa's aide Tomás Urbina.

Kill and Pray (Italian title *Requiescant*) is an Italian-German co-production released in 1967 and directed by Carlo Lizzani. With this movie, Lizzani helms a "politicized" Western, replete with revolutionary "pro-Third World" themes characterizing many Italian movies produced during the late 1960s. Such themes, deriving from the fight for freedom of the oppressed populations, in turn inspired by the so-called "revolutionary Catholicism," are represented in this movie by Juan, the warrior-priest portrayed by Pier Paolo Pasolini, the famous writer and movie director, who (according to Carlo Lizzani) also cowrote the screenplay. Juan, modeled around the personality of the Colombian revolutionary priest Camilo Torres (1929-1966), is the film's true master-spirit. Juan, as a matter of fact, "fuels" the revolutionary "drive" of the main character (played by Lou Castel), a Mexican bandit's son who was orphaned and adopted by a preacher. The boy grows into manhood ignoring his past. He casually discovers his inbred ability with a gun. From that moment onward, he becomes a gunfighter and assumes the name of Requiescant (meaning "Let Them Rest") because he prays over the dead body of his opponents after a showdown. He finds out the truth about his origins when he meets the rebels commanded by Juan in the ruins of an ancient pueblo (a kind of Aztec temple), the same one where their parents and other Mexican people were murdered by Fergusson (Mark Damon), a dark ex-Confederate officer, who steals land from the local Mexican peons with bogus land treaties and his henchmen. The priest and his men help Requiescant in his final gunfight against the villains. After killing Fergusson, Requiescant, accepting Juan's proposal, agrees to lead the revolutionaries, who start their fight anew. Juan, as a Christian, lives the drama of having chosen the violence of the revolution. "I lead them, but, unfortunately, not the way a good shepherd leads his sheep. War is a curse, and woe upon us who fight it!" The authors of a book about Italian cinema published the following statement from the director Carlo Lizzani: "Western movies were the first works to deal with such 'hot' issues as justice, revolt, the 'unrests' of '68. Thus I managed to involve Pasolini in my project who, by the way, had a lot of fun in making the movie, even though he was already a successful man. He didn't do it for the money, but because he loved this way of dealing with certain issues through a 'western' metaphor." But Carlo Lizzani's execution of the material, overflowing with political philosophizing about revolution, racism, and church, is mediocre. *Kill and Pray* is entirely filmed in Italy. It was shot in a suburb of Rome using a quarry and dull country to represent a visually poor Mexico.

Another movie dealing with the Mexican Revolution entirely made in Italy is *Killer Kid* (1967). This Italian production, directed by Leopoldo Savona, features Anthony Steffen (Antonio De Teffé) as lieutenant Morrison, who assumes the identity of an arms trafficking outlaw called the Killer Kid in order to thwart an illegal arms trade. He ends up by siding with the revolutionaries against the "rurales" and the government troops. Spanish actor Fernando Sancho plays the bandit/revolutionary who seems to be in it only for the money, but ends up by displaying an unexpected fit of generosity. Due to the low budget, this movie manages to evoke a Mexican atmosphere using the Mexican village at Cinecittà Studios and a quarry in a suburb of Rome.

The Mercenary (1968), an Italian-Spanish co-production directed by Sergio Corbucci, is set at the start of the Mexican Revolution; there is a hint at Francisco Madero. When the rich mine owner don Alfonso García (the Spanish actor Eduardo Fajardo) is asked if he thinks the insurgent Madero is a threat, he says he is "nothing." The story tells about a Polish mercenary named Sergei Kowalski, known as the Polak (Franco Nero), who is hired to guard silver shipments from the Palo Alto Mine to Texas. When he arrives at the mine, the exploited workers, led by Paco Román (Tony Musante), have taken over. Paco rebels, not through any sense of "revolutionary conscience," but because he has seen his father and brother die in the mine and doesn't want to meet the same fate. The Polak realizes that there is more money to be made siding with the rebels and teams up with them. Also Paco at first is only interested in money. But with the Polak's tuition, Paco and his dozen-strong gang become a force to be reckoned with. His men begin to shout "Viva Paco!" and the Polak claims he can make Paco as world-famous as Villa or Zapata. Soon Paco is inadvertently a revolutionary icon to the Mexican people. But the Mexican authorities, with Don Alfonso García in command, and a sadistic American hired killer named Curly (Jack Palance, who worked extensively in Italy throughout the 1960s), who sides with García, hunt him down. Curly's grenade-filled valise is based on the Hollywood Mexican Revolution movie *Bandido!* (1956), directed by Richard Fleischer, in which Robert Mitchum's laid-back gringo mercenary Wilson is similarly equipped. *The Mercenary* was originally written by Franco Solinas, but then director Sergio Corbucci employed Luciano Vincenzoni (best known for his work with Sergio Leone on the "Dollars" trilogy) to help him adapt the story for the screen. Along the way, the serious politics of the story ended up taking a back seat to the humor as the political message of the film was almost lost among the exhilarating action and comic-strip style. The film's exteriors were shot entirely in Spain (Almería and Madrid areas) by the Spanish cinematographer Alejandro Ulloa, who filmed many Spaghetti westerns. The crew completed filming interiors in Rome. Ennio Morricone's soundtrack is effective and suggestive. *The Mercenary* was released to massive success in Italy in December 1968. It was also successful in Germany. In Spain it was known as *Salario para matar*. It was retitled *A Professional Gun* in the United Kingdom, where it appeared in 1970, and it was released the same year in the United States as *The Mercenary* under the United Artists banner. The film was successful in the U.S. and U.K. markets, and earned some positive reviews.

The impact of European Westerns, in particular the Clint Eastwood films made in Spain and Italy and directed by Sergio Leone, produce a significant resurgence in popularity of the American Western in the second half of 1960s and also some big-budget films related to the Mexican Revolution were made, such as *The Professionals* (1966) by Richard Brooks and *The Wild Bunch* (1968), directed by Sam Peckinpah and shot in Mexico. Three American action films were made in Spain, including Paramount Pictures' *Villa Rides!* (1968), directed by Buzz Kulik and co-scripted by Sam Peckinpah. In 1912, American pilot Lee Arnold (Robert Mitchum), who is smuggling guns into Mexico, agrees to serve as Villa's one-man air force, bombarding government troops with homemade grenades. Villa's success infuriates revolutionary commander General Huerta (effectively portrayed by English actor Herbert Lom), who sends Villa on a suicide mission by ordering him to take the city of Conejos. Arnold secures victory by bombarding the enemy from the air. Later the Anglo again helps Villa to overthrow Huerta, now installed as dictator after having assassinated President Madero (played by Alexander Knox). As usual, the image of the colorful "primitive rebel" Pancho Villa (portrayed by Yul Brynner), trendy and impulsive, is set against that of a taciturn, detached American observer, who becomes increasingly (though sometimes reluctantly) loyal and impressed by the commitment of the revolutionaries as the story progresses. Charles Bronson has a minor role as Villa's aide, the sadistic and fearsome Rodolfo Fierro, and Spanish actor Roberto Vihar plays Tomás Urbina. *Villa Rides!* is an action-packed adventure film in which the complex political and historical issues involved are given rather short shrift. It has several spectacular sequences, including the Conejo battle, which was shot at Escalona (Toledo province).

Also filmed in the Madrid and Almería areas is the American production *100 Rifles* (1969), directed by Tom Gries and cowritten by Clay Huffaker. It is more a "Western-Mexican" adventure film than a movie on the Revolution. In the early 1900s, Yaqui Joe (Burt Reynolds), a mestizo, robs an Arizona bank to purchase 100 rifles for the Yaqui Indians. Then he flees across the border into the Mexican town of Nogales, Sonora, where the governor, General Verdugo (Fernando Lamas), aided by a German military advisory, Von Klemme (Hans Gudegast), is waging a war of annihilation against the Yaqui Indians. Lyedecker (Jim Brown), a black American deputy, is assigned to bring the mestizo back to the States. The two men, joined by Sarita (Raquel Welch), a beautiful Indian revolutionary, are involved in the fight between General Verdugo and the Indians. When this melting-pot movie was released, Raquel Welch's steamy love scene with Jim Brown made a sensation as explicit interracial sex. The fact that Raquel Welch was supposed to be a Yaqui Indian did not alter the impact of showing bodily contact between a black male and white female.

The Mexican Revolution becomes a background for comic interpretations, gags, parodies, and picaresque adventures in the Italian-Spanish coproduction *Train for Durango* (1968), directed by William Hawkins (real name Mario Caiano). There is the usual hunt for a stolen and impregnable gold-filled safe. The characters are two unlucky adventurers, the inept and fearful gringo (Anthony Steffen) and the apparently shrewd Mexican, Lucas (Enrico Maria Salerno). Among the exaggerated characters, we find a credulous "regulares" commander (Spanish actor Aldo Sambrell), bizarre "bandoleros" (Spanish actors Roberto Camardiel and José Bódalo), as well as cynical Yankees, who, as usual, try to make a profit out of the chaos caused by the revolution. This movie was filmed in Almería.

A different approach to the Mexican Revolution is found in *Blood and Guns* (European title *Tepepa*, 1969), an Italian-Spanish co-production, directed by Giulio Petroni. The script was written by Franco Solinas. It has the Cuban actor Tomás Milián in one of the best acting parts of his career as Jesús María Morán, who is nicknamed Tepepa. He is a revolutionary profoundly disappointed in President Francisco Madero for hesitating to implement agrarian reform and having betrayed the revolutionary cause. Tepepa realizes that nothing will ever change for him and his people, so he refuses to lay down his arms. He then organizes his men to assault the government forces. During the fight Tepepa is wounded and calls upon an ambiguous English doctor (English actor John Steiner) who had joined his band to help him. But the English doctor's real mission is to take revenge for the death of his fiancée, the daughter of a Mexican hacendado who committed suicide after being raped by Tepepa when he attacked their hacienda in Morelos in January 1910. Great filmmaker Orson Welles plays the part of the evil colonel Cascorro extraordinarily well; he is the best in the series of the government officers of the Zapata Western subgenre. In Giulio Petroni's movie a psychological drama is framed by a quick-moving action story. The notable and impressive historical reconstruction often is made by means of effective flashbacks, such as the sequence in which Francisco Madero, pursued and exhausted, takes shelter in Tepepa's father country house in 1909; peons lay down their weapons in the presence of President Francisco Madero and General Huerta after the victory against Porfirio Díaz; and the

Rambla de Lanújar in the Almería desert, used in *Train for Durango*

landowner and his family return under the protection of colonel Cascorro at the hacienda, which was occupied by Tepepa and his men. *Blood and Guns*, rich in rhythm and epic inspiration, was beautifully filmed in various locations of Almería province and in the town of Guadix in fall 1968. Petroni commented on his film: "*Blood and Guns* was very successful even in Mexico and really this was rather strange because the Mexicans, like the Italians, are not all that fond of foreigners talking about them. Probably it was my characters and the various situations they find themselves in that were credible and authentic."

Conceived around the model of *The Dirty Dozen* (1967), intermixed with elements of *The Magnificent Seven* (1960), is the Italian film *Five Man Army* (1969), codirected by Italo Zingarelli and Don Taylor, and written by Dario Argento, the "wizard" of Italian horror. A mercenary band of specialists, led by "the Dutchman" (Peter Graves), are hired to rescue a revolutionary (Italian actor Nino Castelnuovo) and then, with his top-secret information regarding a Mexican government train, they steal a load of gold. However, the whole combo will end up by helping the revolutionaries. *Five Man Army* was made in Almería and in Italy, where the train sequences and those concerning the Mexican village (we see in the first part and final part of the movie) were filmed.

After the success of *The Mercenary* (1968), Sergio Corbucci directed another movie set during the Mexican Revolution: *Compañeros* (a.k.a. *Vamos a matar,*

The Iglesia de Santiago in Guadix, used in *Blood and Guns* and *A Fistful of Dynamite*

compañeros, 1970). The story features a Swedish arms dealer (Franco Nero) and a Mexican bandit called El Vasco (Tomás Milián, who is dressed in the style of Che Guevara) who are commissioned by Mongo Álvarez, a greedy Mexican general (played by Spanish actor Francisco Bódalo), to rescue a popular political prisoner, a pacifist, from jail. He is Professor Xantos (Spanish actor Fernando Rey), the only person able to open a safe. It is the beginning of a long adventure during which the two characters have to battle against government troops, the band of a sadistic bounty killer (Jack Palance, again), and finally against General Mongo Álvarez himself in the village of San Bernardino, because the general is more interested in the money than in his people's cause. Accompanied by Morricone's soundtrack, the film has at its center the love-hate relationship between the Swede and the Mexican. Finally El Vasco has become a revolutionary and the European decides to fight at his side. Photographed by Alejandro Ulloa in the Almería and Madrid areas, *Compañeros* is an entertaining movie, but Sergio Corbucci's bizarre touches and slapstick style tend to obscure any "disguised" populist themes and political messages.

Entirely shot in Spain (Madrid area) is the American film *Cannon for Córdoba* (1970), directed by Paul Wendkos, who had made *The Guns of the Magnificent Seven* two years before in Spain. The plot of this "Western-Mexican" adventure film is loosely related to the Pancho Villa raid on Columbus, New Mexico (1916), but the action takes place four years before. In 1912, Héctor Córdoba, a former Mexican army general (played by Italian actor Raf Vallone), attacks a United States army fort a short distance over the border and six cannons fall into the hands of Mexicans. General John Pershing (John Russell) orders captain Douglas (George Peppard) to capture Córdoba and bring him back to the United States for trial. Douglas assembles a small commando band (in *The Dirty Dozen* style) for the dangerous mission into the heart of Córdoba's territory on the Sierra Madre.

The fifth movie made by Sergio Leone in Spain, *A Fistful of Dynamite* (originally *Duck, You Sucker*, 1971), filmed in the Almería and Guadix areas, is backdropped against the Mexican Revolution at the historical moment of Huerta's imminent downfall (1914). But the director points out that the Mexican Revolution is a symbol. His movie celebrates the disillusion that inevitably comes with the revolution. At the heart of his film is the theme of friendship between a naïve Mexican peasant bandit, Juan (Rod Steiger), and Sean (James Coburn), a disenchanted Irish professional revolutionary who is an expert with explosives and has a guilty past. The last part of the film is dominated by a distressing and ineluctable feeling of desperation and death. Sergio Leone is able to infuse an epic dimension into his work and to elevate the scenes of action to the level of great historical spectacle, emphasized by the Ennio Morricone's outstanding accompaniment. Memorable are elaborate action sequences, such as a bridge blowing up while the government troops are crossing, executions of civilians, railroad and crowded depot scenes, and a head-on collision between two locomotives traveling at full speed at the climax. *A Fistful of Dynamite* had a fairly long run in Italy, France, and Germany, but flopped in America.

Bitterness, pessimism, and tragic atmosphere dominate *El bandido Malpelo* (1971), a low-budget, little known Italian-Spanish production directed by

Giuseppe Scotese and filmed in the Almería and Madrid areas. It doesn't contain those comic, satiric, grotesque elements and picaresque spirit that are often dominant in European movies dealing with the Mexican Revolution. As in Sergio Leone's film, the story takes place in 1914, at the time of the chaotic final period of Huerta's dictatorship. It features Diego Medina (George Carvell), the idealist young nephew of a government general, who steals the defense plan concerning the fortress of Zacatecas and sets out on a perilous journey to give it to the constitutionalists led by Pancho Villa on the Sierra Madre. On the way, Diego, pursued by Captain Orozco (Spanish actor José Nieto) and by a ruthless "rastreador" (bounty killer), meets Malpelo (Eduardo Fajardo), a bandit, who at first is only interested in money, but then sacrifices himself for Diego. When Diego finally arrives at a Villista outpost, he is shot on sight without the opportunity to reveal his mission's purpose. There is action in this movie, but the dialogue is more important because it depicts many historical events, characters, and places of the Mexican Revolution.

In the early 1970s, during the final phase of the spaghetti Western boom, the emphasis shifted to comic-strip stories, slapstick comedy, and burlesque. An example of this trend is *Long Live Your Death* a.k.a. *Don't Turn the Other Cheek* (1971), an Italian-Spanish-German co-production directed by Duccio Tessari and filmed in the Madrid area. It's about a treasure hunt by three people:

The Catedral de Guadix (Granada province), used in *A Fistful of Dynamite*

a would-be, self-styled Russian prince (Franco Nero), Lozoya (Eli Wallach), a peasant mistaken for a revolutionary hero, and a gusty Irish journalist (Lynn Redgrave). Once again Eduardo Fajardo is in the role of a wicked general.

In the attempt to compete with the influx of spaghetti Westerns, various British film investors also financed some productions. One of those projects was *A Town Called Bastard* (1971), a British-Spanish coproduction by Robert Parrish, an American director who also made *The Wonderful Country* (1959) starring Robert Mitchum, set during the Mexican Revolution and filmed in Mexico (it's a movie that somehow anticipates some of the themes of Eurowesterns). In the first sequence of *A Town Called Bastard* a group of Mexican revolutionaries led by Águila take possession of a pueblo, break into the church, and kill all the "regulares," civilians and the priest. Years later, a beautiful widow (Stella Stevens), comes to the pueblo, now ruled by a rebel bandit (Telly Savalas). Her purpose is to kill Águila and avenge her husband, who was murdered by Águila for having betrayed the revolution. In the end, the widow finds out that Águila (a common name for the symbolic leaders of the revolution) has become the pueblo's new priest (Robert Shaw). The plot is rather confusing, but it skims over a theme that we find very seldom in the movies related to the Mexican Revolution: a break between the church and state, the strong anti-clerical policy, and the persecution of Catholics. For *A Town Called Bastard* a huge Mexican fortress set was built at Madrid 70 Studios near Daganzo (20 miles east of Madrid) created by the American screenwriter Philip Yordan, who, in cooperation with the producer Bernard Gordon, made several films in Spain.

Partially shot at Madrid 70 Studios in 1971 (but released in the United States in 1974), is *Viva Pancho Villa* (British title *Pancho Villa*; Spanish title *El desafío de Pancho Villa*), a Spanish production, directed by Eugenio Martín and photographed by Alejandro Ulloa. Villa is portrayed by Telly Savalas, who also co-wrote the movie. The cast also includes Clint Walker (as an American arms dealer), Chuck Connors (as Colonel Wilcox), and Anne Francis. The general and his men, after feeling betrayed in a bogus arms deal, cross the Mexican/American border and take possession of the army outpost at Columbus, New Mexico; but this historical episode (March 9, 1916) is depicted by the movie in comical tones. *Viva Pancho Villa* contains several train sequences filmed in the La Calahorra area, east of Guadix (Granada province), but chiefly it is remembered for the amazing two-train collision that takes place in the final part of the movie.

Following the success of *Compañeros*, Sergio Corbucci directed a third film set during the Mexican Revolution, *What Am I Doing in the Middle of the Revolution?* (1972). This time, however, the film is more along the lines of comedy than a political apologue. In order to demonstrate his desire to highlight the comical aspects, he chose a pair of Italian actors who had nothing to do with Westerns, but who were well known for their comedies: Vittorio Gassman and Paolo Villaggio. Guido Guidi (Vittorio Gassman), an Italian actor, selfish and a bit of a coward, arrives in Santa Cruz to play in Shakespeare's *Richard III*. Here, together with Don Albino (Paolo Villaggio), an Italian priest, also a bit of a coward, he becomes unwittingly involved in the revolution led by Emiliano Zapata. The two Italians, after some initial skirmishes due to differences in their characters, end up good friends as they cross Mexico, which is torn apart by violence. In the end, Guidi, paid by an evil government colonel (played again by Eduardo Fajardo) to impersonate Zapata and ruin his image, suddenly becomes politically aware and, risking his life, incites the peons to revolt. But he is killed and dies in the arms of his friend, the priest. *What Am I Doing in the Middle of the Revolution?* is photographed by Alejandro Ulloa in several locations in the Madrid and Almería areas.

The group of films set during the Mexican Revolution made in Spain and Italy from 1966 to 1972 comprises fifteen European coproductions and three American productions. Only three or four of them are really "political" films made by left-wing directors and screenwriters who, through the mythology of the Mexican Revolution, which provides a good context for transplanting a progressive ideology into a popular genre such as the spaghetti Western, attempt to disseminate a productive political discourse. Most of the other movies are adventure/comedy stories of greed and treachery or parodies backdropped against the Mexican Revolution, where the dialectical aspects of the Anglo-Mexican relationship usually become stereotypical, involving a "conversion" on the part of one or the other of the protagonists. Mexican censorship forbade several of those movies, because of their stereotypes, carnivalesque, grotesque and ludicrous aspects, inaccuracies, and distortion of the historical events. At the same time (late 1960s to the early 1970s) there were Mexican films made about

The Plaza Mayor in Tembleque (Toledo province), used in *What Am I Doing in the Middle of the Revolution?*

the Revolution, such as *Lucio Vázquez* (1966); *La Valentina* (1965); *Un dorado de Pancho Villa* (1965); *El centauro Pancho Villa* (1967); the Spanish-Mexican co-production *La guerillera de Villa* (1967); *La soldadera* (1967); *Valentín de la Sierra* (1968); *La marcha de Zacatecas* (1969); *La generala* (1970); *Emiliano Zapata* (1970); *Reed: México insurgente* (1972); but the Mexican Revolution became a very popular theme chiefly through the medium of a popular genre as the European Western, which had a great international impact.

WORKS CITED

Bruschini, Antonio, and Andrea Tentori. *Western all'italiana. Book I, The Specialists*. Firenze: Glittering Images, 1998.

———, and Federico De Zigno. *Western all'italiana. Book II, The Wild, the Sadist and the Outsiders*. Firenze: Glittering Images, 2001.

———. *Western all'italiana. Book III, 100 More Must-See Movies*. Firenze: Glittering Images, 2006.

De España, Rafael. *Breve historia del western mediterráneo. La recreación europea de un mito americano*. Barcelona: Ediciones Glénat, 2002.

Frayling, Christopher. *Once Upon a Time in Italy: The Westerns of Sergio Leone*. Harry N. Abrams, Inc., in association with the Autry National Center, 2005.

———. *Sergio Leone: Something to Do With Death*. London-New York: Faber & Faber, 2000.

———. *Spaghetti Western: Cowboys and Europeans from Karl May to Sergio Leone*. London-Boston: Henley, Routledge and Kegan Paul, 1981.

Gaberscek, Carlo. "Reflejos del western europeo sobre el Americano." *Nosferatu. Revista de Cine*, 41-42 (octubre de 2002): pp.69-78.

———. "Rural Architectural Elements of a Western Style in Spain: The Sixties." *Film Style*. Udine, Italy: XIII Udine International Film Studies, 27-30 March 2006. Forum. 187-201.

———. *Il vicino West. Set e location del cinema western in Spagna*. Udine, Italy; Ribis, 2007.

Giusti, Marco. *Dizionario del western all'italiana*. Milano: Arnoldo Mondadori, 2007.

Hughes, Howard. *Once Upon a Time in the Italian West. The Filmgoers' Guide to Spaghetti Westerns*. London-New York: I.B.Tauris, 2004.

Márquez Úbeda, José. *Almería, Plató de Cine*. Almería: Instituto de Estudios Almerienses, 1999.

Martínez Moya, José Enrique. *Almería, un mundo de película*. Almería: Instituto de Estudios Almerienses, 1999.

Matellano García, Víctor. *Un lugar para el cine: Colmenar Viejo y la Industria Cinematográfica*, Concejalía de Cultura, 2006.

Núñez Marqués, Anselmo. *Western a la europea... Un plato que se sirve frío*. Madrid: Entrelíneas Editores, 2006.

Ventajas Dote, Fernando, and Miguel Ángel Sánchez Gómez. *Guadix y el cine: Historia de los rodajes cinematográficos en la comarca accitana (1924-2002)*. Guadix: Asociación para el Desarrollo Rural de la Comarca de Guadix, 2003.

Weisser, Thomas. *Spaghetti Western, the Good, the Bad and the Violent: A Comprehensive, Illustrated Filmography of 558 Eurowesterns and Their Personnel, 1961-1977*. Jefferson, NC: McFarland, 1992.

Bandoleros, aventureros, guerrilleros

Gonzalo Sobejano
COLUMBIA UNIVERSITY

En el mes de junio del 2007 me visitó en Nueva York mi antiguo estudiante de Columbia y siempre admirado y querido amigo Gary Keller. Siempre que viene a Nueva York me avisa y nos encontramos en casa o en algún restaurante para, dialogando, compartir recuerdos y esperanzas. En esta ocasión me dijo que tenía en proyecto, con sus colaboradores de la Universidad Estatal de Arizona, un estudio amplio sobre la imagen del "bandido generoso" (para decirlo pronto) y sus avatares en la literatura de lengua española. Me trajo copias de algunos grabados o láminas, entre los cuales estaba un retrato de Juan Martín el Empecinado, guerrillero cuyo nombre da título a uno de los *Episodios Nacionales* de Galdós (el penúltimo de la Primera Serie, publicado en 1875). Me habló también del *Quijote*, no sólo por la presencia en el libro de Cervantes de un famoso bandolero catalán, Roque Guinart, que fue lo primero que saqué a relucir en nuestra conversación, sino también por aquellos aspectos que en la conducta del Caballero de los Leones y de su escudero Sancho Panza pudiesen tener relación con la conducta del "bandido generoso".

Quedé con Gary Keller en escribir algo acerca de ese tema, que me parecía y me parece muy interesante pero del que nunca me había ocupado. Objetos de mi ejercicio como profesor, historiador y crítico de literatura española han sido principalmente la poesía lírica y la narrativa del siglo 17, la novela realista del siglo 19 y la novela del siglo 20.

En poesía yo sólo recordaba la "Canción del pirata" de Espronceda: "Veinte presas / hemos hecho / a despecho / del inglés, / y han rendido / sus pendones / cien naciones / a mis pies". "Que es mi barco mi tesoro, / que es mi Dios la libertad, / mi ley la fuerza y el viento, / mi única patria la mar".

En la narrativa mi memoria era menos escasa. Gran parte del relato de Lucio Apuleyo, *El asno de oro*, tenía lugar estando Lucio, transformado en asno, al servicio de grupos de ladrones mancomunados y bien capitaneados para saquear las casas de los más ricos propietarios, y aquellos ladrones se mostraban violentos, sí, pero valerosos. Otro antiguo relato (tan importante para comprender el *Persiles* de Cervantes como *El asno de oro* para comprender la confesión de Lázaro de Tormes y su descendencia), la llamada *Historia etiópica* de Heliodoro, comenzaba "in medias res" con una escena en que unos bandidos se disputaban la prisión y posesión de los jóvenes náufragos Teágenes y Cariclea.

Evoco esto para señalar la antigüedad del tema; pero aquí, como es lógico, voy a ceñirme al *Quijote* y al episodio nacional de *El Empecinado*. En el *Quijote* hay un "bandolero", Roque Guinart, que existió en la realidad histórica, y un caballero andante, Don Quijote, que, como tal caballero andante, y no sedente o cortesano, se va por los caminos a la aventura, o en busca de las aventuras, por lo que podemos clasificarle de "aventurero" sin ninguna intención peyorativa. Y en *Juan Martín el Empecinado* nos refiere Gabriel Araceli —el personaje-narrador de toda la Primera Serie de los "Episodios" galdosianos— una etapa de actividad combativa, en la Guerra de la Independencia, del "guerrillero" Juan Martín, que fue una persona de carne y hueso.

Sin ocultar una cierta afición a la simetría y aun a la consonancia, podría anunciar estas reflexiones bajo el título "Bandoleros, aventureros, guerrilleros" y vayan por delante algunas razones, etimológicas y semánticas.

"Bandido" o "bandolero" son sinónimos para el *Diccionario de Autoridades*: "El que sigue algún bando por enemistad y odio que tiene a otro, y se hace al monte, donde los unos y los otros andan forajidos y hay continua guerra; y también se extiende a los ladrones y salteadores de caminos" (s.v. "bandolero").

En cualquier enciclopedia se pueden encontrar precisiones. En la que tengo más al alcance, la alemana Brockhaus, hallo una referencia a los "banditi" o "bravi" de Italia, proscritos o desterrados que se organizaban en compañías, y preceden a la 'camorra' y a la 'mafia'. Y bajo las entradas "Räubermärchen" y "Räuberroman", la distinción tradicional entre el bandido amable (Schinderhannes, Robin Hood, Fra Diavolo, Francisco Esteban) y el aborrecido delincuente merecedor de castigo, así como referencias oportunas a la combinación de novelas caballerescas y novelas de bandidos que fomentaron en Alemania los iniciales éxitos románticos del "Sturm" de Goethe ("Götz von Berlichingen", el caballero de la mano de hierro) y de Schiller ("Die Räuber").

Sobre "caballero andante" nada hay que precisar aquí, pues Don Quijote mismo, en el libro que cuenta su historia, explica y proclama a cada paso cuál es su profesión y la finalidad de sus aventuras. Lo recordaremos luego.

"Guerrillero", en cambio, es un término no preexistente al personaje, sino coetáneo a él, surgido con él. "Guerrilla" existía como diminutivo, bastante raro, de "guerra" ("guerra de poca importancia"); pero en torno a 1808, tras la invasión napoleónica, se introduce y se afianza "guerrillero", y Corominas, en su diccionario etimológico, remite a Leandro Fernández de Moratín. En el *Vocabulario* de este autor compilado en 1945 por Federico Ruiz Morcuende se registra el siguiente texto de Moratín: "Mande a su amigo y servidor, que no firma para que el *guerrillero* que lea esta carta se quede sin saber quién la ha escrito", y la definición es: "Paisano que sirve en una guerrilla de tropa".

Como es sabido, "guerrilla" y "guerrillero" son vocablos que desde España alcanzaron difusión a otros muchos pueblos e idiomas. Lo que no impide que existan otros casi sinónimos: en español "paisano" y "partidario", y más tarde, "partisano"; en italiano, "partisano"; en francés "maquis"; este término muy extendido también y que el Webster define así: "1. – a zone area around the Mediterranean, used as a hiding place by fugitives, guerrilla fighters, etc. 2. – a member of the French underground fighting against the Nazis in World War II".

Aunque espero llegar a mayores claridades al observar sucesivamente a Roque Guinart, a Don Quijote y al Empecinado, creo oportuna esta distinción elemental: el bandolero (por generoso que sea) comete delitos: asalta con violencia, roba, puede llegar a herir y a matar; sobre todo, el robo es su actividad primaria; el caballero andante o aventurero obra regularmente en nombre de la caridad y de la justicia, por amor, aunque pueda errar, pero no delinquir; el guerrillero lucha por defender la causa de los ocupados, invadidos u oprimidos por un poderoso enemigo mejor armado o legitimado, y en ese batallar es explicable no sólo la violencia del enfrentamiento bélico, sino otros recursos a la agresividad como el asalto, el robo, la trampa, el despojo, la asechanza, la emboscada, cualquier artimaña que acelere la victoria frente al enemigo más fuerte.

Roque Guinart es el más memorable bandolero que recibió un tratamiento literario destacable en el siglo de Cervantes, por el buen retrato que éste hizo de él y porque la persona retratada gozaba de una notoria popularidad. Pero la figura del bandolero o la bandolera aparece con frecuencia relativa en el teatro de la época, y ejemplos de ella son *La Serrana de la Vera* de Lope de Vega y la comedia de igual título de Luis Vélez de Guevara (hacia 1603); la Lisarda de *El esclavo del demonio* de Mira de Amescua; la Ninfa de *La ninfa del cielo* de Tirso de Molina que, despechada por el abandono de un hombre, hace vida bandolera y pretende vengarse en todos hasta que Cristo la rescata; y la rústica Laurencia de *La Dama de Olivar* que repite a su nivel el caso de la Ninfa. Mediante estas conversiones pasajeras a la vida del bandidaje las mujeres atestiguan su despecho y ansia de venganza o reivindicación, como ocurre también en el ejercicio de vida maleante al que se dedica el desconfiado Paulo, despechado contra el cielo por no asegurarle la salvación y condenado por ello, mientras el malhechor Enrico se salva por el único atributo virtuoso de su amor filial. Y recordaré un caso más, el del drama trágico de Calderón *La devoción de la Cruz* (antes de 1633). Eusebio, matador de Lisandro, hermano de su amada Julia, se da a la fuga y capitanea una tropa de bandoleros; saca a Julia del convento donde su padre, Curcio, la había refugiado y la arrastra a su grupo de bandoleros hasta que al fin, bajo el signo de la cruz, se revela la desconocida fraternidad de ambos improvisados salteadores.

Habrá otros ejemplos que pudieran agregarse. Si he mencionado estos es para mostrar la frecuencia del tema en la época y la condición casi siempre accidental, vindicativa o despechada de los bandoleros. No son propiamente estos hombres y mujeres bandidos o ladrones por nacimiento ni vocación o profesión, sino por accidente, como réplica violenta a una situación desesperada. Es lo que explica, si no justifica, su extravío: son pecadores, más que delincuentes.

Y Roque Guinart, luego de haber mostrado ante Don Quijote rasgos de generosidad y larqueza en su auxilio a la desdichada Claudia Jerónima y en su trato con su escudero, le dice, entre otras, estas razones, concordes con las que motivaban a varios de los bandoleros ficticios recién considerados:

> —Nueva manera de vida le debe de parecer al señor Don Quijote la nuestra, nuevas aventuras, nuevos sucesos, y todos peligrosos; y no me maravillo que así le parezca, porque realmente le confieso que no hay modo de vivir más inquieto ni más sobresaltado que el nuestro. A mí me han puesto en él no sé qué deseos de venganza, que tienen fuerza de turbar los más sosegados corazones; yo, de mi natural, soy compasivo y bien intencionado; pero, como tengo dicho, el querer vengarme de

un agravio que se me hizo, así da con todas mis buenas inclinaciones en tierra, que persevero en este estado, a despecho y pesar de lo que entiendo; y como un abismo llama a otro y un pecado a otro pecado, hanse eslabonado las venganzas de manera que no sólo las mías, pero las ajenas tomo a mi cargo; pero Dios es servido de que, aunque me veo en la mitad del laberinto de mis confusiones, no pierdo la esperanza de salir dél a puerto seguro. (981-982)

Roque Guinart, con estas palabras tan comprensivas, tan sinceras, tan bien dichas, yo diría tan elegantes, está explicándole al caballero andante, no justificando, el oficio de bandolero cuyas primeras muestras Don Quijote y los lectores estamos presenciando. Compasivo y bien intencionado —dice— y pecador; pecador, no ladrón ni criminal. Por vengar un agravio que sufrió y asumir las venganzas de otros; consciente de su confesión; esperanzado en salir a buen puerto. Es decir: un hombre bueno.

Recordemos el encuentro de Don Quijote y Roque Guinart. Yendo Sancho Panza a arrimarse a un árbol en el camino hacia Barcelona, siente que le tocan la cabeza "dos pies de persona, con zapatos y calzas" y lo mismo le sucede al arrimarse a otros árboles. Don Quijote responde al asombro y el miedo de Sancho con palabras de involuntaria comicidad: "—No tienes de qué tener miedo, porque estos pies y piernas que tientas y no vees, sin duda son de algunos forajidos y bandoleros que en estos árboles están ahorcados; que por aquí los suele ahorcar la justicia cuando los coge, de veinte en veinte y de treinta en treinta; por donde me doy a entender que debo estar cerca de Barcelona" (974).

Como lector del *Quijote* a mí me resulta bastante extraño que el hidalgo manchego, hasta su primera salida a los caminos supuestamente absorto en las lecturas de sus libros de caballería, se manifieste aquí tan bien enterado de la proliferación del bandolerismo en Cataluña y aun de la fama de su más activo representante. Pues cuando aparecen de súbito cuarenta bandoleros vivos y, al frente de ellos, Roque Guinart, que dice que sus manos son más compasivas que rigurosas, Don Quijote le saluda con admiración: "¡oh valeroso Roque, cuya fama no hay límites en la tierra que la encierren!" (976), y Roque tranquiliza al "valeroso caballero" anunciando en su encuentro un giro de la fortuna que muestre cómo el cielo puede, por extraños rodeos, "levantar los caídos y enriquecer los pobres" (976).

Viene a seguida el caso de Claudia Jerónima, que ha dado muerte al amante que ella piensa le fue infiel, y en la resolución de este caso Roque Guinart se revela comprensivo, valiente y generoso en grado extremo, y todo ocurre ante los ojos de Don Quijote.

Roque Guinart hace devolverle a Sancho Panza los dineros que sus secuaces le habían quitado. Las quejas de Claudia "sacaron las lágrimas de los ojos de Roque, no acostumbrados a verterlas en ninguna ocasión" (979). Y Roque hace que sus criados lleven a enterrar al amante difunto de Claudia, se brinda a acompañar a ésta al monasterio adonde pensaba retirarse y a defenderla de la persecución de los del contrario bando; se asegura de la devolución de lo robado por sus escuderos, y reparte entre estos "todos los vestidos, joyas y dineros" robados últimamente, sin defraudar "nada de la justicia distributiva", alegando ante Don Quijote que: "—Si no se guardase esta puntualidad con éstos, no se podría vivir con ellos" (980-81).

He aquí, pues, la figura del bandido generoso en un ejemplar humano hacia el que Don Quijote manifiesta indisimulada simpatía, por más que en cierto momento arengue a sus seguidores tratando de persuadirles que "dejasen aquel modo de vivir tan peligroso así para el alma como para el cuerpo" (980) y después enderece al propio Roque una breve lección sobre la curación de la enfermedad y la enmienda de los errores: "…y si vuestra merced quiere ahorrar camino y ponerse con facilidad en el de su salvación, véngase conmigo, que yo le enseñaré a ser caballero andante, donde se pasan tantos trabajos y desventuras, que, tomándolas por penitencia, en dos paletas le pondrán en el cielo" (982).

¿Don Quijote caballero andante a lo divino? No, nada de eso: en el mundo y para el mundo, un mundo en el que, a veces, y antes del encuentro con Roque Guinart, ha tenido experiencias en que su conducta ha podido implicar modos de obrar propios del bandolero noble.

Pero antes de pasar a este asunto, recordaré dos cosas. Una es que, antes de desaparecer de la escena, Roque Guinart, mejor dicho, sus abanderados, cometen un acto de asalto y despojo a un séquito donde va con escolta y familia una dama principal, mujer del regente de la Vicaría de Nápoles. Roque manda hacer la cuenta de lo sustraído y, movido a piedad, lo devuelve, pidiendo a los acompañantes y a la Señora doña Guiomar de Quiñones sendos préstamos, "para contentar —dice— esta escuadra que me acompaña, porque el abad, de lo que canta yanta, y luego puédense ir su camino libre desembarazadamente, con un salvoconducto que yo les daré, para que si toparen otras de algunas escuadras mías que tengo divididas por estos contornos, no les hagan daño; que no es mi intención de agraviar a soldados ni a mujer alguna, especialmente a las que son principales" (983). Y, cumplidas estas y otras condiciones, deja a todos "ir libres, y admirados de su nobleza, de su gallarda disposición y estraño proceder, teniéndole más por un Alejandro Magno que por un ladrón conocido" (984).

La otra cosa por recordar es que esta visión en cierto modo ennoblecedora del bandolero, así en la causa de su dedicación (vengar un agravio) como en los modos de conducirse (no olvidar la justicia distributiva) no es sólo una dignificación literaria del escritor de ficciones, sino en gran medida algo que responde a las realidades que el historiador refiere en sus crónicas. Baste como muestra el siguiente botón. En su *Historia de los movimientos, separación y guerra de Cataluña*, el historiador hispano-portugués Francisco Manuel de Melo escribe acerca de las banderías de los catalanes (aún hoy se habla de "venganza catalana" y de "venganza corsa"):

> Habitan los quejosos por los boscajes y espesuras, y entre sus cuadrillas hay uno que gobierna, a quien obedecen los demás. Ya deste pernicioso mando han salido para mejores empleos Roque Guinarte, Pedraza y algunos famosos capitanes de bandoleros, y últimamente Don Pedro de Santa Cicilia y Paz, caballero de nación mallorquín, nombre cuya vida hicieron notable en Europa las muertes de trescientos y veinte cinco

personas que por sus manos o industria hizo morir violentamente, caminando veinticinco años tras la venganza de la injusta muerte de un hermano. Ocúpase en estos tiempos Don Pedro sirviendo al rey católico en honrados puestos de la guerra, en que ahora le da al mundo satisfacción del escándalo pasado. (Melo 110-11)[1]

Don Quijote —como todos sabemos— decide hacerse caballero andante e irse por el mundo con sus armas y caballo "a buscar las aventuras y a ejercitarse en todo aquello que él había leído que los caballeros andantes se ejercitaban, deshaciendo todo género de agravio, y poniéndose en ocasiones y peligros donde, acabándolos, cobrase eterno nombre y fama" (I, 38). Sus ideales son, por tanto, la justicia (deshacer agravios), la caridad (ayudar a los menesterosos, como afirmará repetidamente) y el anhelo de gloria. Jamás entra en sus intenciones el desposeer a nadie de sus bienes o propiedades, o sea, el robo, por desinteresado o equitativo que fuere. Pero, claro está, su esfuerzo por hacer lo que cree justo puede ponerle en conflicto con lo que han establecido como justo la Ley o el Gobierno; y por aquí pueden producirse situaciones que admiten alguna relación con aquellas que el bandido generoso provoca o resuelve.

Cuando, en su primera aventura, Don Quijote libra al humillado Andrés de los azotes de Juan Haldudo el Rico y obliga a éste a pagar al muchacho los dineros que presuntamente le debe, apunta ya una sombra del aludido conflicto. Don Quijote practica la caridad cuando libra al criado del látigo del amo, pero no sabemos si éste le debe a aquel unos dineros, aunque queremos creer que así sea. Más arriesgada es la situación creada por el caballero, ya acompañado de Sancho Panza, cuando empeñado en defender a una mujer que él imagina secuestrada, entra en combate con el vizcaíno y le hiere. Aquí Sancho aconseja retraerse a alguna iglesia porque "según quedó maltrecho aquel con quien os combatistes, no será mucho que den noticia del caso a la Santa Hermandad y nos prendan; y a fe que si lo hacen, que primero que salgamos de la cárcel que nos ha de sudar el hopo". "Calla —dijo Don Quijote—. Y ¿dónde has visto tú, o leído jamás, que caballero andante haya sido puesto ante la justicia, por más homicidios que hubiese cometido? (X, 98). Lo triste de este caso es que, de ser prendido por los guardianes del orden público, éstos tendrían razón, dado que el caballero andante había agredido al vizcaíno creyéndole un raptor de mujeres, aunque Don Quijote sea subjetivamente inocente pues había obrado según lo que su imaginación le hacía ver como real.

Más adelante, en la venta que Don Quijote se imaginaba ser castillo, aparecerá un cuadrillero de la Santa Hermandad que, en nombre de la Justicia, trata de apresar a quienes han apaleado a Don Quijote, a quien el cuadrillero cree muerto. Y la acción se enreda y precipita de tal manera que Don Quijote, huyendo del cuadrillero y del ventero, escapa al galope, sin pagar, porque los caballeros andantes no están obligados a pagar venta o posada y todo honor les es debido por lo mucho que hacen en defensa de todos, pues su oficio "no es otro sino valer a los que poco pueden y vengar a los que reciben tuertos, y castigar alevosías" (XVII, 156). Nuevamente aparece aquí el caballero, al irse sin pagar el hospedaje, como un delincuente, aunque según su quimera no es culpable.

Más se aproxima el caballero andante al salteador de caminos cuando, atacando a los encamisados que llevaban en andas un cuerpo muerto, considerado por Don Quijote el de un caballero cuya venganza a él solo estaba reservada, ataca a la comitiva y Sancho desvalija una acémila del repuesto de los encamisados, y amo y criado comen de aquí (XIX).

En la aventura del yelmo de Mambrino, Don Quijote arrebata la bacía del barbero creyéndola yelmo, pero deja ir al barbero porque: "—Nunca yo acostumbro [...] despojar a los que venzo, ni es uso de caballería quitarles los caballos y dejarlos a pie" (XXI, 195), no obstante lo cual permite a Sancho que se quede con los arreos del caballo del barbero, que se dio a la fuga. Claro que esto no permite calificar a Don Quijote y Sancho de bandoleros ni ladrones, pues falta la dedicación consecuente con una actividad que en Roque Guinart y sus semejantes como más tarde en los guerrilleros y resistenciales tenía un signo *político*.

Sobre la aventura de la liberación de los galeotes poco he de decir habiendo sido tan comentada por tantos doctores. Entre los cuales menciono a Jean Canavaggio, de quien son estas palabras:

> Don Quijote es incoherente cuando libera a los galeotes encadenados que además, le dan una tunda en lugar de hacer caso a sus conminaciones y presentarse ante Dulcinea cargados con sus cadenas, pero objetivamente, no deja de realizar un acto de justicia, liberando a unos condenados víctimas de un castigo inicuo y cuyas penas no pueden compararse con los delitos que han cometido. Según la perspectiva adoptada, el episodio puede leerse de dos formas diferentes, y esas lecturas se completan sin anularse. (249)

Los galeotes a los cuales Don Quijote con serenidad interroga y con vehemente intemperancia desencadena, son víctimas de un castigo desproporcionado a los delitos que han perpetrado; pero han sido condenados a galeras como delincuentes. Mayores eran las acciones violentas de las bandas de bandoleros, pero regidas por un capitán tan valiente y gallardo como Roque Guinart, cobraban —repito— un signo *político* que hacía a sus adalides colaboradores potenciales —y efectivos— de los Gobiernos. Entre los rateros a los que Don Quijote da libertad hay uno, Ginés de Pasamonte, en quien yo creo ver la réplica picaresca del bandolero "heroico" (entre comillas "heroico"). No sé si exagero pero parece que en la figura del "guerrillero" español de la guerra contra los franceses, se dan a menudo, en cierta medida, rasgos entrecruzados de Roque Guinart y de Ginés de Pasamonte.

Recordemos que en los capítulos 29 y 30 del *Quijote* se expone un debate entre el cura y el caballero acerca de la liberación de los galeotes: el cura maldice de quien liberó a tales ladrones y Don Quijote defiende lo que hizo no sólo por las leyes de la caballería, tan otras de las codificadas, sino porque puso los ojos en sus penas y no en sus bellaquerías.

En el pleito de la bacía del barbero (XLV) se suscita, a presencia de todos los congregados en la venta y de varios cuadrilleros que habían entrado al olor de la pendencia, la cuestión de los galeotes. Uno de esos cuadrilleros trae la orden de prender a Don Quijote por la libertad que les dio, y lee el mandamiento; y la respuesta de Don Quijote no tiene desperdicio:

—Venid acá, gente soez y mal nacida: ¿saltear de caminos llamáis al
dar libertad a los encadenados, soltar los presos, acorrer a los mise-
rables, alzar los caídos, remediar los menesterosos? [...] Venid acá,
ladrones en cuadrilla, que no cuadrilleros, salteadores de caminos
con licencia de la Santa Hermandad; decidme: ¿quién fue el ignorante
que firmó mandamiento de prisión contra un tal caballero como yo
soy? ¿Quién el que ignoró que son esentos de todo judicial fuero los
caballeros andantes, y que su ley es su espada, sus fueros sus bríos, sus
premáticas su voluntad? [Etc., etc.] (XLV, 465)

Sin duda, Don Quijote aspira y trasuda la razón de su sinrazón caballeresca
en esta diatriba contra la corrupta policía estatal; pero en la acalorada invec-
tiva se trasluce una crítica del contraterrorismo de entonces y una exaltación
del quijotesco terrorismo compasivo de los caballeros andantes de otro tiempo,
llevados a actualidad por impulso de su generosa locura.

Podría seguir glosando el *Quijote* en estas aproximaciones de su protagonista al ideal del bandido noble y, si hay tiempo, señalaré brevemente otros momen-
tos del libro de 1605 y del libro de 1615 (éste menos aventurero y caminante que
aquél, aunque sea el libro que, en su final, traiga a presencia al aguerrido Roque
Guinart). Baste lo dicho, como invitación al coloquio, y renuncio a algunas
reflexiones sucintas en torno a los guerrilleros, o mejor, a uno de sus más caracterizados ejemplares: Juan Martín el Empecinado. Quede para otra ocasión.

NOTA

[1] En el estudio de Melo, el editor remite a: Lluis Soler y Terol, *Perot Roca Guinarda*
(Barcelona, 1909), y a J. Reglà, *El bandolerisme català del Barroc* (Barcelona, 1966).

OBRAS CITADAS

Canavaggio, Jean. *Cervantes*. Trad. Mauro Armiño. Madrid: Espasa-Calpe, 1987.

Cervantes Saavedra, Miguel de. *Don Quijote de la Mancha*. Texto y notas de Martín de
Riquer. Barcelona: Juventud, 1965.

Melo, Francisco Manuel de. *Historia de los movimientos, separación y guerra de Cataluña*.
Ed. Joan Estruch Tobella. Madrid: Castalia, 1996.

PART TWO

THE

MEXICAN REVOLUTION

OF

1910

AND ITS

CULTURAL LEGACY

Demetrio Macías, el heroico bandido justiciero

Santiago Daydí-Tolson
THE UNIVERSITY OF TEXAS AT SAN ANTONIO

En *Los de abajo* observamos la capacidad sintetizadora del novelista que, siguiendo modelos realistas del narrar, compone un texto de carácter documental (que hoy leemos como histórico) en el que la realidad se ordena y simplifica bajo coordenadas literarias del género narrativo de ficción. Una de estas coordenadas es la que se refiere a la caracterización de los personajes y al valor representativo que cada uno de ellos tiene en la figuración fictícia de la realidad en el plano narrativo. Simplificando el análisis de este aspecto de la novela en vías a dedicarle atención preferencial al protagonista, que es la figura que aquí nos interesa, habría que decir que los personajes de *Los de abajo* son, en esencia, figuras tópicas, o tipos literarios basados en la observación de la realidad y en una interpretación estilizada de la misma (Daydí 8). Es en razón de esta esencialización de los personajes que ha de interpretarse la figura central de Demetrio Macías como "bandolero social", en la terminología de Eric Hobsbawm o, en términos más adecuados a la tradición popular hispana, en "bandido justiciero".

Es evidente en el tratamiento que Azuela hace de los personajes de su novela que no está interesado en desarrollarlos. Todo lo contrario, los quiere simples y claramente definidos en sus mínimos rasgos más típicos, como personajes que son de una historia concebida y contada en términos sumarios, como una narración épica directa y rotunda. Se dividen éstos en grupos claramente delimitados por sus mínimas características encasilladoras. Por una parte están los revolucionarios, encabezados por Demetrio Macías y caracterizados muy toscamente por sus rasgos más directamente relacionados con su condición de hombres y mujeres del pueblo; por otra, están los representantes de la clase media, también apenas bosquejados en trazos tipificadores; por último están los militares federales y los no revolucionarios, que aparecen aún tanto más evidentemente como simplificaciones de tipos sociales que incluso se los podría aproximar a la caricatura.

El protagonista, Demetrio Macías, no difiere demasiado de los demás personajes en la complejidad de su caracterización, sólo que por ser el protagonista tiene un desarrollo acorde con el plan cíclico de la novela. Difiere, eso sí, en el valor positivo de sus rasgos y en el efecto que éstos tienen en la efectividad representativa de su figura icónica de revolucionario popular, hombre del pueblo, honorable y justificadamente rebelde. A diferencia de los demás revolucionarios, particularmente sus subalternos más inmediatos, Demetrio se presenta como el personaje idealizado del bandido justiciero, defensor de los humildes y revolucionario por reacción de rebeldía contra el poder indiscriminado. No lo motiva la política sino una ética esencial, de profunda raíz humana.

Cabe indicar que, como lo observara Gary Keller (Intervención oral), la motivación revolucionaria de Macías y Montañés, campesinos con tierras y animales, puede no ser tanto la de promover cambios sociales en bien de un campesinado empobrecido, como la de defender, en lo que se podría ver como una característica conservadora del hombre de la tierra, sus propios intereses económicos de pequeño agricultor contra los abusos de caciques locales apoyados por la autoridad que controlan desde su posición de terratenientes tradicionalmente adinerados y poderosos. Desde esta perspectiva, más objetiva que la de ver en Macías un defensor del pueblo, la figura del "bandido noble" se entiende aun mejor como idealización de una realidad social.

Esta idealizada figuración del rebelde, que Azuela obviamente recoge de un sentir popular que se remonta a un patrón imaginario tradicional, se logra en la novela, como todo en ella, con sólo dos o tres trazos descriptivos. Componen estos trazos no sólo la configuración del protagonista mismo, sino también las de sus compañeros de hazañas, quienes, por sus importantes diferencias con él, lo hacen destacar más claramente como superiormente distintivo. Se trata de un héroe, de un auténtico protagonista, figura de excepción.

Como todo personaje excepcional, y el "bandido social" es excepcional por definición, Demetrio Macías se distingue precisamente por su contraste con el resto de los miembros de su banda, de los cuales dos o tres aparecen caracterizados en términos que podrían considerarse como explícitamente opuestos a los que definen al héroe. Macías aparece como alguien completamente diferente —su antípoda— al delincuente común, que vive fuera de la ley, escondido en el descampado por haber cometido un crimen contra el poder que, a pesar de parecer un acto justificado por la defensa del honor y los derechos básicos, no lo inspira a adoptar en la ilegalidad una actitud combativa reivindicadora, en la justa rebeldía, de su honor y de la clase oprimida.

Al hablar de este contraste valdría la pena observar que Juan Rulfo, en su cuento "Diles que no me maten", pareciera estar apuntando a esa diferencia fundamental que hay entre el hombre justo, que al convertirse en bandolero por las circunstancias se enaltece en la lucha por la justicia, y el delincuente común que, una vez cometido el acto de justicia, es incapaz de enfrentar su destino de rebelde y se convierte en un fugitivo fuera de la ley. En el análisis comparativo del cuento de Rulfo y *Los de abajo* se hace evidente el carácter excepcional del modelo que Azuela sigue en la caracterización de Macías, y la visión opuesta, antiheroica, crudamente realista que se propone en "Diles que no me maten". No son tantos ni complejos los rasgos necesarios para formular el tipo en cuestión.

Primeramente estaría, sustentando la figura del "bandido justiciero", el suceso delictivo que hace del personaje un fugitivo de la ley. En esto hay ya una diferencia importante entre los dos tipos, si bien coinciden tácitamente en lo que en la historia de Joaquín Murrieta, por ejemplo, se entiende como una justificación para la rebeldía violenta. Tanto Macías como el personaje de

Rulfo se han enfrentado al poder, implícitamente injusto, de la clase dominante, que por exceso del abuso los obliga a reaccionar. La reacción de Juvencio Nava, en el cuento, podría interpretarse como desmedida. Lo que no deja duda es la condición dominante del asesinado terrateniente autoritario:

> Don Lupe Terreros, el dueño de la Puerta de Piedra, por más señas su compadre. Al que él, Juvencio Nava, tuvo que matar por eso; por ser el dueño de la Puerta de Piedra y que, siendo también su compadre, le negó el pasto para sus animales. (212)

Se insinúa un conflicto similar entre un campesino pobre y un terrateniente para explicar la condición de fugitivo de Macías; sólo que en su caso el acto de rebeldía no llega al extremo del crimen violento. Se trata de una acción dictada por el honor ofendido. El delito de Demetrio se reduce a "[u]na escupida en las barbas por entrometido, y pare usté de contar..." (34; sec. I, cap. XIII). Azuela no especifica los detalles de la disputa entre Demetrio y don Mónico, "el cacique que me trae corriendo por los cerros" (5; I, II), como dice Macías; en cambio, deja en claro lo esencial, que el poderoso abusa de su poder: "Pues con eso ha habido para que me eche encima a la Federación" (34; I, XIII), observa Demetrio, apuntando a lo desproporcionado de la reacción del que domina. En conversación con Luis Cervantes, explica sus motivos para andar peleando:

> ¿Sabe por qué me levanté... ? Mire, antes de la revolución tenía yo hasta mi tierra volteada para sembrar, y si no hubiera sido por el choque con don Mónico, el cacique de Moyahua, a estas horas andaría yo con mucha priesa, preparando la yunta para las siembras... (33; I, XII)

Su experiencia muestra, como la del personaje del cuento de Rulfo, la situación de los campesinos en conflicto con los terratenientes y caciques. Con esta explicación Demetrio justifica su decisión de convertirse en revolucionario: lo hace para defender sus derechos y los de su gente que, como él, son víctimas inocentes de la opresión. No tiene otra forma de obtener justicia. En otra instancia en la narración se da a entender que Macías fue encarcelado tal vez por tal escupida, y que eso, en parte, le ha valido el que se lo vea como un bandido: "Yo estuve junto con él en la Penitenciaría de Escobedo" (3; I, I), comenta un soldado en referencia al protagonista, famoso por sus hazañas de rebelde. Queda claro, sin embargo, que Demetrio no es un asesino común ni un oportunista, como parecen serlo otros personajes de la novela y como lo es el del cuento de Rulfo.

Justino Nava, el protagonista de "Diles que no me maten", a diferencia de Macías, reacciona contra el poder abusivo de un modo nada honorable: comete un crimen violento, incluso ensañado: "Luego supe —dice el hijo del asesinado— que lo habían matado a machetazos, clavándole después una pica de buey en el estómago" (217). Entre los dos personajes hay una clara diferencia de carácter, la que se hace aun más evidente en las acciones que siguen a la transgresión. Habría que anotar aquí como otro contraste distintivo el que entre los compañeros de Macías hay varios que se han unido a la revolución huyendo de un crimen que poco o nada tiene que ver con la justicia social, la defensa del honor o la lucha reivindicadora de los derechos del pueblo. "Sí, ya me acuerdo, Codorniz, de que andas con nosotros porque te robaste un reloj y unos anillos de brillantes" (26; I, X), le reprocha Venancio, acusado él mismo de andar con ellos por haber envenenado a su novia. Anastasio Montañés, por su parte, también campesino, huye de la ley por haberle dado "un navajazo a un capitancito faceto" (31; I, XII).

Azuela no se ocupa de explicar cómo Macías llega a convertirse en el jefe de una banda de insatisfechos y delincuentes. Le basta poner en boca de unos federales la palabra que lo define frente a la ley y mostrarlo en su acción de cabecilla: "—Ud. ha de conocer al bandido ése, señora..." (3; I, I), le pregunta el soldado a la mujer de Demetrio en las primeras páginas de la novela. Poco después se lo muestra a Macías convocando a los suyos en una escena de sugerencias épicas:

> Demetrio se detuvo en la cumbre; echó su diestra hacia atrás, tiró del cuerno que pendía a su espalda, lo llevó a los labios gruesos, y por tres veces, inflando los carrillos, sopló en él. Tres silbidos contestaron la señal, más allá de la crestería frontera. (5; I, II)

Mientras Macías encuentra en la sierra la compañía de un grupo de rebeldes como él y celebra el ritual magnífico de una comida en común, el asesino de Rulfo se escabulle a solas por el campo, a medio morir de hambre:

> Y yo echaba pal monte, entreverándome entre los madroños y pasándome los días comiendo sólo verdolagas. A veces tenía que salir a la medianoche, como si me fueran correteando los perros. Eso duró toda la vida. No fue un año ni dos. Fue toda la vida. (214)

A la figura heroica y cuasi mitológica de un Demetrio de pie en lo alto de un risco monumental llamando a los suyos con un cuerno, se opone la del que huye a escondidas, como una alimaña perseguida.

Hay, precisamente, en el porte de los personajes, y en sus movimientos, una indicación de su carácter. Macías se presenta en las primeras escenas como la figura idealizada del hombre de la tierra, el noble indígena americano: "Alto, robusto, de faz bermeja, sin pelo de barbas, vestía camisa y calzón de manta, ancho sombrero de soyate y guaraches" (1; I, I). Más adelante en la novela se vuelve a anotar su estirpe: "...sus ojos recuperaban su brillo metálico peculiar, y en sus mejillas cobrizas de indígena de pura raza corría de nuevo la sangre roja y caliente" (40; I, XV). Algunos de sus compañeros, en cambio, por eso del contraste ya comentado, se describen en términos muy diferentes. "El Manteca", por ejemplo, aparece como un tipo brutal, "de ojos torvos de asesino" (10; I, III). Se lo describe como "una piltrafa humana: ojos escondidos, mirada torva, cabellos muy lacios cayéndole a la nuca, sobre la frente y las orejas; sus labios de escrofuloso entreabiertos eternamente" (19; I, VI). Pancracio, por su parte, se caracteriza por la "inmutabilidad repulsiva de su duro perfil de prognato" (10; I, IV) y por "la frente roma y oblicua, untadas las orejas al cráneo y todo de un aspecto bestial" (18-19; I, VI). ¿No son éstos los rasgos del bandido prototípico? Junto a ellos, la figura de Demetrio Macías se enaltece como la del "bandido social", virtuoso, digno, hierático.

El personaje de Rulfo, por otra parte, es un viejo desgastado en los trabajos inútiles de la constante huida. Su aspecto, "con aquel cuero viejo, con aquellas piernas flacas como sicuas secas, acalambradas por el miedo de morir" (215), es signo de su indignidad: "su cuerpo había acabado por ser un puro pellejo correoso curtido por los malos días en que tuvo que andar escondiéndose de todos" (214).

Al aspecto físico, robusto y alto, de Demetrio le corresponde un moverse parsimonioso y digno. Cuando al principio de la narración tiene que dejar su casa para evitar a los soldados que llegan, lo hace caminando lentamente: "Salió paso a paso, desapareciendo en la oscuridad impenetrable de la noche" (2; I, I). Y poco antes, al oír que se aproximaban los soldados, reacciona calmadamente: "sin alterarse, acabó de comer; se acercó un cántaro y, levantándolo a dos manos, bebió agua a borbotones. Luego se puso en pie" (1; I, I). Hay varias otras escenas en la novela, como la de la llamada con el cuerno ya comentada, en que se reafirma esta cualidad connatural al héroe. En contraste, sus compañeros se mueven y actúan descuidada y violentamente. Justino Nava, en el cuento, se mueve de un modo totalmente diferente, completamente opuesto a la dignidad que le corresponde a Demetrio. Recuerda un animal destinado al matadero: "amarrado en un horcón... No se podía estar quieto" (212). Lo habían traído caminando, sin necesidad de atarlo, porque "anduvo solo, maniatado por el miedo" (215). Y al final, ya definitivamente condenado, actúa sin ninguna dignidad, como un desesperado: "Estaba allí, como si lo hubieran golpeado, sacudiendo su sombrero contra la tierra. Gritando" (218).

Además de moderado en sus movimientos Macías es parco de palabras. Sus compañeros, en cambio, hablan de más y fanfarronean a voz en cuello. El personaje de Rulfo, entretanto, no cesa de suplicar y justificarse. El contraste en este caso es también notable en cuanto adscribe al héroe la virtud clásica de la parsimonia, signo de un espíritu equilibrado, mientras a los demás los rebaja al parloteo, la bravuconada, el insulto y el lamento acobardado, todas manifestaciones de personalidades deficientes.

Relacionada con el porte digno, la acción mesurada y el hablar con medida está la actitud de Demetrio con respecto a la violencia. Frente al regusto que sus compañeros demuestran por toda acción destructiva, la postura de éste resulta notablemente diferente. A los soldados que vienen a buscarlo en su casa de Limón sólo los enfrenta y atemoriza, a pesar de que su mujer le dice que los mate: "Demetrio se quedó mirándolos y una sonrisa insolente y despreciativa plegó sus líneas" (4; I, I). Cuando mucho después se enfrenta con su enemigo, el cacique que le ruega de rodillas que no lo mate, lo deja ir también sin hacerle daño y no permite que nadie saquee la casa. Es cuando uno de los suyos no obedece que actúa violentamente y con su propia mano lo detiene en la puerta con un disparo (78; II, V). La orden de prenderle fuego a la casa, por otra parte, se ha de entender en términos de una justicia superior. Obviamente su gente no lo entiende: "Cuando dos horas después la plazuela se ennegrecía de humo y de la casa de don Mónico se alzaban enormes lenguas de fuego, nadie comprendió el extraño proceder del general" (78; II, V).

De Macías se sabe desde un comienzo que tiene fama de rebelde. "—¿Con qué aquí es Limón?", se pregunta el sargento que ha venido a la casa de Demetrio, "¡La tierra del famoso Demetrio Macías! ... ¿lo oye mi teniente? Estamos en Limón" (3; I, I). A la admiración que el soldado siente por el héroe popular se opone la fama de cobarde del personaje de Rulfo:

> Pero los demás se atuvieron a que yo andaba exhortado y enjuiciado para asustarme y seguir robándome. Cada que llegaba alguien al pueblo me avisaban:
> —Por ahí andan unos fuereños, Juvencio.
> Y yo echaba pal monte... (214)

En su caso, además, se ve lo opuesto a la fama cuando al llevarlo preso pensaba que a lo mejor no era a él al que buscaban: "Tal vez ellos se hubieran equivocado. Quizá buscaban a otro Juvencio Nava y no al Juvencio Nava que era él" (215). La negación de la propia identidad, su anonimato, tiene su correlato al final del cuento, cuando el hijo lo subió al burro, le "metió su cabeza dentro de un costal" (218) y le habló: "Te mirarán a la cara y creerán que no eres tú. Se les afigurará que te ha comido el coyote, cuando te vean con esa cara tan llena de boquetes por tanto tiro de gracia que te dieron" (219).

Contrasta este final guiñolesco del cadáver sin rostro, cruzado como un saco sobre el burro, con la visión épica, cinematográfica a lo Eisenstein, de un Demetrio Macías al final de la novela convertido en una estampa idealizada del bandido heroico, inmortalizado en la imagen casi religiosa de su ideal:

> Y, al pie de una resquebrajadura enorme y suntuosa como pórtico de vieja catedral, Demetrio Macías, con los ojos fijos para siempre, sigue apuntando con el cañón de su fusil... (119; III, VII)

OBRAS CITADAS

Azuela, Mariano. *Los de abajo*. Ed. John Englekirk and Lawrence B. Kiddle. 1971. Long Grove, IL: Waveland, 1992.

Daydí, Santiago. "Characterization in *Los de abajo*." *The American Hispanist* 2.11 (Oct. 1976): 8-11.

Hobsbawm, Eric (J). *Bandits*. 4ª rev. ed. New York: New Press, 2000.

Keller, Gary. Intervención oral en el encuentro sobre los "bandidos nobles" celebrado en el Hispanic Research Center, Arizona State University, 13 de febrero del 2008.

Rulfo, Juan. *Pedro Páramo y El llano en llamas*. 3ª ed. Barcelona: Planeta, 1973.

Race and Social Class in Azuela's Characterization of the *Bandido*

Santiago Daydí-Tolson

THE UNIVERSITY OF TEXAS AT SAN ANTONIO

I n his article "La novela mexicana frente al porfirismo" John Brushwood observes that Mariano Azuela's *The Underdogs* was seen by most Mexicans as a novel that, having captured the essence of the revolutionary commotion that followed the fall of Porfirio Díaz, had the function to define the Mexican nation. ["Cuando los mexicanos se dieron cuenta de que Mariano Azuela había captado en *Los de abajo* la esencia de las conmociones revolucionarias que siguieron a la caída de Porfirio Díaz, la novela comenzó a desempeñar con plena seguridad su función de intérprete de la nación mexicana" (Brushwood 7).] A document that virtually antecedes the journalistic and graphic reports of contemporary wars, *The Underdogs* was conceived and presented as "Pictures and Scenes of the Present Revolution" ["Cuadros y escenas de la revolución actual" (Robe 123)], that is, as a realist depiction of what was happening in Mexico at the time. The novel narrated the same events that were being reported and commented on in the pages of *El Paso del Norte*, the Spanish-language newspaper in El Paso, Texas, that published the novel in *folletín* form in 1915. As such, *The Underdogs* gave a fairly true account of the social forces that were the cause, in part, of what for the author had turned out to be a failed revolution.

Disenchantment with politics and revolution is the essential thematic element of *The Underdogs*, and that can be seen in its three-part narrative structure that represents in its development Azuela's own intellectual experience with the revolution: his initial idealized optimism, followed by the sobering experience of his direct involvement in the military action and, finally, the sense of disillusionment and doom that took hold of him when he faced the political reality and the human egotistical interests behind the revolution. In order to express his loss of faith in what he had thought was a revolutionary movement for the betterment of the Mexican underdogs, Azuela had to weave the story of an ideal betrayed by the practical ways of the world: a literary representation of his own intellectual and moral story of a mistaken revolutionary, someone who fought not for himself but for the others, his people, the ones he knew had lost all hope of a change for the better. Azuela "observed at first hand the wild excitement, the bewilderment, the brutality, the hopes, the frustrations of the people of the sierras, of the underdogs" (Hendricks xvii) and depicted them as realistically and directly as he knew how to do, being the experienced realist writer he was: a keen observer of his society.

Basically, in *The Underdogs* Azuela constructed a narrative that tells the classical story of the hero, the ideal embodiment of justice and social virtue, who naively confronts the evils of the world, those injustices created by the society of men, only to be disappointed and defeated by the ones who, being in power, are disdainful of justice and of the commonwealth. In his view, the pragmatics of politics practiced by the ones above, "los matricidas" (OC III, 1266), as he calls them, always prevail over the ideals of the reformer who fights for social justice. Faced with the reality of the day, and obviously responding to the cultural constructs responsible for it, Azuela could not avoid dealing with the issues of class and race that had been so prevalent in the nineteenth century, when independent Mexico, a country that recognized three distinctly different racial groups, was fighting violently for establishing a national identity.

Almost half of the 15 million Mexicans at the time of the revolution belonged to the illiterate population, the underdogs, as attested by the census of 1910. A majority of them must have been among the 40 percent of Indian, with a lower proportion among the 40 percent mestizo sector of the population. Azuela himself belonged to the 20 percent of white Mexicans of European origin, most of them educated Creoles, but he had an affinity for the lower classes he knew well as a medical doctor. He might have had some Indian ancestry, though, as suggested by Stanley Robe when describing the physical appearance of the novelist at the time he joined the revolution: "He was approximately five feet eight inches tall and stockily built, with light brown skin that revealed some Indian ancestry" (13). His clientele in his home town of Lagos de Moreno, where he lived and practiced general medicine until becoming engaged in revolutionary activities by October 1914, were mostly members of the other 80 percent of the population, mestizos and Indians. Azuela knew their ways and sided with their interests.

> Azuela's practice was that of a general physician, providing treatment for the townspeople and the farmers and ranchers from the outlying areas. He had long shown a personal and professional sympathy for these people, most of whom were from the less affluent levels of society. From his earliest years Azuela had enjoyed their company; his family origins were modest, springing from farmers and small shopkeepers, and he was comfortable when he was with them. (Robe 8)

In his novel Azuela depicts them very well, those ranchers and townspeople of the lower classes, some of them probably of pure Indian extract. He takes care not to generalize or stereotype the members of this group, showing how among them are different, individually peculiar types that represent an ample variety of characters.

> He evidences a strong feeling of sympathetic understanding for the countrymen of Jalisco and Zacatecas "whose eyes were those of children and whose hearts were wide open" as a consequence of his having shared with them "many of their joys, many of their longings, and much of their bitterness." Years later when all of them had disappeared, he expressed the wish to pay homage to "each indomitable member of the indigenous race, generous and uncomprehending . . ."

writes Hendricks (xix), translating Azuela's own comments about his human interest in the ranchers he served as a doctor: "Compartí con aquellos rancheros de Jalisco, Zacatecas —ojos de niño y corazones abiertos— muchas de las alegrías, muchos de los anhelos y muchas de sus amarguras . . . quiero dedicar estos renglones a esa casta indómita, generosa e incomprendida" (*OC* III, 1268).

His own social group he also knows well, of course, and represents it mostly through two distinctly opposite types of individuals: Luis Cervantes, "el seudorrevolucionario y logrero" (*OC* III, 1081), the one specifically described as white, is the figure of the *tejón*, the "badger," or political opportunist, as Azuela refers to this type of person later in his retrospective writings (Robe 7), while Alberto Solís, the disillusioned officer, obviously from the middle class and supposedly white, could be seen as the idealist who is doomed to succumb to the forces of pragmatism and political expediency. In fact, this character represents Azuela's own disenchantment with the revolution: "[M]i situación fue entonces," says the novelist in one of his commentaries about the composition of *The Underdogs*, "la de Solís en mi novela" (*OC* III, 1081).

Solís, though, was not the character Azuela needed to narrate the story of his disillusionment. Although the young army officer was an idealist and Azuela's literary alter ego, he did not serve the novelist as well as other characters would to depict the violent and pointless actions of the revolution as Azuela experienced them. The disenchanted white army officer lacked the class and race markings and the revolutionary motivation and zeal to be a war leader. In his cynical view of the political situation Solís speaks better for Azuela himself, who had abandoned politics even before serving the revolution as medical officer and director of public education. "Disillusion follows," comments Hendricks about Azuela's experience, "expressed in the words of the officer Alberto Solís who reflects Azuela's own situation at the time he wrote the novel" (xx). Solís is neither the opportunistic *tejón*, nor is he the enraged man of action who takes up arms in the name of justice.

In spite of the fact that traditionally and historically the bandit has been a white or mestizo from the middle class, Azuela opted for a different characterization, turning his attention to the actual fighters as he knew them from direct experience. He centered, then, the action of his novel on a character that encompassed in his persona all the qualities of a rebel as seen in real life and in the popular literary traditions. Demetrio Macías, his hero, a noble bandit of sorts, the true revolutionary, is not a representativé from the middle class, nor is he a white man or a mestizo; he is an Indian, a true underdog from the lowest class and the "inferior" race. Azuela explains at length how the different characters of his novel are taken from real individuals (*OC* III, 1082-1086), but he also observes that "los mejores personajes de una novela serán aquellos que más lejos estén del modelo" (*OC* III, 1082).

That is the case with Demetrio Macías, who is a composite of real individuals and literary characters. It has been said that Azuela chose General Julián Medina, for whom he served as medical officer, as the model for his protagonist. "Julián Medina me dio la impresión de ser un revolucionario por convicción y de sanas tendencias," Azuela explains, suggesting a liking for the real person as representative of the type of hero he needs to express his disenchanted views. "Era el tipo genuino de ranchero de Jalisco, valiente, ingenuo, generoso y fanfarrón" (*OC* III, 1079), not unlike Demetrio Macías, his fictional hero. As a novelist, though, Azuela insists on the literary character of his revolutionary leader, only partially taken from the real person: "Me desentendí de Julián Medina, para forjar y manejar con amplia libertad el tipo que se me ocurrió" (*OC* III, 1080).

The type he created, Demetrio Macías, also has another inspiration from real life, also a member of Medina's group: "Manuel Caloca . . . muchacho de unos veinte años, alto, flaco, olivado, tipo un tanto mongoloide . . . sucedió a Julián Medina en la sustitución de mi personaje" (*OC* III, 1080). Thus, Macías becomes a true literary figure, a creation of his own: "To draw him," observes Luis Leal, "Azuela combined the personalities of two revolutionary leaders, General Julián Medina and Colonel Manuel Caloca" (101). In addition, Azuela adds the racial characterization of Macías as an Indian, an element not necessarily taken from reality, as neither Medina nor Caloca seemed to have been from that ethnic group.

From the first scenes in the novel Macías is represented as the idealized figure of the man from the land, the noble American Indian. At the very beginning of the novel he is shown as a "tall, robust man with a ruddy, beardless face" (*Three Novels* 163); a few lines later he reappears as a "white form" filling "the dark opening of the door" (*Three Novels* 165). This is a visual reference to what has been described before as his being dressed in a "shirt and pants of rough white cloth" (*Three Novels* 163), the "unbleached muslin" produced by the textile mill in Lagos de Moreno, "which was the type of cloth most used by the rancheros and those of limited resources" (Robe 4). ["Alto, robusto, de faz bermeja, sin pelo de barba, vestía camisa y calzón de manta, ancho sombrero de soyate y guaraches" (I, I, 1)]. Later in the novel there is another, even more direct reference to Demetrio's race: "The hot, red blood in his coppery cheeks that revealed his purely indigenous origin pulsed with renewed force" (*Three Novels* 195) ["en sus mejillas cobrizas de indígena de pura raza corría de nuevo la sangre roja y caliente" (I, XV, 40)].

The characterization of Demetrio as an Indian is not stressed by the narrative beyond those three references to his appearance, perhaps because Azuela was not being historically correct. As pointed out before, neither the man for whom Azuela served as chief medical officer nor the younger revolutionary he took as partial models for his hero was of pure Indian extraction. When Azuela on another occasion describes Medina, the historical figure, he uses almost exactly the same words he used to describe Macías in the novel: "tall, well built, of ruddy complexion, his eyelids slightly drooping, thick lips, with little facial hair" (Robe 14). In his dress, though, Medina differs from Macías; instead of the simple white muslin shirt and pants of the farmer, he uses "tight-fitting trousers and a deerskin jacket trimmed with braid and without a necktie" (Robe 14), more akin to the garments of the charros. In the case of Manuel Caloca, his having an olive-hued skin and a mongoloid-type face are not sufficient proof of his not being a mestizo instead of an Indian. The fact that the American consul in Guadalajara at the time of Villa's triumphal entrance in the city identifies Medina as an Indian is not proof of Medina's race, either. In a letter reporting his visit to Medina, who had been installed as governor, the consul writes: "General Medina looks the Indian—General Medina acts the Indian—General Medina is an Indian—and, worst of all, an untutored Indian" (Robe 21). In his description of the revolutionary general the consul is basically following the stereotype of the Mexican commonly held in those days in the United States (Evans 69-75).

A possible explanation for Azuela's characterization of Demetrio Macías as a pure Indian could be suggested by looking at other Mexican novels dealing with bandits and sociopolitical turmoil in previous periods of revolutionary upheavals. Very briefly one could compare how in *El periquillo sarniento* the bandits are all Creole mestizos, "consistent with Lizardi's social hierarchy in which indigenous people are too degraded to be men of action" (Frazer 103-4), while years later, at another period of revolutionary fighting, in *El Zarco*, by Ignacio Altamirano, class and race are much of the essence in this novel's proposal of a national new order. The mestizo, in this case, is the negative character, while the Indian appears as the forceful defender of justice. The bandit, El Zarco, is, as his own given name indicates, a blue-eyed white man or a mestizo, as suggested in his physical description by the "blanco impuro" of his skin:

> El joven no tenía mala figura: su color blanco impuro, sus ojos de ese color azul claro que el vulgo llama *zarco*, sus cabellos de un rubio pálido y su cuerpo esbelto y vigoroso, le daban una apariencia ventajosa; pero su ceño adusto, su lenguaje agresivo y brutal, su risa aguda y forzada, tal vez le habían hecho poco simpático a las mujeres. (25)

To his physical aspect are added some elements of his character, "Su organización grosera y sensual, acostumbrada desde la juventud al vicio . . ." (24), that make of him a negative figure, the opposite of the heroic bandit.

In contrast with this white bandido, the figure of the Indian Nicolás appears as the personification of virtue:

> era un joven trigueño, con el tipo indígena bien marcado, pero de cuerpo alto y esbelto, de formas hercúleas, bien proporcionado y cuya fisonomía inteligente y benévola predisponía desde luego en su favor. Los ojos negros y dulces, su nariz aguileña, su boca grande, provista de una dentadura blanca y brillante, sus labios gruesos, que sombreaba apenas una barba naciente y escasa, daban a su aspecto algo de melancólico, pero de fuerte y varonil al mismo tiempo. Se conocía que era un indio, pero no un indio abyecto y servil, sino un hombre culto, ennoblecido por el trabajo y que tenía la conciencia de su fuerza y su valer. (*Zarco* 11)

That Azuela decided in favor of creating an Indian hero is probably due to his own views as a turn-of-the-century Mexican on the qualities of the Indian in comparison with the other national racial groups and their political agency. It seems that by his characterization of Macías as an Indian, Azuela was pointing not so much to the qualities of the Indian as a natural man free from the vice of modern society, as to the fact that Mexico was badly served by its elites, whose interests were far from the interests and needs of most of the population. In spite of the realistic documental character of his "Pictures and Scenes of the Present Revolution," Demetrio is, more than a real character, a literary creation, an idealization, perhaps, of a real man, but most of all, an artistically effective representation of a political elusive hope in the future of a nation with a complex social structure in which race and class dictate the individual destiny of millions.

The final scene of the novel lingers in the memory of the Mexican reader as a revolutionary poster cum sacred image, the icon of the good bandit, the revolutionary and freedom fighter, the noble Indian, the man of the land whose sacrifice should not be forgotten and would not have been in vain:

> The smoke of the firing was still hanging in the air. Locusts sounded their imperturbable and mysterious song; from crannies in the rocks doves sang lyrically; cows placidly grazed.
>
> The mountain range displayed its fairest aspect. Over its inaccessible peaks the brilliantly white clouds fell like a snowy veil over the head of a bride.
>
> At the foot of the great hollow as impressive as the portico of an old cathedral, Demetrio Macías, with his eyes forever fixed, continued to aim the barrel of his rifle. (*Three Novels* 261).

WORKS CITED

Altamirano, Ignacio M. *El Zarco: La Navidad en las montañas.* Introducción de María del Carmen Millán. México: Porrúa, 1966. Print.

_____. *El Zarco: The Blue-eyed Bandit.* Introduction by Christopher Conway. Trans. Ronald Christ and Sheridan Phillips. Santa Fe, New Mexico: Lumen Books, 2007. Print.

Azuela, Mariano. *Los de abajo.* Edited John Englekirk and Lawrence B. Kiddle. Prentice-Hall, 1971. Long Grove, IL: Waveland, 1992.

_____. *Obras completas.* 3 vols. México: Fondo de Cultura Económica, 1960. Print.

Brushwood, John. "La novela mexicana frente al porfirismo." *Una especial elegancia: Narrativa mexicana del porfiriato.* México: UNAM, 1998. Rpt. in *Historia Mexicana* VII, 3 (ene-mar, 1958). Print.

Evans, James Leroy. *The Indian Savage, the Mexican Bandit, the Chinese Heathen: Three Popular Stereotypes.* Austin: U of Texas P, 1967.

Frazer, Chris. *Bandit Nation: A History of Outlaws and Cultural Struggle in Mexico, 1810-1920.* Lincoln, NE: U of Nebraska P, 2006.

Hendricks, Frances Kellam. Introduction. *Three Novels by Mariano Azuela.* San Antonio, TX: Trinity UP, 1979. xvii-xxv.

Leal, Luis. *Mariano Azuela.* New York: Twayne Publishing Inc., 1971.

Robe, Stanley L. *Azuela and the Mexican Underdogs.* Berkeley: U of California P, 1979.

Three Novels by Mariano Azuela: Trials of a Respectable Family, The Underdogs, The Firefly. Trans. Frances Kellam Hendricks and Beatrice Berler. San Antonio, TX: Trinity UP, 1979.

"Por camino torcido"
LIMINAL IDENTITIES IN THE NOVEL, SCREENPLAY, AND FILM VERSIONS OF *LA NEGRA ANGUSTIAS*

Laura Kanost
KANSAS STATE UNIVERSITY

F rancisco Rojas González's *La negra Angustias* (1944) is recognized as the first—and, to my knowledge, still the only—novel to center on a female Afro-Hispanic protagonist who is a leader in the Mexican Revolution of 1910. The trailblazing Angustias, modeled after an actual person Rojas González had met, attracted the interest of another Mexican female pioneer, screenwriter and director Matilde Landeta. When Landeta adapted the novel for the screen, she chose to change key aspects of the original story—most notably the ending—in both her original screenplay[1] and the 1949 film she directed. A parallel reading of Rojas González's and Landeta's depictions of this iconoclastic Mexican female revolutionary brings to light the conflicting values the three versions project regarding gender and politics.

At the outset, the novel, screenplay, and film largely coincide. "La Negra" Angustias Farrera, a figure who is marginalized because of her ethnicity, her father's reputation as a bandit, and her refusal to marry, is finally forced to flee her rural Mexican community when she kills a man who attempts to sexually assault her. The mule-train drivers who find Angustias in the wilderness also threaten to rape her, but an enamored protector helps her to escape. Taking advantage of her father's legacy as a Robin Hood figure, as well as her own charisma as a speaker, Angustias spearheads an uprising, and her devoted followers declare her their *coronela* as they join the ongoing Revolution. Although she is a highly successful leader, Angustias meets her downfall when she decides to hire a light-skinned, urban, bourgeois man to teach her to read.

In refusing to be sexually objectified, rejecting motherhood, taking a commanding role in the Revolution, and hiring a private reading teacher, la Negra Angustias defies Mexican sociocultural norms, but she eventually returns to an expected female role after she falls hopelessly in love with her teacher. Angustias and her *hechicera* mother figure use the phrase "por camino torcido"[2] to refer to her unconventional trajectory. This "crooked path" is common to the three versions of Angustias's story, but its contours and ultimate destination vary markedly. In comparing these twists and turns, we will see that the screenplay projects the highest degree of acceptance of Angustias's liminality, and by extension, of the liminal qualities of the Revolution as a whole and of Landeta's position as a woman filmmaker.

The concept of liminality, borrowed from Rojas González's professional field of anthropology, brings into focus the transformative potential of social "in-betweenness." Early twentieth-century French ethnographer Arnold van Gennep proposed that a rite of passage has three stages: a person is first separated symbolically from the community, then passes through a liminal or transitional phase, and finally is reincorporated into the group. Anthropologist Victor Turner compares the "liminal" state to the subjunctive mood in language, describing it as

> a unidirectional move from the "indicative" mood of cultural process through culture's "subjunctive" mood back to the "indicative" mood, though this recovered mood has now been tempered, even transformed, by immersion in subjunctivity [. . .] In preliminal rites of separation the initiand is moved from the indicative quotidian social structure into the subjunctive antistructure of the liminal process and is then returned, transformed by liminal experiences, by the rites of reaggregation to social structural participation in the indicative mood. The subjunctive, according to *Webster's Dictionary*, is always concerned with "wish, desire, possibility, or hypothesis"; it is a world of "as if," ranging from scientific hypothesis to festive fantasy. It is "if it *were* so," not "it *is* so." (Turner 163)

In all three versions of the Negra Angustias story, the protagonist is not merely marginal or an outsider, but rather occupies just this sort of in-between, or liminal, position with regard to her society. Through her participation in the Revolution—a "subjunctive" moment in the national imagination—Angustias is able, at least temporarily, to transgress the conventional divisions of her society and imagine another possibility: an innovative hybrid identity.

As her story begins, young Angustias is introduced for the first time to her elderly bandit father, "el Negro" Antón Farrera, who has just returned to his home after serving a long sentence in prison camp. Doña Crescencia, the witch who has raised Angustias since her mother died in childbirth, sadly returns the girl to her father, and years pass as Angustias devotes herself to tending to her father and their home. The novel, in particular, repeatedly describes the amount of time that Angustias spends each day making tortillas, going for water, and doing the washing. Angustias conforms to her expected feminine activities in this respect, but rejects them in others. Since childhood, she has harbored a strong aversion to heterosexual sex and motherhood, which apparently began when she watched her favorite goat become pregnant and later die giving birth. Landeta chooses to open her screenplay and film with these events, further emphasizing their importance.

Although Angustias and her father are seen in the community as different because of Antón's past and their darker skin, they are not shunned until Angustias rejects a marriage proposal that explicitly places her as a commodity to be exchanged between families. Her "unfeminine" behavior draws the wrath of the townswomen, who attempt to stone Angustias. The novel goes into further detail on the ensuing gossip, which includes accusing Angustias of having an incestuous relationship with her father and being a predatory lesbian. Angustias reiterates her refusal to be objectified by repeatedly fending off a violent would-be rapist named Laureano. The separation from her community, which constitutes Angustias's liminality, becomes complete when she kills Laureano in self-defense. Antón gives his knife to Angustias in the novel, but in both versions by Landeta, Angustias takes it from him while he is sleeping. Whether she has her father's blessing or not, Angustias uses this phallic object to punctuate in very physical terms her rejection of her expected feminine role as sexual object, and now she has no choice but to physically remove herself from her community.

So Angustias begins to forge her liminal path. In the in-between spaces of the wilderness and the Revolutionary encampments, she frees herself from the expectation to conform to a traditional feminine gender role.[3] Among the group of mule-train drivers who find her is fawning admirer Güitlacoche, who helps Angustias to escape from the rape threatened by his womanizing boss, Efrén "el Picado." Upon escaping, Angustias immediately dominates her smitten savior, their uneven power relationship comically apparent as Angustias leads the way on a tall horse and Güitlacoche follows behind on a much smaller mare. When she subsequently transforms into a *coronela*, Angustias draws on her father's legacy of stealing from the rich to abate poverty. In an instant, she changes the way others see and interpret her, and this transition is particularly evident in Rojas González's narrative, when Angustias commands an elderly innkeeper to look at her and corrects him when he first perceives her as an attractive woman:

> El mesonero [. . .] miró al rostro moreno de la joven, sonrió un poco y hasta murmuró:
> —¡Buena moza! . . .
> —Veme más, viejo, más, hasta que . . .
> Pero los ojos del "huéspere" se habían redondeado y su lengua, paralizada por el asombro, no atinaba a moverse [. . .] (80)

At Angustias's instruction, the old man recognizes that her pretty face is also inscribed with her father's features; in this liminal social space, others are willing to accept her hybrid gender characteristics. From this point on, *la coronela* Angustias commands the respect and obedience of her male followers.

Although in the novel and screenplay Angustias dresses in men's clothing[4]—a charro suit confiscated from Güitlacoche—and in all three versions takes on many conventionally masculine behaviors such as leading, fighting, drinking, and smoking, Angustias does not merely trade in the prescribed feminine role for the masculine one. Rather, on several occasions, she uses her "masculine" leadership role to counteract machismo and the sexual objectification of women. Perhaps the most famous of these actions comes early in her military career when she apprehends Efrén "el Picado" and orders his castration on behalf of all the women he has abused. Later, when a pregnant woman begs Angustias to let her take the place of her boyfriend, who has been sentenced to death, Rojas González's Angustias punishes this stereotypical feminine self-sacrifice by stripping the woman naked and commanding Güitlacoche to beat her. In this disturbing tableau, the woman suffers and is exploited, but Güitlacoche suffers, too, because Angustias's control renders him powerless to act sexually. Ultimately, the force driving the beating is Angustias, another woman, therefore exposing the role women play in perpetuating their own exploitation (116-17).[5] Landeta chose to omit the beating in both

Photo still from the film *La negra Angustias* (1950), directed by Matilde Landeta, showing María Elena Marqués in the title role

the screenplay and the film; instead, she had Angustias take pity on the woman and her unborn child, granting a pardon. In a third example common to all three versions, when some of her men drunkenly use a prostitute's shoe as a target in a shooting competition, Angustias gives the betting pool not to the best shot, but to the prostitute, explaining to the men, "Esas merecen más respeto que todas las otras; cobran por soportar la peste y la brutalidad" (sc. 323; similar quotation in Rojas González 129). As long as Angustias remains in her liminal role as *coronela*, she is able to take on conventionally masculine characteristics while also working to undermine the social structures that perpetuate the dominance of men and abnegation of women.

Her decision to add a new component to this identity—that of literacy— finally upsets the balance. Despite her lifelong aversion to heterosexual relationships, Angustias quickly falls in love with Manuel de la Reguera, the effeminate, white, urban, bourgeois mama's boy she hires to teach her to read and write. From the time she allows him to guide her hand to help her trace out the correct shapes of the letters, Angustias is smitten with her "Manolito." In the screenplay, Angustias shows up to her very next session dressed in feminine attire, having decorated the barracks with flowers in order to please Manuel (sc. 363-372). In the novel, it is not until Angustias writes her first unassisted word ("Manolo") that she bathes, puts ribbons in her hair, and uses makeup and perfume before attending her lesson (172). In either case, this sudden and

unprecedented turn, so closely intertwined with the process of achieving literacy, begs further attention.[6] Perhaps Angustias is attracted to Manuel precisely
because he is her opposite in terms of color and gender attributes or because he
shows no interest in her sexually[7]; perhaps what she is really in love with is the
power of literacy itself; perhaps by submitting to a bourgeois and by purchasing
an education she upsets the Revolutionary underpinnings of her hybrid identity.
At any rate, when Angustias allows Manuel to guide the writing instrument in
her hand, she cedes many of the "masculine" traits that she has wielded hand-
ily ever since taking up her father's knife. Upon the death of Manuel's mother,
Angustias suggests that as his wife she could take care of him, and when a hor-
rified Manuel responds that society would consider such a union "una cruza
absurda" (Rojas González 176, Landeta sc 387), Angustias is devastated.

It is here that Rojas González and Landeta begin to diverge. In the film version, Angustias quickly snaps out of her lovesickness when Güitlacoche is killed.
She instantly returns to her role of *coronela*, indefinitely prolonging the relative
freedom of her liminality at the cost of abandoning the notion of becoming a wife
or mother. Her liminal status permits her to take on many "masculine" qualities,
to avoid sexual objectification, and to subvert machismo, but it cannot absorb
the roles of student and wife, rooted as they are in society. Within the film, then,
there is a limit to the degree of gender hybridity available to Angustias, but in the
end she is pleased with the in-between status in which she has chosen to make her
home. As Elissa Rashkin points out in her study of Mexican women filmmakers,
Angustias's triumph in the film softens the novel's harsh critique of the postrevo-
lutionary establishment's betrayal of *los de abajo* (52-53). Implicitly, however,
Angustias's liminal status as *coronela* will end with the Revolution and the return
to an "indicative" framework (how things really are). By suspending Angustias
and the nation in a perpetual "subjunctive" mood capable of perceiving what
might be, Landeta's film underscores the potential for social change inherent in
both Angustias's unconventionality and the Revolutionary project.[8]

In the novel and the screenplay, by way of contrast, Angustias takes a final
"masculine" action, kidnapping Manuel and taking him home to her village
to be her husband. But once she returns to the domestic sphere, Angustias
abandons her liminal identity and falls back into her expected feminine role.
Manuel, too, is transformed, now a domineering macho.[9] Soon becoming pregnant, Angustias even agrees to move to the capital and officially surrender to
the new government so that they can draw a stipend, which Manuel squanders
while she toils away in a sad little tenement house. The novel ends with Manuel
bragging to a drinking buddy that this is only "la casa chica [. . .] sin mis cui-
dados y huérfana de mi apoyo, quién sabe qué sería de ella," while an oblivious
Angustias tends to the housework (226-28). Although her temporary liminality
allowed her to act transgressively, Rojas González's Angustias has now been
brought firmly into line with the social expectations for her as a woman.[10] In
the final lines, as Manuel and the narrator flaunt their ability to speak about
Angustias, the voice that had powerfully barked orders through much of the
text has now lost all power to communicate, reduced to motherly songs that
intertwine in the house with the warbling of a caged blackbird (228).

Elizabeth Salas, in her study *Soldaderas in the Mexican Military*, reads the novel's ending as the author's prescription for what 1940s psychologists viewed as a social ill: the absence of men from the home as they fought in the Revolution afforded an unprecedented amount of power to women within the family structure, just as Angustias's power as a military leader is seen in the novel as unnatural and unhealthy (87). In Salas's reading, it follows that "the best cure for her sick personality is to love, marry, and serve a man. In submitting to the teacher, she discovers her true identity as wife and mother" (87). Susan Dever echoes Salas in asserting that mainstream post-Revolutionary Mexican cinematic representations of female agency—and Rojas González's novel—aim to put women back in their place "and thus reconstruct the broken national family. 'Feminizing' the woman who had been excessively 'masculinized' by her participation in the war or by her dominion at home in the absence of a man was the task of mainstream melodrama" (84-86). Dever points to Landeta's film adaptation as a notable exception to this rule.

The resolution of Landeta's currently unpublished screenplay diverges from the novel and even more firmly rejects mainstream representations of women by explicitly overturning them. In the screenplay, Angustias overhears her husband's drunken conversation and becomes aware of his perception of her. Downing a big swig from his bottle, she confronts him in front of his friend and announces she has decided to "volver a ser la coronela Angustias Farrera" (sc. 462). Grabbing her baby boy in one arm and a gun in the other, she leaves Manuel in order to reunite with her fellow revolutionaries, and the final words of the text are her own: "Razón tenía Doña Crescencia: jallé pero por camino torcido . . ." (sc. 464). It is only in the screenplay, then, that Angustias finds her own way by combining her roles as literate mother and revolutionary leader. This return to a liminal position is not imposed on her as it was when she fled her village after killing the rapist Laureano. This time, it is a deliberate choice that Angustias explicitly identifies as her rightful place in life. Just as this return to the subjunctive state of liminality is "tempered" by her previous experiences, it seems clear that, with the end of the Revolution, Angustias and her compatriots will return to the "indicative" mood with an altered perspective on their society.

To my knowledge, existing interviews and studies do not address the significant changes Landeta made when completing the film version of her screenplay. Length may have been a factor; the film version omits the last several pages of a sixty-three-page screenplay. Whatever the reason, the fact remains that only the screenplay ends with an Angustias who is able to return to her "masculine" and feminist revolutionary activities, while still maintaining her role as mother and her ability to read and write. It does not seem coincidental that Angustias is allowed this willful return to liminality only in the screenplay, itself an interstitial genre that falls outside the conventions for more fixed forms like novel and film. Landeta's screenplay, a nearly invisible threshold between the acclaimed novel and landmark film, is the only space in which Angustias can reconcile the traditionally masculine and traditionally feminine aspects of her identity.

Like her protagonist, Landeta embraced the challenge to negotiate ingrained social expectations by creating an unconventional role for herself in the male-dominated Mexican film industry. As Rashkin observes, "Like Angustias, Landeta adopted masculine dress to carry out her work and adapted to pre-existing models (of filmmaking rather than revolution) while retaining a strong sense of self and of her identity as a woman. She was politically active [. . .] she relied on a network of male allies [. . .] without playing the conventional roles of wife and mother" (although she did get married and had a child who died in early infancy) (54-55). Indeed, Landeta herself saw parallels between her own path and that of Angustias. When asked in 1995 by interviewer Isabel Arredondo about her decision to change the novel's ending in her film, Landeta explained:

> Rojas González me dijo que lo que pasaba en su novela, antropológicamente, era lo lógico: la mujer perdía su carácter cuando se enamoraba. Pero a mí me parecía que La negra no iba a dejar de existir porque se hubiera enamorado. Yo nunca creí que una mujer decente pudiera perder su temple, su ideología, por haberse enamorado. [. . .] Yo tenía mucho carácter y, a pesar de haberme enamorado, pude hacer toda una revolución para lanzarme a dirigir películas. (201)

Nor did the historical Angustias simply conform to a preset masculine or feminine gender role. In an interview with Carmen Huaco-Nuzum in the late 1980s, Landeta described a 1948 meeting that Rojas González arranged for her with the black female revolutionary colonel who inspired his novel:

> There she was, smoking a cigar. She appeared older than her sixty years and lived alone in the mountains of Guerrero in a little hut. She had a sharp tongue, malhablada y llena de picardías (profane and mischievous wit), as she remembered the revolution and her role in it. Angustias married, had a son (Manuelito, a mestizo who became a teacher) and lived in Mexico City until the end of the revolution, after which time she returned to her mountain village in the state of Guerrero. (Huaco-Nuzum 92)

The participation of Landeta, the historical Angustias, and her fictional counterparts in their respective liminal revolutions may have been finite, but their activities enacted a lasting change in perspective, an awareness of potentiality. Likewise, although Landeta's screenplay was hidden away in an archive for decades, it has always been an influential layer in the palimpsest of history, novel, and film.

NOTES

[1] I want to express my gratitude to Marcela Fernández Violante and the Mexican Cineteca Nacional for making Matilde Landeta's unpublished screenplay available for study and translation.

[2] This phrase is used in the screenplay version. Near the end, the *hechicera*, Doña Crescencia, remarks that Angustias took a crooked path to find her proper place as wife and mother (sc. 440). In the final words of the screenplay, Angustias ironically echoes her mother figure by reiterating the phrase—"jallé, pero por camino torcido"—referring to her decision to abandon her domineering husband (sc. 464).

[3] Although her approach is psychoanalytic, Carmen Huaco-Nuzum makes a similar observation that, in the film, "Angustias oscillates between female and male identification positions, but finds within the revolution a place of sanctuary that signifies her escape from assigned gender" (102).

⁴ The novel emphasizes that the masculine attire actually exaggerates Angustias's femininity: "el varonil traje de charro le daba un aspecto curioso: por más que quería ser hombruno, la línea relajada de las carnes ubérrimas, aprisionadas en la estrechez propia del atavío, realzaban la feminidad, desbordándose en curvas desproporcionadas" (110-11).

⁵ At the end of this ritualistic scene (118), Angustias reiterates words spoken by her adoptive mother following the cleansing performed on Angustias earlier in the novel. The beating Angustias has just performed is an inversion of the former purification ritual, which was meant to cast out the evil spirits causing Angustias to rebel against norms for feminine behavior.

⁶ Landeta explained in an interview that what most caught her attention about the novel was the fact that Angustias was the only one of her revolutionary peers who wanted to learn to read. In 1940, Landeta recalled, the government had initiated a nationwide literacy campaign, calling on every literate citizen to teach another how to read (Arredondo 199).

⁷ Huaco-Nuzum surmises, "Angustias' attraction to Manolo is that he poses no threat to her. He represents difference, class and race" (101).

⁸ Although her point is quite different, Raquel Chang-Rodríguez, in her study of the novel, also notes the parallel trajectories of Angustias and the Revolution: "Tanto Angustias como los revolucionarios se lanzan a una lucha que temporalmente los hace dueños de su destino. Pero es un tiempo medido, una posesión efímera, matizada por el aparecer y reaparecer de señales que cambiarán el curso de la Revolución y de Angustias" (102).

⁹ To be precise, in the novel, this inversion takes place immediately after Manuel submits to Angustias's demand for sex, which in wording and location parallels Laureano's fatal attempt to rape Angustias (200).

¹⁰ See Janet J. Hampton's feminist critique of the novel. Interestingly enough, Rojas González himself ostensibly foregrounds feminist issues by using Sor Juana's words as the epigraph to his novel: "Siempre tan necios andáis, / que con desigual nivel / a una culpáis por cruel / y a otra por fácil culpáis."

WORKS CITED

Arredondo, Isabel and Matilde Landeta. "Entrevista a Matilde Landeta Ciudad de México, 10 de julio de 1995." *Mexican Studies / Estudios Mexicanos* 18.1 (2002): 194-204.

Chang-Rodríguez, Raquel. "Trayectoria y símbolo de una revolucionaria: *La Negra Angustias* de Francisco Rojas González." *Revista de Crítica Literaria Latinoamericana* 7.13 (1981): 99-104.

Dever, Susan. *Celluloid Nationalism and Other Melodramas.* Albany, NY: SUNY Press, 2003.

Hampton, Janet J. "*La Negra Angustias*: Flawed Hero or Tragic Victim?: A Feminist Reading." *Afro-Hispanic Review* 10.3 (1991): 27-32.

Huaco-Nuzum, Carmen. "Mestiza Subjectivity: Representation and Spectatorship in Mexican and Hollywood Films." Diss. U California Santa Cruz, 1993.

La negra Angustias. Screenplay by Matilde Landeta. Dir. Matilde Landeta. TACMA, 1949.

Rashkin, Elissa. *Women Filmmakers in Mexico: The Country of Which We Dream.* Austin: U of Texas P, 2001.

Rojas González, Francisco. *La negra Angustias.* Second ed. Mexico City: EDIAPSA, 1948.

Salas, Elizabeth. *Soldaderas in the Mexican Military: Myth and History.* Austin: U of Texas P, 1990.

Turner, Victor Whitter. "Social Dramas and Stories About Them." *Critical Inquiry* 7.1 (1980): 141-68.

van Gennep, Arnold. *Rites of Passage.* Chicago: U of Chicago P, 1960.

Santa Teresa de Cabora (and Her Villainous Sister Jovita)
A SHAPE-SHIFTING ICON OF MEXICO'S NORTHWEST BORDERLANDS*

Robert McKee Irwin
UNIVERSITY OF CALIFORNIA, DAVIS[1]

Teresa Urrea is an iconic figure of the U.S.-Mexican borderlands, well remembered—albeit in distinct ways—on both sides of the border. A *curandera* popularly known as "la Santa de Cabora," her name is often associated with the 1892 rebellion in Tomóchic, Chihuahua, an important precursor to the Mexican Revolution of 1910. Her alleged role in borderland uprisings, most particularly a Mayo Indian revolt in the town of Navojoa, Sonora, also in 1892, led to her deportation that same year to Arizona, where she began collaborating with fellow exile and revolutionary militant Lauro Aguirre. Teresa Urrea's "astonishing story" has been reconstructed with la Santa cast as a warrior (the Mexican Jeanne D'Arc), a "living saint," an "Indian girl," and a sideshow attraction, depending on the context of her deployment: the Mexican borderlands, Mexican national culture, the U.S. (Anglophone) Wild West, the Chicano Southwest, etc. This dynamic trajectory suggests that her borderland context expands the range of cultural uses of the Latin American rebel outlaw beyond those posited by Juan Pablo Dabove in *Nightmares of the Lettered City*, allowing her even to cross into the realm of the borderland bandit lore made popular by late nineteenth-century dime novels, as I will show in my reading of the little known *Santa Teresa: A Tale of the Yaquii Rebellion*, a novel by William Thomas Whitlock published in 1900.[2]

Teresa Urrea, also popularly referred to as la Santa de Cabora

THE LIFE OF LA SANTA DE CABORA

Before I flesh out my arguments, let me present a biographical sketch of Teresa Urrea.[3] Teresa was born in 1873 in Ocorini, Sinaloa, the illegitimate daughter of the wealthy *hacendado* Tomás Urrea and a young

---

*Additional visual material for this article may be seen at http://noblebandits.asu.edu/Topics/GoodBandits2009.html

Tehueco Indian woman, Cayetana Chávez, an employee on his ranch. She was raised by her mother and an aunt on the ranch until Tomás was forced for political reasons to move to his San Antonio de Cabora ranch in Sonora in 1880. In 1888, the audacious young Teresa convinced her father to invite her to move into his house and allow her to use his last name. A year later, she suffered a cataleptic attack that left her unconscious for thirteen days and then sent her into a trance for several months. When she emerged from her trance, she began to heal the sick and handicapped. Her miraculous powers began to attract attention, first locally, and then nationally and even internationally. Local admirers—and the press— dubbed her "la Santa de Cabora." Soon her father's ranch became a major destination for pilgrims, some of whom accepted her as a Catholic miracle worker, while others believed that her Catholic façade masked the application of indigenous traditions, and still others understood her powers through the fashionable concept of spiritism.[4] Young Teresa's abilities extended beyond curing; she was also a charismatic speaker who openly criticized both the Mexican government and the Catholic Church for their mistreatment of the poor and disenfranchised.

One of the most prominent "living saints" of the late nineteenth-century Mexican borderlands, Teresa, whose activities turned into a major media spectacle in the early 1890s, provoked concern among Mexican authorities. In 1892 a band of Mayo Indians staged an armed insurrection in the town of Navojoa, Sonora, rallying to the war cry "Viva la Santa de Cabora." Meanwhile, a group of citizens from the town of Tomóchic, Chihuahua, who were engaged in a series of disputes with both government and church authorities, had traveled to Cabora to meet Santa Teresa, whose likeness they had displayed in their town church. Federal troops were called in, but were embarrassed in a series of skirmishes with the *tomoches*, as they were called.[5] At this time, mid-1892, Teresa and her father were arrested and soon afterwards deported to Nogales, Arizona. Meanwhile federal troops laid siege to the town of Tomóchic, basically leveling it and annihilating its residents. Dramatized in a novel by the federal soldier Heriberto Frías, the massacred townsfolk became heroes, and the battle would later go down in history as a major precursor to the Mexican Revolution.[6] Although la Santa de Cabora had already been exiled at the time of the armed conflict, the Tomóchic story would forever be associated with the name of Teresa Urrea, who was portrayed as a figure of inspiration to the insurgents in Frías's novel.

During her exile, Urrea became increasingly involved in the propagandistic activities against the Porfirio Díaz regime in Mexico of family friend Lauro Aguirre, with several articles under her name eventually being published in his newspaper in El Paso, Texas. While Teresa was living in El Paso en 1896, a group of Yaqui rebels attacked the customs house in Nogales, Sonora. Among the articles found on the bodies of rebels killed on the scene were documents implicating Teresa Urrea. Mexican authorities attempted to have her extradited for prosecution, but U.S. authorities refused to cooperate.

Following this incident, the Urreas left Texas, distancing themselves from Aguirre and his politics. All the while she continued curing the many pilgrims who sought her attentions. In 1900, she married a Mexican miner who attempted to convince her to return to Mexico and subsequently threatened to kill her; she would later claim that he was a spy sent by the Mexican government to assassinate her. He was institutionalized and they were divorced several years later. Around the time of his arrest, Teresa Urrea visited San Francisco, where she was hired to conduct a national tour, performing her miraculous cures all over the United States. During her travels to places such as New York City, she gave birth to two daughters, the father being a teenage friend of the family who was accompanying her as a translator (they never married). Eventually she returned to Arizona, where she died in 1906.

THE MEMORY OF LA SANTA CABORA

One of the arguments I make about the borderland icons that I study in my book *Bandits, Captives, Heroines and Saints: Cultural Icons of Mexico's Northwest Borderlands*, is that these legendary figures take shape largely outside of lettered culture, and therefore are slow to enter any kind of "official" historiography. This makes them particularly malleable figures, and so borderland icons such as la Santa de Cabora have been reshaped to suit the diverse needs and desires of the many contexts in which they have traveled (xvii-xxiii).

Teresa Urrea, for example, took on initial meanings in the press of the borderlands, which saw her as something of an embarrassment and mostly represented her as a fraud, probably in response to the Mexico City press's mocking representations of her and what it portrayed as the superstitious naïveté of her overzealous followers, affirming urban Mexico's prejudices of the borderlands as a place of ignorance and fanaticism. The Anglophone press in the United States, meanwhile, took her up as pure entertainment, reflecting prejudices not about the borderlands, but about Mexico in general. The journal that took her most seriously in the early years was the Mexico City-based *La Ilustración Espírita*, for which Lauro Aguirre was correspondent.

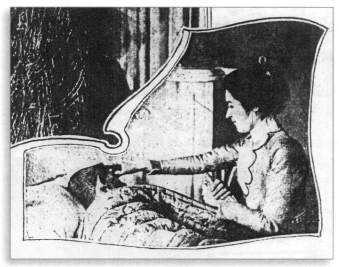

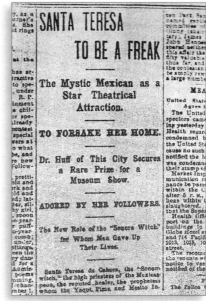

Above: La Santa de Cabora in San Francisco. *Right:* Newspapers in the United States presented Teresa as a form of entertainment.

A mocking representation of Teresa Urrea by José Guadalupe Posada

When in 1892 she became a symbol or possible instigator of insurgence in the eyes of Porfirio Díaz's government, the local press played down the politics, adopting the ironic tone that Mexico City had been using with her. In Mexico City her exile was not even covered by major newspapers. U.S. newspapers likewise did not portray her as a political dissident but as a charismatic quasi-religious figure who had become dangerous for her tendency to rile up superstitious Indians who might follow through on their zealotry in irrational and unpredictable ways. Once exiled, Urrea was largely forgotten by the Mexican press even as she continued to garner headlines, mostly as a "sensational crazy saint" in the U.S. press. The place in which she took on the most political relevance was in the journalism of Lauro Aguirre, who published, with Teresa herself listed as coauthor, a booklet titled "¡Tomóchic! ¡Redención!" in El Paso in 1896, which made Teresa out to be a central figure behind the Tomóchic uprising.

Later representations included those that portrayed her with great affection, such as her 1978 biography by William Curry Holden, who infantilizes her (its title is *Teresita*) and voids her image of any political meaning, and others that made her a symbol of peasant resistance to the tyranny of Porfirio Díaz, as occurred with "La Santa de Cabora y la insurrección de Tomóchic en 1892," published serially in Los Angeles and San Antonio in the Spanish language daily *La Opinión/La Prensa* in 1937 (Valadés). Following the revolution, she would enter Mexican national historiography as a Joan of Arc-like figure (Gill), an image that would be revived in Chihuahua in 1992 at the centennial of the Tomóchic rebellion.[7] In the United States, early scholars of Chicano studies embellished her biography with stories of involvement in railroad strikes and indigenous-inspired use of hallucinogenic mushrooms in her healing activities, fashioning her into what one major reference source called "a symbol of resistance to oppression for contemporary Chicanos" (Mirandé and Enríquez 86).[8] Meanwhile, Arizona newspapers periodically hauled her out in stories that conjured her up as another eccentricity of the Old West. Two recent high-profile novels reshaped her yet again, including the well researched *La insólita historia de la Santa de Cabora*, by Brianda Domecq, which emphasizes the extraordinary nature of her accomplishments in the public sphere as an illegitimate mixed-race girl born to an uneducated and impoverished single mother, with special weight on her role as a woman. More recently a relative, Luis Urrea, recounted the story of her early years in *The Hummingbird's Daughter*, and plans to flesh out some of the less well-known periods of her life in the United States in a sequel that will incorporate Urrea family lore.

I have presented these multiple and conflicting images of Teresa Urrea to demonstrate the degree to which she has been if not exactly a palimpsest, definitely a malleable figure that has served conflicting political needs for diverse authors on both sides of the border. The reason for this is that there is no authoritative representation of her from her lifetime. Newspaper stories are full of not just mockery, but errors. Some called her a "Yaqui girl"; others claimed she eloped with a cowboy, or that she once escaped from a Mexican firing squad by willing the earth at the last second to swallow up her would-be executioners.[9] In other words, it is difficult to assign the press much more credibility with regard to its ability to represent the "truth" of Urrea's story than one might to oral legend. In fact the most widely cited early source on Teresa Urrea is not of a textual genre generally associated with mimesis, but the "fictitious" account of the Tomóchic saga as represented in Heriberto Frías's 1893 novel.

By the time she entered historiography, it was really too late for her life to avoid politicized reshaping. If she was made into a protorevolutionary heroine in many texts, including those that represent a perspective of Mexican national history, or one of the regional history of Chihuahua, a state that she never visited, in her home state of Sonora, historiography has treated her mostly with disdain.[10] Just as the official newspaper of the state, *La Constitución*, for the most part kept her out of its news reports, including those on Tomóchic and other incidents of political importance in which she was implicated, major historians have tended to write her out of local history. While some do introduce hers as a "story determined by the hysteria of an abnormal woman" (Sobarzo 64), some important works including two major editions of a grade-school textbook leave her out entirely. The six-volume *Historia general de Sonora*, published in the 1980s, mentions her name only once (Figueroa Valenzuela 160). Teresa Urrea does not become the folk hero one might expect her to be for Sonoran historiographers, who remain perhaps discomfited by her reputation as a spriritist, *curandera*, or even fraud for which she had so often been ridiculed. *Mestiza* Santa Teresa, friend to *indios salvajes* and emblem of religious fanaticism and superstition that recalls a barbarous indigenous past, is best left out of official history.

BORDER BANDITRY: WHITLOCK'S *SANTA TERESA*

anta Teresa de Cabora was called a faith healer, a revolutionary insurgent, a visionary, a nurse, an actress, a freak, a fraud, and a beauty queen—but never a bandit. Yet as a popular celebrity viewed with suspicion among Anglo Americans and Mexico City elites, but adored by Mexican subalterns on both sides of the border, she shared many characteristics with other iconic borderland figures such as Joaquín Murrieta, Pancho Villa, or Jesús Malverde. Interestingly, another study currently being carried out by Desirée Martín, does not cast la Santa de Cabora as a bandida, but instead probes the images of Malverde and Villa, along with Teresa Urrea, as "border saints."

In any case, writing from New York, where distorted reports of Urrea's activities undoubtedly piqued the imagination of readers of dime novels such as Joseph Badger's popular "Joaquin" series of the 1880s (*Joaquin, the Terrible*; *Joaquin, the Saddle King*; *The Pirate of the Placers; or, Joaquin's Death Hunt*) and other adventure tales of the Wild West, William Thomas Whitlock published the novel *Santa Teresa: A Tale of the Yaquii Rebellion* in 1900. The novel complicates the already chaotic landscape of the still untamed West, with its competing Anglo American, Mexican, indigenous (in this case, Papago, Yaqui, and Apache), and independent bandit interests now intersected by women with the capacity to seduce and charm and make possible otherwise unlikely alliances.

In the novel Teresa Urrea is not a bandit. An old "teamster, miner, ranchero, trapper and Indian fighter" Arizonan named Neely McBride narrates: "You know them Papago and Yaquii Injuns believe that some day one o' their old chiefs is to come back from down in Mexico and make 'em rulers o' this land, jest like they were 'fore white man came here . . . Well, they're whisperin' round now that he's comin', only that it's in a woman's form" (10). The novel's protagonist, John Deware, a New York stockbroker sent to Arizona by his parents to cure a chronic cough, soon meets Santa Teresa and falls in love with her at first sight. However, Deware soon admits, "If there were no church, no poor people to be cured of diseases, I might be the happiest man in the world" (50), but Teresa is not willing to give up her calling for mortal love.

However, a more important complication takes the form of Teresa Urrea's sister, Jovita. Jovita, introduced at the very beginning of the novel, had been married off as a teenager to "old man Carrios," apparently against her will. Familial injustice and not racism or xenophobia is the determining force of the beautiful Jovita's life. According to Neely McBride, "Less'n a year after [Jovita was married to Carrios] . . . she killed him with a knife. They couldn't prove it on her, but everybody knowed she done it. She never denied it herself" (9). Jovita promptly became a bandit, leading "a band o' the most lowdown people ye ever saw," taking lovers among them, and sometimes seducing her enemies, including police authorities, into alliances with her.

The complication for John Deware is that Jovita falls in love with him, declaring, "Before I hated all Americans, and now I love one of them. We were made for each other" (29). When Jovita discovers that he is pursuing her sister, Teresa, at the Bosque ranch, she writes a letter to Teresa that the nosy Señora Estrella opens, reading: "It might be best for you to leave the Bosque ranch at once. Do not see *him* again. *I love that man* . . . Not even you shall win him from me" (67). Teresa then disappears, and soon after Jovita appears. Deware naïvely asks her to take him to Santa Teresa, but she refuses, proclaiming to him, "You must be mine" (77). When he rejects her, she tries to stab him, but only manages to injure his manservant.

Jovita then becomes determined to bring down her sister. She shows up at a mass gathering of Teresa's followers, announcing to them: "You are dupes, fools. You believe this woman to be a saint? *She is my sister.* Can one of my race have supernatural powers except for evil?" (90). The crowd then turns on Teresa, who somehow manages to escape with her father. Meanwhile, Jovita seduces a marshal, giving her band free reign to wreak havoc in the region. Someone (the narrator attributes this to either Jovita or Teresa's father) has incited the Papagos and Yaquis against the Mexican government. However, Teresa herself has completely disappeared from sight, and in fact is rumored to be dead.

Deware eventually tracks down Teresa's father, who confirms that she has died, and presents Deware with a crucifix as a memento. Soon after this, Deware decides to return to the tranquility of New York: "But still another pang was to be endured before we could leave that Spanish-tainted section of our country"—another meeting with Jovita. By now, she had taken up with a new lover, the Mexican American Alonso Bosque: "There was nothing to do, however, but to ride on and leave the enchantress with her latest victim" (168). The novel closes with an epilogue, a news story on a Yaqui rebellion in Mexico, apparently inspired by "a mysterious woman" named Santa Teresa (169), implying then that Teresa may have survived after all.

The bandida trope of course lends itself marvelously to the sketchy biography of Teresa Urrea. What is interesting is not so much whether she herself is cast as a bandit, but rather the dual images of power-wielding women that her image evokes in the imagination of Whitlock. Teresa is a powerful charismatic figure, capable of essentially ruling the life of John Deware during the entire course of his stay in the West, and more importantly able to incite besieged indigenous peoples to defend their territories. She possesses miraculous healing powers, an ability to escape from near death situations at will—and even, apparently, rise from the dead in a true messianic fashion. Jovita gets almost everything she wants (everything except the love of John Deware), using her beauty and charm to seduce men, engaging in banditry and violence with impunity, and even challenging the divine powers of her saintly sister. No male characters in the novel are as powerful or influential as the two larger-than-life Mexican sisters. It would seem, in fact, that the entire novel is an adventure fantasy in which the male protagonist, with whom the reader is presumably meant to identify, is dominated by women, whether a *devoradora de hombres* like Jovita, or a woman so purely good as to be unreachable.

Thus, unlike many dime novels that play out male fantasies of adventure, romance, and conquest in the Old West, *Santa Teresa* allows male readers back in the urban East, where the book was marketed,[11] to fantasize about adventures in the Wild West not by imagining themselves as victors in heroic battles with savage enemies, but in the more masochistic role of the protagonist, a man who is successful neither in wooing his love (Santa Teresa) nor in subduing her indomitable sister. As the publicity for the book calls it "a romantic tale" and compares it to Cooper's romantic classic, *The Last of the Mohicans*, it is certainly conceivable that unlike the case of many dime novels (such as Badger's Joaquin series), this book's publishers targeted both male and female readers, the latter of whom would likely appreciate the strength of the female characters. Sickly, Deware returns empty handed to New York while the novel's two female leads ride off into the sunset, with new boy toy in tow (Jovita) or heading toward Mexico to lead a rebel insurgency (Teresa).

LATIN AMERICAN BANDIT NOVELS

I want to close by juxtaposing my reading of this borderland novel (and I might have constructed similar arguments for other narrative constructions of border banditry, whether in novels, *corridos*, historiography, or popular legends) with the paradigms of banditry in Latin American literature as studied in Juan Pablo Dabove's *Nightmares of the Lettered City*, an important critical reading of the central role of banditry in Latin American literature in the nineteenth and early twentieth centuries. I have argued a bit with Dabove about the importance of banditry not only as a national trope, but also as a borderland trope, and maintain that the reading of Latin American banditry is incomplete without taking into account the roles Latin American bandits assume outside of their national spaces, most especially in the U.S. Southwest (review of *Nightmares*).

Summarizing (and simplifying a bit), Dabove would argue that bandits serve in different ways to affirm or destabilize national cultures, functioning as 1) outside threats (threats of rural, illiterate classes) to national modernizing projects whose suppression is paramount to national consolidation; 2) critiques of national modernizing projects (tropes representing injustice, resistance); or 3) the suppressed (rural, illiterate) "origin" of national culture. Where I take issue with Dabove is in his insistence in confining his study to literary representations contextualized in narrowly defined national terms. Nonetheless, when in his introduction he refers to nonliterary representations of Latin American banditry through *corridos* and various forms of "popular" literature, contrasting these "popular appropriations of the bandit figure" (9) with deployments of the bandit trope within *la ciudad letrada* (the lettered city), the two examples on which he focuses at greatest length are Jesús Malverde and Joaquín Murieta [*sic*] (9-12), both bandits who operate not within a closed national space, but within the dynamic and unstable space of the U.S.-Mexican borderlands. As such, their trajectories are not limited to any one national tradition—Murrieta, for example, protagonizes well-known works produced and disseminated in the United States, Mexico, and Chile.[12]

Borderland bandits (or similar figures) such as Jovita (or Santa Teresa) are more complex than—or at least different from—the national heroes or antiheroes analyzed by Dabove (e.g., Juan Moreira, El Zarco, or Antônio Conselheiro) because they must be read from the borderlands, i.e. from dynamic transnational contexts. Teresa Urrea, for example, well known as a protagonist of Mexican novels (Frías's *Tomóchic* and Domecq's *La insólita historia/The Astonishing Story*) is equally prominent as a protagonist of U.S. novels (Urrea's *The Hummingbird's Daughter* and Whitlock's *Santa Teresa*) and intertextualities are inevitable. There is no doubt, for example, that both Domecq and Urrea read and drew from Frías. While Whitlock likely was unfamiliar with Frías's Spanish-language text, his Teresa shares numerous characteristics with that of Frías as both protagonists are undoubtedly based on the sensationalist newspaper coverage she generated in the 1890s. While their geographical locations differ, both Teresas get mixed up in frontier violence (Jovita's banditry and Tomóchic's insurgency, respectively) while retaining a saintly innocence. Both are mysterious figures, admired but never really understood by the battered male protagonists (a Mexican soldier engaged in the siege of the town of Tomóchic in the case of Frías's text). In a way, each Teresa (along with Jovita) might be thought to represent a frontier exoticism that challenges the national cultures represented in the male protagonists, each of whom hails from his nation's largest city and represents a modern, urban sensibility that clashes with frontier culture.

Each of the two more recent novels, both of which focus on Teresa's life from her birth in 1873 to her withdrawal from politics in 1896,[13] technically belongs to a particular nationally defined literature (Urrea's is a novel of U.S. literature; Domecq's is Mexican), yet any allegories produced in either are difficult to articulate in terms that are merely national. Unlike frontier spaces of Dabove's national novels: the Brazilian *sertões*, the Argentine *pampa*, the Venezuelan *llano*, all of which are circumscribed in national terms, Teresa Urrea's frontier is the borderlands, and she never ceases to produce meaning (albeit often conflicting meanings) pertinent to both national contexts. Just as Domecq's Mexico cannot be understood without taking into account the U.S. borderlands as a space of militancy against the Díaz regime, Whitlock's U.S. Southwest is defined in part by the Mexicans and Mexican Americans—including exotic saints and bandits—who live there. The borderlands, again, are a space that destabilizes notions of national unity or integration, and Teresa Urrea as a woman of and from the borderlands, always a liminal figure, whether curing the Mayo infirm and enchanting spiritists in Sonora or hosting press conferences in Tucson or San Francisco, never ceases to destabilize notions of unified U.S. or Mexican national identity.

Regarding Whitlock's novel, there is clearly a failed national romance in the turbulent love triangle of Deware, Jovita, and Teresa that implies, five decades after the acquisition of California, Arizona, and the rest of the Southwest, a failure to integrate Mexican Americans into U.S. culture—despite their powerful presence in the Southwest. However, while Jovita and Teresa's powers seem to make them both a destabilizing force in the Southwest, they remain distant from the center of U.S. culture in New York, where they are little more than fanciful figures of outlandish newspaper headlines—i.e., national culture is not threatened as long as it is defined around its financial and cultural center of the northeast, and does not seek to integrate the otherness of the Southwest. Meanwhile, Teresa's influence on and alliances with recalcitrant borderland indigenous groups, which might initially seem to make her a threat to U.S. Indian removal policy, ultimately has ramifications only in Mexico, where national stability becomes uncertain in the novel's epilogue. Once again, the threat is not to the nation's core; instead, the Mexico City core of Mexican national culture remains stable only by relegating the tumultuous borderlands, with their roving *bandidas* and Yaqui rebellions, to the periphery of the national imaginary.

Nonetheless, while Mexicans as a group are repeatedly denigrated in Whitlock's novel as foul smelling, excessively passionate, and ultimately incapable of self-rule, the real destabilizing force to either national culture would appear to be the Indians, who remain unassimilated to if not in open rebellion against national cultures. However, they seem to lack the wisdom to save themselves from extinction, as illustrated in the case of Cholla, Neely McBride's Indian servant who in one scene defends Deware from an attack by an English lover of Jovita, killing the assailant. Cholla is tried and sentenced to death since the law dictates that punishment for any Indian who kills a white man, regardless of the circumstances. It is, however, a symbolic sentence since the authorities ultimately believe that Cholla's actions were justified, and they have no intention of enforcing the sentence. However, it seems that Indians are incapable of dishonesty: "his tribe would never forgive him should he fail to keep his word on an occasion like this" (163-64), so he shows up of his own will on the appropriate date, forcing the authorities to hang him. These Indians, who do not think like New Yorkers or even like white southwesterners (undoubtedly their thinking is equally at odds with that of Mexico's urban center) once again are borderland figures who are not imagined in such a way as to fit them neatly into national narratives. Their prominence in the borderlands again serves to undermine national projects, and their adherence to Teresa Urrea in Whitlock—or in Domecq and Urrea—once again demonstrates how border icons—like Urrea, or Joaquín Murrieta, to name another—tend to thwart any allegorical readings defined in neatly national terms.

At the end of the novel, both Jovita and Teresa apparently survive, and future national implications of their survival are uncertain—Teresa leads a borderland war against Mexico; Jovita continues to wreak havoc with impunity in the U.S. borderlands. What is certain is that the multicultural West, while never a threat to national unity for the United States, remains in 1900 a scenario for the explorations of fantastic scenarios of troubling international and interracial alliances—and as such remains exotic and unassimilated into the national mainstream.

Borderland bandidas and bandidos are difficult to tie down; they generate multiple, often contradictory meanings that point to the instability of borders as cultural barriers, and the borderlands as a contact zone, a space of never-ending intercultural dialogue. For this reason Santa Teresa de Urrea is as alive now in the novels of Luis Urrea and Brianda Domecq or the works of borderland performance artist Elena Díaz Björkquist as she was during her lifetime in Heriberto Frías's *Tomóchic*, Lauro Aguirre's "¡Tomóchic! ¡Redención!", or William Thomas Whitlock's *Santa Teresa: A Tale of the Yaquii Rebellion*.

NOTES

[1] The research for this paper was made possible by a Title VI Library Travel Grant from the University of Arizona's Center for Latin American Studies.

[2] The most complete biographical study on Teresa Urrea's life in Mexico from her birth in 1873 until her deportation in 1892 and her early years in exile in Arizona and Texas, culminating in the 1896 raid on the Nogales, Sonora customs house, in which Teresa was implicated, is Domecq's "Teresa Urrea." I piece together the trajectory of her public persona during those years as well as during her exile in the United States (where she died in 1906) in *Bandits* (195-261). The reference to Teresa's "astonishing story" is a nod to the importance of Brianda Domecq's 1990 novel, *La insólita historia de la Santa de Cabora*, translated to English as *The Astonishing Story of the Saint of Cabora*. Urrea was first referred to as the Mexican Joan of Arc in Aguirre and Urrea; on her collaborations with Aguirre, see my *Bandits* (224-32). On the concept of "living saints" in the late nineteenth-century Mexican northwestern borderlands, see Domecq, "Teresa Urrea" (20-21), Aguirre and Urrea (120).

[3] It should be noted that any "biography" of Teresa Urrea is inseparable from her legend. This sketch (based principally on Domecq, "Teresa Urrea" and summarized from my *Bandits* 195-249) does not pretend to separate one from the other.

[4] The most complete early biographical information on Urrea was recorded in the Mexico City-based spiritist journal *La Ilustración Espírita*. At least some of this information was gathered and reported by Lauro Aguirre (see my *Bandits* 208-12).

[5] Frequent references both in the press and in official Mexican government documents to *tomoches* or *tomochitecos* implied that the rebels were an indigenous group when in reality Tomóchic was a *mestizo* town whose indigenous population (of *tarahumaras*) had long since been expelled (see my *Bandits* 215-22).

[6] See especially Valadés and Gill.

[7] Several essays on Urrea appeared in Vargas Valdez, including, notably, Domecq's "Teresa Urrea."

[8] See my analysis of the work of Carlos Larralde's *Mexican American Movements* and "Santa Teresa" (*Bandits* 257).

[9] See my summary (*Bandits* 200-48).

[10] See Irwin, *Bandits* (204-5, 213, 218, 220, 252-53).

[11] This novel has, to my knowledge, never been treated critically, nor even mentioned by biographers of Urrea or historians of the Old West. The only evidence I have been able to find of its dissemination is an ad in the *Brooklyn Eagle* (2/16/00: 3).

[12] For an analysis of Murrieta's trajectory as a border icon, see my *Bandits* (38-90).

[13] Although Domecq's novel covers Urrea's entire life, up to her death in 1906, those last ten years are treated in more sketchy terms than are the prior two decades; Luis Urrea's novel ends quite suddenly in 1896.

WORKS CITED

Aguirre, Lauro and Teresa Urrea. "¡Tomóchic! ¡Redención!" [1896]. *Tomóchic: la revolución adelantada*, vol. 2. Comp. Jesús Vargas Valdez. Ciudad Juárez: Universidad Autónoma de Ciudad Juárez, 1994: 91-193.

Badger, Joseph. *Joaquin, the Saddle King*. New York: Beadle and Adams, 1881.

———. *Joaquin, the Terrible*. New York: Beadle and Adams, 1881.

———. *The Pirate of the Placers; or, Joaquin's Death Hunt*. New York: Beadle and Adams, 1882.

Dabove, Juan Pablo. *Nightmares of the Lettered City: Banditry and Literature in Latin America 1816-1929*. Pittsburgh: University of Pittsburgh Press, 2007.

Domecq, Brianda. *The Astonishing Story of the Saint of Cabora*. Trans. Kay García. Tempe: Bilingual Press/Editorial Bilingüe, 1998.

———. *La insólita historia de la Santa de Cabora*. Mexico City: Planeta, 1990.

———. "Teresa Urrea: la Santa de Cabora." *Tomóchic: la revolución adelantada*, vol. 2. Comp. Jesús Vargas Valdez. Ciudad Juárez: Universidad Autónoma de Ciudad Juárez, 1994: 9-65.

Figueroa Valenzuela, Alejandro. "Los indios de Sonora ante la modernización porfirista." *Historia general de Sonora*, vol. 4: *Sonora moderno: 1880-1929* [1985]. Coord. Cynthia Radding de Murrieta. Hermosillo: Gobierno del Estado de Sonora/Instituto Sonorense de Cultura, 1997: 139-63.

Frías, Heriberto. *Tomóchic* [1893]. Mexico City: Consejo Nacional de la Cultura y las Artes, 1998.

Gill, Mario. "Teresa Urrea, la Santa de Cabora." *Historia Mexicana* 6.24 (1957): 626-44.

Holden, William Curry. *Teresita*. Owing Mills, MD: Stemmer House, 1978.

Irwin, Robert McKee. *Bandits, Captives, Heroines and Saints: Cultural Icons of Mexico's Northwest Borderlands*. Minneapolis: University of Minnesota Press, 2007.

———. Review of *Nightmares of the Lettered City* by Juan Pablo Dabove. *Revista Iberoamericana* 74.223 (2008): 586-88.

Larralde, Carlos. *Mexican American Movements and Leaders*. Los Alamitos, CA: Hwong Publishing, 1976.

———. "Saint Teresa: A Chicana Myth." *Grito del Sol: Chicano Quarterly* 3.2 (1978): 5-114.

Martín, Desirée. "Bordered Saints: Unorthodox Sanctity Along the Border in Mexican and Chicana/o Literature." Doctoral Dissertation, Duke University, 2004.

Mirandé, Alfredo, and Evangelina Enríquez. *La Chicana: The Mexican-American Woman*. Chicago: University of Chicago Press, 1979.

Sobarzo, Horacio. *Episodios históricos sonorenses y otras páginas*. Mexico City: Porrúa, 1981.

Urrea, Luis Alberto. *The Hummingbird's Daughter*. New York: Little, Brown, 2005.

Valadés, José C. "La Santa de Cabora y la insurrección de Tomóchic en 1892." Serialized weekly in *La Opinión* nos. 166, 173, 180, 187, 194, 201, 208, 215, 222, 229, 236, 243, Segunda Sección. 2/28/37-5/16/37.

Vargas Valdez, Jesús, comp. *Tomóchic: la revolución adelantada*. 2 vols. Ciudad Juárez: Universidad Autónoma de Ciudad Juárez, 1994.

Whitlock, William Thomas. *Santa Teresa: A Tale of the Yaquii Rebellion*. New York: Town Topics Publishing, 1900.

Kristín Guðrún Jónsdóttir
UNIVERSITY OF ICELAND

Yo peleo por la justicia,
también por la libertad,
y la quiero para el Pueblo
por toda la eternidad.

Para el Pueblo sagrado
para el pueblo tan sufrido
que por siempre ha vegetado
por los grandes oprimido.

Corrido de Pancho Villa

San Pancho Villa, tú que haces milagros,
te estoy rogando vengas a darme ayuda
en esta tribulación que me agobia, para
que reciba los consuelos y socorros del
cielo en todas mis necesidades.

Gran novena a Pancho Villa

Los campesinos le rezan novenarios
cuando les falta el frijol y la tortilla
que falta le hace que reviva Pancho Villa.

Corrido de Francisco Villa,
Jorge Saldaña

INTRODUCCIÓN

Querido hermano [...] a ti invoco de todo corazón, así pues, te sirvas darme valor, tú que fuiste guía de los desamparados y sufridos, dadme tu pensamiento y tu osadía. Así sea." Estas palabras provienen de una oración a Francisco Villa o Pancho Villa, el gran héroe revolucionario ("Oración al espíritu de Pancho Villa"). Pancho Villa es, sin duda, uno de los íconos culturales más importantes de México. Una infinidad de corridos cantan sus hazañas, cientos de libros y artículos han salido sobre el héroe, se han producido numerosas películas sobre él y es muy visible en la iconografía mexicana tanto oficial como popular.

*Additional visual material for this article may be seen at http://noblebandits.asu.edu/Topics/GoodBandits2009.html

Pero detrás de la imagen oficial hay otra no tan conocida que no forma parte del discurso oficial de la mexicanidad: es la imagen religiosa de Pancho Villa.

Como bien se sabe la vida de Pancho Villa está rodeada de un aura de misterio donde el mito y su vida se mezclan a tal grado que es difícil separar la ficción de la "verdad", lo cual le convierte en mito y realidad a la vez. Ha sido representado tanto como el asesino más vil y sanguinario hasta como el bandido generoso por excelencia que obró a favor de los desheredados. La figura de Pancho Villa como bandido generoso y noble es la que interesa aquí. Nuestra investigación sobre el gran héroe revolucionario apunta que es precisamente ese factor que ha incitado a la *vox populi* a llevarlo a los altares, al nivel de santo popular.[1]

"EL CENTAURO DEL NORTE": BANDIDO GENEROSO POR EXCELENCIA

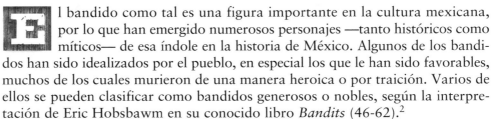

l bandido como tal es una figura importante en la cultura mexicana, por lo que han emergido numerosos personajes —tanto históricos como míticos— de esa índole en la historia de México. Algunos de los bandidos han sido idealizados por el pueblo, en especial los que le han sido favorables, muchos de los cuales murieron de una manera heroica o por traición. Varios de ellos se pueden clasificar como bandidos generosos o nobles, según la interpretación de Eric Hobsbawm en su conocido libro *Bandits* (46-62).[2]

Conforme a Hobsbawm, el bandido generoso de "gran corazón" es un arquetipo universal cuya figura ha surgido en numerosas culturas siendo Robin Hood el más conocido, sin lugar a dudas, a quien podríamos considerar el prototipo del bandido generoso. En su estudio clásico sobre el bandolerismo, Hobsbawm (19-33) examina la universalidad de la figura y cómo se reproduce con asombrosa uniformidad en distintas épocas y países. En general, son figuras empujadas al margen de la ley a causa de las injusticias cometidas por las autoridades, que se manifiestan fundamentalmente en la distribución desigual de riquezas. La figura, símbolo de resistencia ante el orden injusto, ha sido convertida en héroe de los que se encuentran en la periferia de tal orden: los subalternos. A consecuencia de sus actos "heroicos y generosos" el bandolero ha sido admirado mediante centenares de leyendas, canciones, corridos, romances, coplas, poemas, cuentos y novelas, pero llevar a tal figura a la santidad por parte de la *vox populi* no es tan común, lo que hace el caso de Pancho Villa singular, por lo menos dentro de México. Hay, sin embargo, otro bandolero mexicano que la *vox populi* ha llevado a los altares: Jesús Malverde, oriundo de Culiacán, Sinaloa, a quien se refiere muchas veces como narcosantón.

Según Hobsbawm, las características principales del bandido de "gran corazón" se resumen en nueve puntos (47-48).[3] De acuerdo con la imaginación popular, la figura de Pancho Villa concuerda con la mayoría de las características y categorías de Hobsbawm. Aquí queremos mencionar cinco de ellas para subrayar tres que nos parecen determinantes en cuanto a su santificación: el motivo de bandidaje forzado causado por una injusticia, su acto generoso de robar a ricos para distribuir el saqueo entre los necesitados, ser justiciero, su invisibilidad y su muerte trágica; son factores que se podrían sintetizar en tres palabras: víctima, justiciero y mártir. Estas características son también las principales en la elevación a santidad de Jesús Malverde, el otro bandido canonizado por la *vox populi* en México.[4] Los rasgos mencionados se reflejan en la tradición oral, en los cantos y corridos a Pancho Villa.

La voz popular sostiene que de joven, Villa se vio obligado a huir a la sierra, donde anduvo prófugo durante años, constantemente perseguido por la justicia que le calificó de "bandido" y "delincuente". Su huida fue causada por haber herido o matado al dueño de la hacienda (o al hijo, depende de la leyenda) donde trabajaba cuando trataba de defender a su hermana, agredida por éste. En otras palabras, Villa fue víctima del despotismo de los hacendados y obligado a obrar de esa manera para luego huir a la sierra. El corrido "Historia y muerte del general Francisco Villa" dice:

> Trabajó por mantener
> a su madre y a su hermana
> y luchó por obtener
> de trabajador la fama.
>
> Pero el hijo del patrón,
> con su dinero y poder
> burló a la hermana del peón
> que al fin era una mujer.
>
> Pero Pancho era muy hombre,
> y en prueba de su valor,
> lavó con sangre su nombre
> malhiriendo al burlador.
>
> (*The Mexican Revolution*)

Ese hecho corresponde a los años prerrevolucionarios de Pancho Villa. Muchos factores de su vida, sobre los cuales no se sabe mucho, son tema de controversia, en especial su época de bandidaje. Friedrich Katz, en su extenso estudio sobre el caudillo *The Life and Times of Pancho Villa* (2-8), habla de tres versiones básicas sobre los años prerrevolucionarios del caudillo: la leyenda blanca, la leyenda negra y la leyenda épica. La primera versión, que se basa sobre todo en *Memorias de Pancho Villa*, libro editado por Martín Luis Guzmán, lo pinta como víctima del sistema económico y social del porfiriato. Como indica la denominación, la leyenda negra encierra la versión del asesino despiadado exento de cualidades buenas que mata por puro gozo. Y finalmente, la leyenda épica se basa en la tradición oral mediante corridos y leyendas que surgieron a partir de la Revolución, la cual enfatiza más la importancia política prerrevolucionaria de Villa que las otras dos leyendas. Pero todas esas "leyendas" provienen de "reminiscences, popular ballads, rumors, memoirs, and hearsay" como señala Katz (2); se solapan y son difíciles de separar del todo. En su "autobiografía" *Memorias de Pancho Villa*, él mismo narra cómo se vio empujado hacia la vida bandolera por haber herido a su patrón, quien intentó violar a su hermana (14-16), lo que subraya la leyenda blanca. Según Katz, no existen fuentes fidedignas que corroboran esta historia (Bolado Muñoz). Paco Ignacio Taibo II menciona varias versiones de la historia en su libro *Pancho Villa: Una biografía narrativa* (23-25), una de las cuales dice que el propio Pancho Villa inventó la historia. Pero la veracidad histórica no interesa tanto aquí, más bien lo que sostiene la voz popular, que normalmente lo pinta como víctima, tanto durante los años prerrevolucionarios, es decir, su época de bandidaje, como durante su época de general, incluso despúes de la Revolución. La "Gran novena a Pancho Villa" subraya ese factor: "…tú que fuiste encarcelado, herido, perseguido por soldados extranjeros, asesinado, cortada y robada tu cabeza". Y, tras su muerte Pancho Villa no se libera de la persecución. Su tumba fue profanada tres años después de su muerte, en 1926, cuando su cuerpo fue decapitado.[5] El misterio que rodea la profanación de la tumba y la localización del "verdadero" lugar de descanso del revolucionario puede haber desempeñado un papel importante en su santificación.[6]

Otro rasgo hobsbawmniano del bandido noble atribuible a Villa que consideramos una extensión del ya mencionado es la invisibilidad o la invulnerabilidad en la persecución que sufrió por las autoridades. Se sabe que anduvo prófugo cerca de dos décadas, durante las cuales fue imposible de capturar. Esa historia se repetirá durante la Expedición Punitiva, la persecución del general Pershing con su cuerpo de miles de hombres y un escuadrón de aviones. Buscaron al "centauro del norte" durante meses sin localizarlo.

Por lo que se refiere al rasgo justiciero y el de robar sólo a los ricos para dar a los pobres, Villa los encarna también. Mediante la tradición oral la *vox populi* exalta ese factor benevolente, tanto durante su vida "bandolera" prerrevolucionaria como en épocas posteriores. Reitera que anduvo prófugo en la sierra durante su vida "bandolera" prerrevolucionaria, donde a menudo robó a los ricos para distribuir entre los pobres; de allí surgió el epíteto "el amigo del pobre", del que goza. Incluso recibió el apodo "el Robin Hood mexicano" entre los norteamericanos (Reed 123). Un sinnúmero de leyendas y corridos cantan su generosidad hacia los pobres, donde Villa es "valiente y noble de corazón" ("Historia y muerte del general Francisco Villa", *The Mexican Revolution*). El corrido "De la salida de los gachupines de la ciudad de Torreón" canta:

> Con Villa no anda la infamia,
> menos la calamidad;
> antes socorre a los pobres,
> que le piden caridad.
> (Mendoza 46)

Algo semejante se manifiesta en el corrido "General Francisco Villa":

> Francisco Villa nació,
> con el valor mexicano
> para ayudar a los pobres
> contra el yugo del tirano.
> (*The Mexican Revolution*)

Villa es el protector de los necesitados:

> Al pobre lo ha protegido
> Y a los ancianos también
> Y quien le pide auxilio
> nunca se vuelve sin él.
> (Simmons 267)

Y el corrido de Patricio Corral dice:

> Pancho Villa se llamaba

el valiente guerrillero.
Él no robaba los pobres
antes les daba dinero.
(Corral)

Contrario a la memoria colectiva sobre la generosidad hacia el necesitado, igual que en el caso del bandidaje forzado, la "verdad histórica" niega esos factores. Katz sostiene que: "In 1910 Villa was neither the much-wanted murderer his enemies have made him out to be nor the legendary Robin Hood, the idol of the peasants" (71). Taibo II habla de cómo se elaboró el mito de Pancho Villa: "En sus acciones hubo poca generosidad hacia los pueblos; robó a los hacendados, pero no los confrontó; mató rurales, pero no organizó su destrucción; robó a los ricos, pero pocas veces para entregar a los pobres" (45). Pero las *Memorias de Pancho Villa* contradicen ese juicio donde el propio Villa dice explícitamente que nunca robó al pobre, ni para sí, sino que despojaba al rico y al avaro para repartir entre los "hermanitos", que tantas angustias padecían. Sus propias palabras: "Y así sucesivamente: en el término de ocho a diez meses todo lo que me sobraba de los cincuenta mil pesos lo fui dedicando a socorrer gentes faltas de ayuda" (20). Como hemos visto, la tradición oral exalta ese factor tanto como los "textos religiosos". La "Auténtica oración al Espíritu Mártir de Pancho Villa" dice: "Así como ayudaste en el mundo terrenal a los NECESITADOS" y la "Gran novena a Pancho Villa" repite algo semejante donde habla del general como "siervo fiel y defensor del pueblo […] amado defensor de los que sufren". Lo que parece importante aquí en la santificación profana es el mito y el misterio que rodea la vida del centauro del norte, no lo que sostiene la historia "verdadera". Con razón Halldór Laxness señala en su libro *Vettvangur dagsins* (1943) que "Munnmælin eru vitrari en sagnameistararnir" o "la leyenda sabe más que los historiadores" (7). El factor de la generosidad-no generosidad es fundamental en el discurso popular sobre San Pancho Villa, donde queda explícita la bipolaridad ellos-nosotros, poder-no poder, rico-pobre, legal-al margen de la ley, como veremos más adelante.

El último rasgo que queremos destacar es la muerte violenta y trágica del sujeto; como es harto sabido, Villa murió en una emboscada o "por traición". Este rasgo lo consideramos decisivo en cuanto a la santificación del sujeto, pues lo convierte en mártir: Pancho Villa muere sacrificándose por los suyos.[7] En ese respecto refleja la muerte del santo mártir primitivo. Pancho Villa fue "víctima" y luego mártir que sufrió una muerte injusta por las autoridades. Aparte de haber sufrido como "nosotros", Pancho Villa representa lo que debería encarnar la autoridad, la justicia. Es la muerte injusta y brutal, el martirio que sufre Pancho Villa lo que justifica sus acciones y hace posible su elevación a la santidad popular. Según ese criterio Pancho Villa es un mártir que muere injustamente, pero es purificado por la sangre.

Llevar una vida ejemplar suele ser el elemento fundamental en la canonización oficial de un personaje, pero en el caso de Pancho Villa (y otros santos populares) los actos poco ejemplares —los robos por ejemplo—, son disculpados por la injusticia que sufrieron los "pobres". Pancho Villa se ve obligado a obrar de manera ilegal y es empujado a actuar fuera de la ley. La vida ejemplar cristiana no parece tener importancia porque en el fondo Pancho Villa representa la justicia y la justa repartición de los bienes.

SAN PANCHO VILLA

n su libro *Bandit Nation: A History of Outlaws and Cultural Struggle in Mexico, 1810-1920*, Chris Frazer menciona cómo el estado mexicano le negó a Pancho Villa sus méritos revolucionarios durante casi medio siglo después de su muerte. Finalmente, es reconocido a nivel oficial, lo cual convirtió a Pancho Villa en héroe nacional (2-4). A pesar de la "negación", el pueblo seguía elogiando a su gran héroe, al bienhechor de los desheredados, durante esos años, convirtiéndolo con el tiempo en San Pancho Villa. Nuestra investigación atestigua que Pancho Villa ha llegado a los altares de sus "hijos" y según parece la veneración va aumentando con el correr de los años. Nos hemos topado con su presencia religiosa muy a menudo en nuestros recorridos por la región fronteriza (el norte de México y el sudoeste de los Estados Unidos). En su mayoría, las yerberías, tiendas religiosas y mercados visitados tienen señales de veneración religiosa al "centauro del norte": artículos para su culto religioso que consisten en estampas, oraciones y novenas; veladoras con su oración que lo figuran con cananas de cartuchos cruzadas sobre el pecho o en su caballo típico; jabón ritual y escapularios. Además, existen aguas purificadas, aceite curativo, sal legítima espiritual, amuletos, perfumes para uso protector y su estatua o imagen en yeso para poner en altares.[8]

Según hemos encontrado, existen dos oraciones y una novena a Pancho Villa. Las estampas, de varios tamaños, lo representan de distintos modos sea en fotos o en dibujos. (Hay por lo menos diez versiones distintas). Ambas oraciones resaltan la oposición dicotómica poderoso/rico-pobre. La "Auténtica oración al Espíritu Mártir de Pancho Villa" dice:

> En el nombre de Dios nuestro Señor, invoco a los espíritus que te protejan para que me ayudes. Así como ayudaste en el mundo terrenal a los NECESITADOS. Así como venciste a los PODEROSOS. Así como hiciste retroceder a tus ENEMIGOS. Así te pido tu protección espiritual, para que me libres de todo mal y me des el ánimo necesario y el valor suficiente para enfrentarme a lo más difícil que se me presente en la vida. Amén. (Mayúsculas presentes en el texto citado)

Y sigue una recomendación para el devoto: "Rece esta oración nueve días seguidos con fe al caer la tarde. Y consérvela siempre al lado del corazón para su protección". Como vemos se pone énfasis en los términos "necesitados", "poderosos" y "enemigos" (es decir, "nosotros") contra "ellos" o los enemigos. Y se pide el ánimo y valor relacionados al héroe para poder seguir adelante. La "Oración al espíritu de Pancho Villa", aunque hay referencia a los "enemigos", no alude tan explícitamente a la contraposición dicotómica, pero habla de Pancho Villa como "guía de los desamparados y sufridos":

> Querido hermano, tú que supiste vencer a tus más fieros enemigos, haz que triunfe en mis más difíciles empresas. Me socorras en mi negocio y penalidades; a ti invoco de todo corazón, así pues, te sirvas darme valor, tú que fuiste guía de los desamparados y sufridos, dadme tu pensamiento y tu osadía. Así sea. (Se rezan tres Padres Nuestros y tres Ave Marías.)

Fuera de la oposición mencionada vemos que las dos oraciones resaltan los poderes específicos de los que dota Villa: su "osadía" y su fuerza para luchar contra la injusticia y el hacer lo imposible. La "Gran novena a Pancho Villa" enfatiza también ese valor: "se te honra e invoca como incansable, combatiente y victorioso" además de resaltar el discurso dicotómico pobre-poderoso, nosotros-ellos (nosotros los que sufrimos vs. explotadores), utilizando los términos pueblo y pobres contra explotadores y traidores (asesinos traidores contrarrevolucionarios). Pero el texto parece más explícito y alude, aunque sea indirectamente, a hechos históricos: Pancho Villa es un revolucionario a quien los traidores contrarrevolucionarios encarcelaron; fue perseguido por soldados extranjeros y finalmente asesinado; lo decapitaron y robaron su cabeza. La novena empieza de la manera siguiente:

> Oh, Gloriosísimo revolucionario San Pancho Villa, siervo fiel y defensor del pueblo, tú que fuiste encarcelado, herido, perseguido por soldados extranjeros, asesinado, cortada y robada tu cabeza; Tú que con la bondad de tus hazañas, derrotando a los asesinos y traidores contrarrevolucionarios y castigando a los explotadores, hiciste poderosos y fieles a los pobres, nunca serás olvidado porque mucho se te quiere; por eso se te honra e invoca como incansable, combatiente y victorioso, santo patrón de los casos difíciles y desesperados.

Aparte de ser Pancho Villa "siervo fiel y defensor del pueblo" y "amado defensor de los que sufren", es decir, de "nosotros", es también el "santo patrón de los casos difíciles y desesperados" que el pueblo quiere y necesita porque no es como los santos "prepotentes y soberbios", como dice la novena. Aquí hay una clara referencia a los santos ortodoxos, pero las palabras "prepotentes y soberbios" sorprenden en realidad, porque normalmente el devoto no hace una distinción entre el santo oficial o extraoficial, y los santos oficiales siempre tienen su lugar al lado de los extraoficiales. Estas palabras pueden expresar cierto resentimiento ante la negativa de la Iglesia a reconocer a Pancho Villa como santo, como "el ángel del pobre" que no es "peor" que los santos ortodoxos. Dichos vocablos manifiestan cierta duda ante la expresión oficial, ya que el pueblo tiene experiencia propia de lo milagroso que es Pancho Villa: "nosotros los que sufrimos, sabemos de los muchos milagros que haces". Se puede decir que de esa manera se contrapone a los santos reconocidos. Sigue la novena:

> San Pancho Villa, también te queremos porque eres bueno como el pueblo y no recurres para que se crea en ti, a la amenaza de que será maldito en el cielo y en la tierra quien dude de tus milagrosos dones como en algunas oraciones rezadas a santos prepotentes y soberbios, dice amagadoramente. Sobre todo nosotros los que sufrimos, sabemos de los muchos milagros que haces sin andar amenazando a los creyentes.[9]

La alusión a los "santos prepotentes y soberbios" puede también indicar que Pancho Villa va adquiriendo la función de los santos oficiales, muy venerados en la región, que tradicionalmente se han ocupado de los pobres, de los desesperados y de los casos imposibles como San Judas Tadeo, San Martín de Porres y San Francisco, santos que normalmente poseen su espacio en las capillas de santos profanos en la región. San Judas Tadeo es "patrono de los casos difíciles y desesperados" como le califica su oración ("Oración a San Judas Tadeo"), San Martín de Porres es "patrono de los enfermos y los pobres" que "tan solícito fuiste en socorrer a los necesitados" ("Oración a San Martín de Porres") y San Francisco es "patrono de los pobres" ("Oración a San Francisco de Asís").

Tal vez se puede decir que San Pancho Villa compite ahora con ellos, incluso con la misma Virgen guadalupana. María Elena Ruiz, propietaria de la yerbería Oaxaca en Ciudad Victoria, Tamaulipas, habla de un aumento impresionante en cuanto a preferencias de sus clientes y dice que Pancho Villa se ha convertido en uno de los santos más populares junto con la Santa Muerte, incluso vende más veladoras a los dos santos mencionados que a la Virgen de Guadalupe (Cruz Zapata).

La tumba de Pancho Villa ubicada en Parral, Chihuahua, acaso no ha producido un centro de peregrinaje como es el caso de otros santos populares, por ejemplo Jesús Malverde, pero no cabe duda de que sus devotos acuden a su "santo" allí a juzgar por las veladoras, los exvotos, fotografías, certificados y cartas de agradecimiento que se encuentran alrededor de su tumba. Aunque no tenemos noticia de ninguna capilla dedicada al héroe nacional, nos hemos encontrado, en nuestros recorridos por "espacios sagrados" en el norte de México, en las tierras fronterizas y en el suroeste de los Estados Unidos, con sus veladoras ardiendo en varias capillas entre diversas imágenes de santos ortodoxos.[10] A diferencia de otras tumbas de santos populares, que en su mayoría se han convertido en santuarios, en la de Pancho Villa ni hay milagritos ni placas de agradecimiento prefabricadas. Eso puede indicar que aún no hay tanta comercialización y negocio relativo a este aspecto de la expresión religiosa a Pancho Villa. Abundan, sin embargo, certificados, tarjetas y carnets de varios tipos. Las cartas expresan en su mayoría agradecimientos por protección y curas de enfermedades.

Examinando los textos encontrados se puede ver la procedencia de los devotos: Monterrey, Matamoros y Nuevo León, principalmente. Conforme a Pedro Perales Herrera, propietario de la yerbería El Niño Fidencio ubicada en Monterrey, el culto a Pancho Villa se concentra en los estados norteños Chihuahua, Coahuila, Nuevo León y Tamaulipas y en el estado sureño de Texas (Cedillo). Nuestra investigación apunta que su veneración se ha extendido a más lugares, como los Estados Unidos. Esto lo confirma su presencia en las tiendas religiosas en dicho país. También lo confirman algunas de las oraciones, donde el texto viene tanto en español como en inglés. Patricio Corral, quien ha cuidado la tumba de Pancho Villa durante más de tres décadas, sostiene que además de los mexicanos, muchos "del otro lado", chicanos/mexico-americanos, le rinden culto y visitan la tumba (Jónsdóttir, entrevista personal 2005). También se empieza a notar su presencia en la capital de México, donde se pueden adquirir artículos religiosos asociados a su culto en mercados populares, por ejemplo, el de Sonora (Ramírez).

Es difícil saber exactamente cuándo se inició la veneración a Pancho Villa. Ramírez Ortiz, miembro de una familia propietaria durante décadas de una yerbería ubicada en la ciudad de Durango, informa que la devoción a Pancho Villa nace por lo menos 30 ó 35 años atrás; eso quiere decir que se remonta a los sesenta o los setenta del siglo pasado (P.M. Hernández). Pedro Perales Herrera, propietario de la yerbería El Niño Fidencio en Monterrey, sostiene algo semejante. Dice que lleva treinta y cinco años en el negocio y se venera a Pancho Villa desde que empezó con la yerbería (Cedillo). En ese contexto es importante el título de las oraciones a Pancho Villa, donde aparece el término "espíritu", lo cual asocia la veneración

a cultos espiritistas. Alberto Salinas, curandero y "materia" (receptor de la espiritualidad y los poderes curativos), quien trabaja con el espíritu de El Niño Fidencio, informa que "Pancho Villa es visto como un espíritu ayudador por personas que conocen el mundo del curanderismo, en el ramo del espiritismo [...] existen materias que lo comunican" (correo electrónico 26 de mayo de 2009). James S. Griffith habla en su libro *Saints of the Borderlands* sobre los estudios que realizó la antropóloga Isabel Kelly cerca de Torreón, en 1953, sobre curanderos y creencias populares donde entra la invocación del espíritu del héroe nacional (100-101). Sabemos también mediante el libro de Ruth Behar *Translated Woman: Crossing the Border with Esperanza's Story*, que su invocación dentro de círculos espiritistas sigue vigente en la actualidad (203-222). Tal vez no sorprende que exista una escuela psíquica con su nombre: Escuela de Estudios Psíquicos Doroteo Arango Arámbula en San Juan del Río, Durango. De esa información podemos deducir que la invocación a Pancho Villa en círculos espiritistas no es reciente tanto como su veneración.

A excepción de Jesús Malverde, no hemos encontrado indicios de culto a otros bandidos generosos mexicanos que hayan tenido el valor de oponerse al orden dominante con el fin de ayudar a los "desamparados y sufridos". En el continente americano, lo más cercano a la veneración mexicana del bandido generoso es el culto a los distintos gauchos en la Argentina.[11] Martín Pascual clasifica ese tipo de devoción como "cultos anómicos" en *Religiosidad popular en la Argentina* (Chapp et al. 62). Según él, son personajes famosos por su desprecio al orden o bandoleros generosos que han "mostrado su capacidad y su audacia de oponerse al orden" en los que el devoto encuentra un "héroe liberador, una potencia a la cual acudir en una perpetua reivindicación del desorden contestatario" (62). Consideramos esa interpretación fructífera para entender la devoción al bandido generoso. Los devotos mediante Pancho Villa encuentran un liberador, un protector o un "amado defensor de los que sufren" ("Gran novena a Pancho Villa")

Arriba: Patricio Corral, el señor que cuida la tumba de Francisco Villa, Parral, Chihuahua

Centro: Carta de agradecimiento, tumba de Francisco Villa

Abajo: Objetos religiosos dedicados a Pancho Villa (Fotos de Kristín Guðrún Jónsdóttir)

a quien pueden acudir en su situación social, económica y personal difícil; situación donde "nosotros", es decir, los que siempre sufren, no pueden, por causa de la injusticia y desigualdad social, participar plenamente en lo que ofrece la sociedad. Taibo II dice que "Hay villistas hoy en día por todos lados clamando: 'Retorna mi general'" (212), así pidiendo el cambio de la desigualdad, como en los tiempos revolucionarios. Katz habla de la muerte de Pancho Villa como "un crimen de estado" (Bolado Muñoz); es decir, cuando lo mataron fue el único sobreviviente de la revolución al lado de la gente, la última esperanza de poder cumplirse los ideales revolucionarios. No obstante, Pancho Villa sigue hoy en día "al lado de la gente" encarnando la esperanza justiciera pero desde el más allá, glorificado por sus actos terrenales.

La veneración a Pancho Villa es una realidad actual. Va creciendo, cobrando nuevos aspectos, difundiéndose. Es una expresión que nace y se desarrolla exclusivamente fuera del discurso oficial, tanto del ámbito secular como del religioso. Pancho Villa forma parte del panteón profano mexicano. La creciente popularidad de Pancho Villa como santo puede, tal vez, relacionarse con los tiempos difíciles y violentos que vive la sociedad mexicana en la actualidad. La *vox populi* ante sus dificultades materiales y espirituales, invoca al centauro del norte, al "siervo fiel y defensor del pueblo", al "santo patrón de los casos difíciles y desesperados" pidiéndole la ayuda y justicia que le parece negada aquí en la vida terrenal.

NOTAS

[1] Un santo popular es un sujeto que el pueblo ha "canonizado", pero no es reconocido por la Iglesia Católica. Para más información sobre los santos venerados en el norte de México, ver Jónsdóttir, "Santos populares".

[2] Hobsbawm clasifica lo que llama "bandidos sociales" en tres grupos: la figura del bandido noble, el guerrillero y el "vengador". El rasgo de este último no es tanto ayudar a los pobres sino vengar a los opresores como los "haiduks" húngaros.

[3] Son los siguientes: 1) comienza su carrera de rebelde no con un crimen sino como víctima de la injusticia o por ser perseguido por las autoridades a causa de un acto que consideran delictivo, pero no el pueblo; 2) es justiciero; 3) roba a los ricos para dar a los pobres; 4) nunca mata sino en defensa propia o justa venganza; 5) si sobrevive, vuelve a su pueblo como ciudadano honrado y miembro (respetado) de la comunidad; 6) es admirado, ayudado y sostenido por su gente; 7) muere invariablemente y solo a traición ya que ningún miembro honorable de la comunidad ayuda a las autoridades contra él; 8) es, por lo menos en teoría, invisible e invulnerable; y 9) el rasgo final: no es enemigo del rey o del soberano (la fuente de justicia), sino de la pequeña aristocracia local, el clero u otros opresores (*Bandits* 47-48).

[4] Para más información sobre Jesús Malverde ver Jónsdóttir, "Voces de la subalternidad"; Quinones, *True Tales*; y Griffith, *Folk Saints*.

[5] Hay varias versiones sobre el destino de la cabeza. Una dice que fue entregada a un millonario norteamericano, Emil Holmdahl, mientras otra dice que terminó en la sociedad universitaria de Yale University "Skull and Bones". Ver Taibo II, *Pancho Villa*, 832-40 y Jiménez Carillo, *Anecdotario villista*, 191-94.

[6] Existen numerosas leyendas en torno a dónde descansan verdaderamente los restos del héroe. Muchas dicen que después de la profanación trasladaron el cuerpo de Pancho Villa de la tumba 632 del cementerio de Parral al número 10 por miedo a otro sacrilegio. En 1976 cuando

las autoridades exhumaron el cuerpo de Pancho Villa para enterrarlo en el Monumento Revolucionario de la Ciudad de México, llevaron el cuerpo de otra persona según la voz popular. Eso significa que los restos de Pancho Villa están todavía en el cementerio de Parral. Ver Jiménez Carillo, *Anecdotario villista* 195-99 donde se habla de cuatro sepelios de Pancho Villa. Hay una historia interesante que narra todos los años Felipe Cárdenas, residente de El Paso. Él sostiene que su padre, José Cárdenas Ponce, el dueño de la única funeraria de Parral al morir Pancho Villa, enterró dos veces al héroe: al morir y por segunda vez después de la profanación. Y para evitar futura profanación utilizó cemento. Ver Bracamontes, "Son recounts family's part".

[7] En el caso de varios santos populares de América Latina parece que una muerte trágica o violenta es suficiente para la elevación a la santidad, por ejemplo, el caso de la cantante Gilda de Colombia y las "animitas" de Venezuela.

[8] Empezamos nuestra investigación sobre santos populares y extraoficiales en 2000. Desde entonces hemos recorrido numerosas yerberías, tiendas religiosas, mercados y comercios turísticos en varias ciudades fronterizas: Lukeville/Sonoyta, San Luis/San Luis Río Colorado, Algodones/Andrade, Mexicali/Calexico, Sásabe/El Sásabe, Douglas/Agua Prieta, Naco, Arizona/Naco, Sonora, las dos Nogales, Laredo/Nuevo Laredo, El Paso/Ciudad Juárez. Además, en Phoenix, Mesa y Chandler, Arizona, y en Hermosillo, México, y tales negocios mediante el Internet. También visitamos la tumba de Pancho Villa en Parral, Chihuahua.

[9] La novena termina así: "San Pancho Villa, tú que haces milagros, te estoy rogando vengas a darme ayuda en esta tribulación que me agobia, para que reciba los consuelos y socorros del cielo en todas mis necesidades, muy particularmente en (aquí es donde deben hacerse las súplicas especiales de lo que se quiere) y para que bendigas a Dios contigo y con todos los escogidos por la eternidad, te prometo, amado defensor de los que sufren San Pancho Villa, acordarme siempre, siempre, hasta el día de mi muerte, de este gran favor y nunca dejaré de honrarte como mi muy personal y poderosísimo protector y de hacer que aumente la devoción por ti todos los días; daré copias de esta oración a quien la pida, también a quienes no la pidan, por donde vivo y cuando esté de viaje; esto haré y todo lo demás que pueda. Amén."

[10] En cuanto a los "espacios sagrados", queremos mencionar la capilla del santo popular Pedro Jaramillo en Falfurrias, Tejas, y el "altar" dedicado al *Tiradito* en Tucson, Arizona.

[11] Para más información sobre la veneración de los gauchos ver Chumbita, *Jinetes rebeldes*; Coluccio, *Devociones populares*; y Bocconi y Etcheverry, "Chamigo Gil".

OBRAS CITADAS

"Auténtica oración al Espíritu Mártir de Pancho Villa". Estampa.

Behar, Ruth. *Translated Woman: Crossing the Border with Esperanza's Story*. Boston: Beacon Press, 1993.

Berumen, Miguel Ángel. *Pancho Villa. La construcción del mito*. Ciudad Juárez: Berumen y Muñoz, 2005.

Bocconi, Diego Oscar, y María Paula Etcheverry. "Chamigo Gil". *Símbolos y fetiches religiosos en la construcción de la identidad popular*. Coord. Rubén Dri. Buenos Aires: Editorial Biblos, 2003.

Bolado Muñoz, Roberto. *El rostro oculto de Pancho Villa*. Canal 11, IPN, 2003. Web.

Bracamontes, Ramón. "Son recounts family's part in Pancho Villa interment". *El Paso Times* 19 de julio 2009. Web.

Cedillo, Juan Alberto. "Pancho Villa: Santo y milagroso". *Revista La Guia.com* 3.36, junio 2003. Web.

Chapp, M. E., M. Iglesias, M. Pascual, V. Roldán y D. J. Santamaría. *Religiosidad popular en la Argentina*. Buenos Aires: Centro Editor de América Latina, 1991.

Chumbita, Hugo. *Jinetes rebeldes. Historia del bandolerismo social en la Argentina*. Buenos Aires: Javier Vergara Editor, 2000.

Coluccio, Félix. *Devociones populares argentinas y americanas*. Buenos Aires: Corregidor, 2001.

Corral, Patricio. "Corrido a Pancho Villa". Hoja suelta recibida del autor en el Panteón de Dolores, Parral, en 2005.

Cortez, Juan. "Cuida Pancho Villa a 'El Rey' Santos". *El Mañana* 27 de octubre 2007. Web.

Cruz Zapata, Benny. "Negocios esotéricos a la alza". *Noticias de Tamaulipas al minuto* 29 de octubre 2007. Web.

Frazer, Chris. *Bandit Nation: History of Outlaws and Cultural Struggle in Mexico, 1810-1920*. Lincoln/London: U of Nebraska P, 2006.

"Gran novena a Pancho Villa". Estampa.

Griffith, James S. *Folk Saints on the Borderlands. Victims, Bandits & Healers*. Tucson: Rio Nuevo, 2003.

Guzmán, Martín Luis, ed. *Memorias de Pancho Villa*. México, D.F.: Compañía General de Ediciones, 1966.

Hernández, Lizbeth. "Otros tiempos, otros santos". *El Universal* 11 de abril 2009.

Hernández, Perla Mónica. "Crece el culto por Francisco Villa". *El Universal* 20 de noviembre 2004. Web.

Hobsbawm, Eric. *Bandits*. New York: New Press, 2000.

Jiménez Carillo, Gilberto, comp. *Anecdotario Villista. Hechos, Relatos y Sucesos de mi General*. Durango: Gobierno del Estado de Durango, 2007.

Jónsdóttir, Kristín Guðrún. Entrevista personal con Patricio Corral. Parral, 20 de octubre 2005.

———. "Santos populares del norte de México". *Revista de las fronteras* 3 (2005): 5-10.

———. "Voces de la subalternidad periférica. Jesús Malverde y otros santos profanos de México". Tesis doctoral, Arizona State University, 2004.

Katz, Friedrich. *The Life and Times of Pancho Villa*. Stanford, California: Stanford UP, 1998.

Laxness, Halldór. *Vettvangur dagsins*. Reykjavík: Helgafell, 1962.

Mendoza, Vicente T. *El corrido mexicano*. México, D.F.: Fondo de Cultura Económica, 1976.

The Mexican Revolution. CD, Vol. 1-4. Archoolie Productions 7041-7044, 1996.

Montes, José María. *El libro de los santos*. Madrid: Alianza, 1996.

"Oración al espíritu de Pancho Villa". Estampa.

"Oración a San Francisco de Asís". Estampa.

"Oración a San Judas Tadeo". Estampa.

"Oración a San Martín de Porres". Estampa.

Osorno, Diego Enrique. "La carretera de la Santa Muerte". *Milenio.com* 12 de septiembre 2008. Web.

Quinones, Sam. *True Tales of Another Mexico*. Albuquerque: U of New Mexico P, 2001.

Ramírez, Bertha Teresa. "Francisco Villa regresa a la capital, pero en forma de culto esotérico". *La Jornada* 15 de septiembre 2008. Web.

Reed, John. *Insurgent Mexico*. New York: Internacional Publishers, 1969.

Saldaña, Jorge. "Corrido de Francisco Villa". *The Mexican Revolution*. CD.

Salinas, Alberto. "Re: Saludos y pregunta desde Islandia". Correo electrónico al autor. 26 de mayo 2009.

Simmons, Merle E. *Mexican Corrido as a Source for Interpretative Study of Modern Mexico (1870-1950)*. Bloomington: Indiana UP, 1957. New York: Kraus Reprint, 1969.

Taibo II, Paco Ignacio. *Pancho Villa: Una biografía narrativa*. México, D.F.: Editorial Planeta, 2006.

La negra Angustias, preámbulo a una revolución trunca

EL ELEMENTO AFROMEXICANO EN LA NARRATIVA DE LA REVOLUCIÓN*

Margarita López López

LOS ANGELES VALLEY COLLEGE

The African presence in Mexico as a whole has historically been minimized, if not ignored or even denied.

Francis D. Althoff, Jr.

En 1944, Francisco Rojas González publicó su primera novela, *La negra Angustias*, la cual ganó el Premio Nacional de Literatura. Sus rasgos etnológicos son aportaciones significantes a la narrativa de la Revolución mexicana.[1] Aún más de sesenta años después de publicarse, *La negra Angustias (LNA)* se distingue como preámbulo inconsecuente de una revolución trunca —la revolución por incorporar y reconocer la herencia africana en la ideología de mestizaje nacional, en la literatura, en la historia, en el arte y en otros registros culturales de México—. En lo general, según declara el antropólogo Aguirre Beltrán cuya extensa obra etnológica se concentra en la población afromexicana, tanto antropólogos como intelectuales mexicanos han mantenido deliberadamente una ideología de identidad nacional exclusiva que sumerge al negro en el subconsciente. Afirma Aguirre Beltrán:

> Cuando los hombres de letras discurren sobre las raíces de nuestra nacionalidad se refieren única y exclusivamente al indio y al blanco... Si se ocupan del mestizaje y proponen la fusión de razas están pensando una vez más en el indio y el blanco; los conservadores con el propósito premeditado de blanquear el país, los liberales tal vez con el mismo fin, aunque no lo manifiestan. *Ni unos ni otros discuten la mezcla con el negro, antes bien la rehuyen.* (1969, 53; énfasis mío)

De manera que, en un esfuerzo posrevolucionario por estudiar y reinterpretar la herencia nacional, Rojas González y otros intelectuales tratan de definir en términos propios, trascendental e inauguralmente, la identidad de la nueva nación mexicana. Dicha obra se manifestó como campaña nacional y como esfuerzos individuales. Por un lado, la campaña nacional instituye sistemáticamente la ideología de mestizaje entre indio y europeo como identidad nacional.[2] De gran influencia en dicha campaña y en el desarrollo del México moderno, se distingue José Vasconcelos, cuya obra famosa *La raza cósmica* expone su ideología de mestizaje:

> *Los tipos bajos de la especie serán absorbidos por el tipo superior.* De esta suerte *podría redimirse, por ejemplo, el negro, y poco a poco, por extinción voluntaria,* las estirpes más feas irán cediendo el paso a las más

---

*Additional visual material for this article may be seen at http://noblebandits.asu.edu/Topics/GoodBandits2009.html

hermosas. Las razas inferiores, al educarse, se harían menos prolíficas, y los mejores especímenes irán ascendiendo en una escala de mejoramiento étnico, cuyo tipo máximo no es precisamente el blanco sino esa nueva raza. (Vasconcelos 42-3; énfasis mío)

Por otro lado y para fines de este estudio, la novela *LNA*, con su trayectoria identitaria de la mulata revolucionaria, se considera como manifestación literaria del esfuerzo individual de Rojas por compensar el mestizaje homogeneizador y borroso reafirmando ahora al negro como agente activo en el devenir histórico de México.

Este estudio expone que *LNA* se ha mantenido en una laguna de omisión como resultado de la ideología del período nacionalista de aquella época y de su trascendencia en la literatura. En base a esto, el presente análisis parte de las siguientes dos premisas: 1) la especificidad de *LNA* corresponde al período nacionalista en que vive Rojas; y 2) las características distintivas del perfil etnológico y literario de Rojas demuestran su compromiso social para con las clases destituidas de México.

Siguiendo la corriente de sus contemporáneos, Rojas plantea el mestizaje en el trasfondo de la Revolución, pero se desvía del tradicional héroe revolucionario para crear la primera novela de este movimiento enfocada en el desarrollo individual de la heroína afromexicana. Por lo tanto, se examina esta obra como un dialogismo de ideologías de la identidad nacional embutidas en un discurso racial y feminista centrado en la protagonista Angustias como agente afromexicano activo en cuatro ambientes en que se (des)envuelve: 1) bajo el amparare de la india Crescencia; 2) bajo el tutelaje de su padre, el negro Antón; 3) como coronela zapatista y 4) en su relación con el catrín Manolito.

Conspicuamente, la trayectoria identitaria de Angustias afirma la complejidad de creencias y tradiciones sobre las razas o castas en México.[3] Primero, Angustias se inicia en un ambiente marcado por la crianza indígena recibida de la pobre y vieja bruja, doña Crescencia. En la pobreza, la niña Angustias "trabaja de sol a sol" desenvolviéndose bajo tradiciones aprendidas de la viuda Crescencia (Rojas, 12). *In medias res*, el lector es integrado a un ambiente en que feliz y naturalmente cohabita la protagonista, quien "lavaba y cantaba" (9). La mulata está suscrita a la naturaleza mexicana y a una domesticidad que inculca recalcadamente el papel sumiso de la mujer —blanca, negra o india— para con el hombre. La india Crescencia, primero, y su padre, el negro Antón, después, insisten en infundirle que como mujer "está mocha" y un hombre la haría completa. En última instancia, el desenvolvimiento psicológico de la protagonista observado en sus subsiguientes facetas, revolucionaria y matrimonial, esclarece el nexo ideológico del autor entre la realidad social y la ficción literaria, evidenciado en un discurso racial y feminista.

En cuanto a la raza de Angustias, por medio de doña Crescencia se dan a conocer tempranamente sus antecedentes blancos maternos y negros paternos. Al regresar el padre de Angustias después de diez años de prisión, Crescencia le reafirma a éste su parentesco subrayando su carácter y color al decirle: "—¡Válgame Dios, Antón Farrera! ... No más véale *la color. Mulata como usted.* La *madre*— ... *era blanca* y fina; de ella sacó Angustias las facciones y de usted los ademanes, *la resolución y lo prietillo"* (13; énfasis mío).

Es por el color que Antón reconoce a Angustias como su propia hija y la lleva a vivir a su lado, determinando así un nuevo rumbo en la vida de la mulata. A saber, la separación de la herencia blanca al morir la madre, la inicial crianza indígena y la segunda y decisiva crianza bajo el padre negro son claves en la primacía que da el autor al origen racial —indio y negro— en el movimiento revolucionario.

Cabe aquí subrayar que, en contraste con la conocida obra de la Revolución *La muerte de Artemio Cruz* (Fuentes, 1962), en que el origen negro del protagonista lo somete al margen de la historia en el argumento, en *La negra Angustias* se subraya un mestizaje en que dicho origen establece precedentes.[4] Si en la obra de Fuentes, mueren ambos mulatos —madre Isabel e hijo Artemio— excluyéndolos así del devenir histórico, en la obra de Rojas, ambos, padre e hija Farrera, se instalan en la historia revolucionaria como agentes activos —el negro Antón como bandido heroico de numerosas hazañas, inmortalizado en el corrido de la Revolución, y la hija mulata como coronela en las tropas zapatistas.[5]

La atmósfera de historicidad de *La negra Angustias*, con héroes nacionales como Zapata, ayuda a inclinar emocionalmente al lector y a darle mayor verosimilitud a la protagonista. De manera que lo emotivo y dinámico del revolucionario afromexicano, subrayado como herencia en la novela, esclarece, a manera costumbrista, el desarrollo y la inscripción de la coronela Angustias como agente histórico en la etapa sangrienta de la Revolución. Dicho trasfondo de violencia se despliega, paralelamente, de comienzo a fin de la novela, a un dialogismo ideológico racial y feminista entre los personajes, con la mulata como figura central.

A primera instancia, lo animalista y erótico exagerado, estereotípico de descripciones del negro, se manifiesta desde la niñez de Angustias pero aunado a un cuestionamiento de la omnipotencia viril bestial.[6] Describe el narrador:

> Angustias Farrera se iba transformando en otro ser. Los arrieros de tierra caliente, cuando pasaban cerca de ella, la miraban de muy particular manera y algunos tenían ciertas palabras dulces y hasta algunos ademanes provocativos... la mulata recordaba la horrible inquietud que se adueñaba de los machos cabríos. (Rojas, 20)

Y explica la experiencia espantosa de Angustias contra uno de sus perseguidores:

> Siguió el acoso lúbrico y terco... la perseguía diciéndole frases rotas por carcajadas nerviosas... la muchacha tropezó y rodó por el suelo. Laureano, rápido, echóse sobre ella; ... la niña logró desasirse del bestial atacante y huir. (21)

En cuanto al "dominio sobre los hombres, la derrota por el hombre culto y la vuelta a la nada de la protagonista", Seymour Menton iguala a Angustias con doña Bárbara (Gallegos) en un estudio comparativo en que trata el carácter dominante y erótico en la trayectoria de ambas protagonistas.[7] No concuerdo con esta afirmación ya que Angustias no es como doña Bárbara y su poder erótico único que ejerce sobre el hombre. Primeramente, Angustias ejerce su dominio sobre los hombres para el beneficio del movimiento revolucionario y para defender a la mujer del abuso, en tanto que doña Bárbara lo ejerce para beneficio personal. Segundo, la derrota de doña Bárbara por el hombre culto simboliza el bien sobre el mal, pero la derrota de Angustias por Manuel simboliza el dominio de la inmoralidad. Y finalmente, doña Bárbara desaparece en la nada al final, pero Angustias vuelve a la condición femenina tradicional de su época.

En *LNA*, la mulata muestra pugna ante el acoso abusivo del macho hacia la hembra indefensa y sufre la violencia viril y discriminación social por luchar contra tal acoso. Tal es el caso cuando la comunidad la juzga injustamente al encontrar el cuchillo del padre Antón en el cadáver de Laureano. Porfiado en su acoso, Laureano muere apuñalado al defenderse Angustias de ser su víctima. Como resultado de la afronta femenina y el castigo mortal contra dicho machismo, Angustias se ve forzada a abandonar al padre y huir al monte por acuchillar a quien trata de violarla. Irónicamente, en su fuga cae bajo el poderío del don Juan de El Rondeño, quien casi la convierte en su enésima violación sexual a no ser por la esposa que le ayuda a escapar.

Aún antes, cuando el rico ganadero Eutimio Reyes se presenta ante el negro Antón para pedir la mano de la mulata para su hijo, Angustias se siente acosada y sólo piensa en el pretendiente como "uno de tantos machos hinchados de vanidad y empecinados de repugnante lujuria" (Rojas, 27). Después responde Angustias, "[m]entira… Esa es mentira, yo no quiero para nada a los machos…" cuando el padre le dice "ya estás pidiendo a gritos un macho que te quebrante y te *acomplete*", reafirmando éste las creencias de la india Crescencia (29; énfasis mío).[8]

Aunque su rechazo del joven acomodado no es de carácter racial, la comunidad entera responde como si lo fuera y muestra su discriminación hacia ambos negros vociferando infamias al "horrible mulato de antecedentes vergonzosos" y a la "mulata [que] despreciaba a los machos porque las mujeres la atraían en forma pecaminosa" (30), a quien "pretendían haber visto… desgreñada y jadeante, correr tras una niña y rodar abrazada de ella presa de un diabólico frenesí" (31).[9] Como resultado, el antes heroico negro ahora es forzado al aislamiento, y a Angustias la apedrean casi a punto de matarla, a no ser por Crescencia quien logra salvarla con una simbólica intervención y limpia espiritual en que hace partícipes a varias mujeres de la comunidad misma.

Más aún, bajo el tutelaje del padre Antón, Angustias llega a formarse y compartir con éste una memoria de un pasado común. La ambivalencia de la comunidad en aceptar el carácter rebelde de padre e hija se concibe dentro del trasfondo de la Revolución. De manera que la exclusión, el racismo y los estereotipos sufridos por ambos, son compensados por el reconocimiento de sus contribuciones revolucionarias.[10] En este hilo, el orgullo y aprecio por el generoso bandido protector de los pobres son observados como derechos y deberes del negro Antón como miembro de la comunidad. Además, la valentía y negritud heredadas del padre —claves en el (des)envolvimiento revolucionario de Angustias— junto con su rebeldía contra la sumisión ante el hombre, llegan a ser apreciadas por la comunidad como parte de este carácter revolucionario.[11]

Irónicamente, la serie de fugas del acoso masculino literalmente llevan a la protagonista a la acción revolucionaria. Una vez que escucha al pueblo de Real

de Ánimas hablar de hazañas revolucionarias y cantar el corrido sobre su heroico padre, Angustias se forma una visión de su propia condición étnico-cultural
que la lanza a convertirse en coronela, seguir el ejemplo de su padre e impartir
justicia entre los pobres.[12] Cabe aquí subrayar que la inclusión explícita del
corrido sobre el negro Antón en *LNA* no sólo establece una fuerte vinculación
con el pueblo en la narrativa, en tanto que utiliza su propio lenguaje sencillo,
sino que además, como forma de memoria popular, genera y reafirma una
identidad colectiva nacional que contrarresta la sistemática de borrar al negro del
concepto de mestizaje indoeuropeo instituido por la campaña nacional cultural.[13]
Canta la voz fresca de una muchacha:

> Antón Farrera el mulato
> era un ladrón justiciero
> jamás robaba a los probes,
> antes les daba dinero... (81)

Resuelta, Angustias se enrola en la tropa zapatista que reconoce su linaje heroico y la toma como coronela. En un estudio feminista de Angustias, Poniatowska
declara que huyendo del asedio de los "revolucionarios", la protagonista se hace
coronela y gana el respeto de éstos.[14] Su rebeldía y dominio sobre los hombres
ahora la convierten en personaje espectacular, y la ambigüedad social asume un
matiz positivo manifestado en el respeto hacia la mulata castigadora del hombre
que abusa de la mujer. Además, como revolucionaria mexicana, Angustias lleva al
extremo su papel sexual e invierte muchos estereotipos. No sólo se viste de hombre
al hacerse coronela, sino que reafirma su castigo severo del abuso de los hombres
para con la mujer, primeramente, al juzgar a nombre de las mujeres al Don Juan
de El Rondeño, haciendo que lo castren (71).

Aunque las "soldaderas" se han representado de muchas formas en la literatura, la historia y el arte, las de herencia afromexicana son escasas. Los autores
de la novelística de la Revolución han constatado esto. Su obra literaria, vasta y
variada estilísticamente, ha complementado los documentos históricos para reve-
lar algo más allá, algo que ayuda a determinar lo que apreciaba o despreciaba la
sociedad de la época.

En cuanto a la imagen que se le dio en el arte a la soldadera en esa época,
Poniatowska comenta que:

> José Clemente Orozco pintó a las soldaderas en forma despectiva y
> caricaturesca, borrachas, el rebozo caído, desaliñadas fodongas al lado
> de sus hombres muy bien uniformados, viva imagen de la Pintada.
> Mientras Silvestre Revueltas compone *La Coronela*, Rufino Tamayo
> retrata a las soldaderas en un fragmento de su mural *Revolución* y
> Siqueiros las muestra de pie junto a sus Juanes. Diego Rivera pintó a
> una soldadera en su *Sueño de un domingo por la tarde en la Alameda*
> ensombrerada y con su rifle al hombro. (Poniatowska 25)

Asimismo, el hidrocálido José Guadalupe Posada incluye grabados de calaveras
revolucionarias, algunos de ellos negros.[15] Más aún, Elizabeth Salas trata la presencia de soldaderas afromexicanas en su obra *Soldaderas in the Mexican Military:*

Arriba: Calavera de don Folías y el negrito de José Guadalupe Posada

Abajo: Calavera revolucionaria de José Guadalupe Posada

Myth and History (Salas 87). Poniatowska, por su parte, cita una numerosa lista de nombres que ofrece su personaje Jesusa (*Hasta no verte Jesús mío*) y otra lista de Salas (*Soldaderas*) para concluir que "[a]hora las etiquetamos por igual, sin distinción de bandos, como 'adelitas'". Después explica Poniatowska: "El que nunca hayan tenido un nombre específico o una participación clara en la milicia se debe al tradicional ninguneo de la mujer en México y al temor de los jefes militares a que ascendieran y llegaran a ocupar cargos de relevancia dentro de las fuerzas armadas" (Poniatowska 22).

En el caso de *La negra Angustias*, Rojas mira más allá de la crueldad deshumanizadora de la Revolución y embute un discurso racial sobre la heroína afromexicana y su lugar en la sociedad mexicana. La etapa revolucionara en la vida de la protagonista crea una apertura para dicho discurso en la narrativa. De este modo, Rojas logra enfocar el interés novelístico en la contemplación de lo afromexicano como parte de la personalidad mexicana.[16] En este hilo, el autor retrata y exhibe en la protagonista intrepidez y liberalidad impropias de lo que la cultura mexicana entiende por roles femeninos adecuados. Totalmente comprometida, la mulata declara sus ideales en la lucha de los de abajo: "Los probes tienen que ser menos probes..., los ricos tienen que ser menos ricos. Deberían, pues, pelear todos hasta llegar a cristalizar la ilusión. Entonces los que vienen detrás, los niños sucios y enfermizos, los niños ateridos y los hambrientos, encontrarían un mundo mejor" (94).

La mulata se caracteriza por su simpatía con el movimiento de los sufridos pobres contra los ricos opresores. Mediante la protagonista Angustias, el autor comprometido esclarece un punto de contacto entre la realidad de la sociedad angustiada y el llamado a la lucha del pueblo unido. Por la fuerza dramática e interés humano de Angustias es fácil entender la lealtad con que la siguen sus tropas. Les dice un viejo a sus hijos al entregárselos a la coronela:

> —¡Bien haiga lo fino! —dijo entusiasmado el viejo, para luego dirigirse a sus hijos—: ¡Síganla con fe y con respeto. Cuídenla y defiéndanla... Trae en sus venas sangre de peleadores y en su pecho ganas de remediar sus males. Llegó ahoy el momento que esperamos desde hace muchos años; no lo desperdicien, por vi'Dios... ¡Lástima de ser tan viejo! (85)

Con su reciedumbre, Angustias reta, además, la noción de superioridad masculina al defender a una prostituta a quien no se le iba a pagar. El sensible Bicicleto observa el carácter de la protagonista y asevera "[l]ástima que el más hombre de todos sea mujer" (129). Por consiguiente, el carácter abusivo del hombre realza en Angustias su reciedumbre como virtud, y el esperado papel del hombre como protector no sólo lo desempeña ahora una mujer, sino que, según observa el Bicicleto, lo hace mejor que el hombre mismo. De este modo, el discurso feminista y racial glorifica las virtudes de la coronela mulata y la fija como agente activa en el grupo revolucionario.

Subsiguientemente, el ritmo acelerado de la acción revolucionaria apuntala los cambios y transiciones en el desarrollo final de la protagonista. Las trayectorias de la Revolución y del desenvolvimiento de la mulata eventualmente llegan a un punto de contacto. En esta instancia, el texto se abre a un esencial develamiento de pensamientos y actitudes de la burguesía, los filósofos científicos revolucionarios y la plebe. La peroración ideológica del autor con respecto a estos tres grupos es fundamental para entender el destino de Angustias puesto que devela una serie de prejuicios hacia las clases marginadas asociada con la desilusión de la Revolución en la narrativa.

Primeramente, en un momento de debilidad, amargura y decepción del grupo de Angustias, se introduce el científico revolucionario Enrique Pérez Gómez quien los escucha para luego hablarles con voz fuerte, explicándoles el porqué de su desilusión:

> ...En realidad, no es de extrañar que cierta amargura y algo de decepción se hayan apoderado de ustedes; ... La desconfianza de la masa en sus propias conquistas se patentiza a medida que *la ignorancia, o la falta de información... es más peculiar de la misma masa...* ; esta

revolución trae un defecto de origen que debemos remediar: es de padres desconocidos. (146-7; énfasis mío)

Explica Pérez Gómez, además, que su propio despecho al régimen dictatorial lo ha llevado a las masas, "a los que la soberbia ignorancia del licenciado Enrique Pérez Gómez, Senior llama *latrofacciosos y robavacas*" (énfasis mío). El filósofo político se muestra a sí mismo ofendido por la actitud de su familia burguesa y porque es juzgado injustamente por el pueblo.[17] Considerándolo necesario, esclarece su verdadero propósito reafirmando que está "[D]ispuesto a imprimir a este movimiento un cauce científico, en el verdadero sentido de la palabra, no en el que el pueblo ha dado a ese grupo de encumbrados hasta ayer en torno de la figura de Porfirio Díaz" (148).

Aunque no logra persuadir al grupo, Pérez Gómez no se desanima y se retira para continuar en su propio rumbo revolucionario, pero no sin haber plantado en Angustias la semilla de la curiosidad por el conocimiento. La negra toma mayor conciencia de su propia situación y su necesidad de aprender. Reflexiona la mulata en voz alta: "—Hay que saber para saber… Bien dijo el catrín que ayer nos echó el discurso. Nosotros así como estamos no semos para el caso… ¡Hay que saber para saber!" (157).

En esta faceta narrativa, el análisis del papel de las mujeres asume mayor importancia dentro del discurso de identidad nacional y los ideales de la Revolución. Mediante una marcada yuxtaposición de 1) respuestas y comportamientos de Angustias ante el profesorcito Manuel de la Reguera y Pérez Cacho y 2) el carácter revolucionario de ésta, se expone eventualmente la desilusión de la Revolución aunada a la sumisión de la protagonista. Explícitamente, la llegada permanente del profesorcito a la vida de Angustias marca la trayectoria final de la protagonista.

En sus primeras clases de alfabetización, Manuel establece su postura en cuanto a la mujer y trata de descartar a la mulata de su papel en la Revolución al sugerirle que "el oficio que… ha escogido no es propio para mujeres… ¡Deje usted a los hombres que arreglen el mundo!" (160). A lo cual responde Angustias, "[E]l día en que las mujeres téngamos la mesma facilidad que los calzonudos, pos entonces habrá en el mundo más gentes que piensen, y no es lo mesmo que piense uno a que piensen dos… ¿O qué opina?" (160).

La revolucionaria reafirma sus ideales feministas, pero en lugar de disputar los prejuicios de Manuel se abre a su opinión porque, según ella, puede aprender de él. Este punto vulnerable de la protagonista es presagio de la subsiguiente caída en la trampa de su patrañero. Ante el desprecio que le manifiesta Manuel por no ser de su clase, explicando éste que su unión con ella "sería considerada por la gente más que como un matrimonio como una cruzada absurda" (176), Angustias parece defenderse a dicha ofensa:

No, hijo, nada de cruzas absurdas. Es necesario que sepas que yo siento un asco terrible por los hombres; que los detesto y los odio por crueles y ordinarios, pero que me siento cabal para ser amiga de algunos y de soportarlos cerca de mí; no para que me empreñen sino de esos que sepan enseñarme algo de lo mucho que tú sabes de letras y de geografía… Por eso resolví cargar contigo y con tus melindres de señorita. (190)

No obstante, a fin de cuentas, aunque se casa con el profesorcito, su sombrío devenir se hace notar, aun en la naturaleza:

> El gris del atardecer era en todas partes... ; mientras que la araña, terminado hasta el último detalle de su falaz ingenio, dejaba, somnolienta, a la imprudencia de los insectos la posibilidad de una cena tierna y apetitosa... Angustias volteó la cara en busca de su maestro... que había abandonado sigilosamente el salón. La mujer, con el cuerpo y el espíritu quebrantados, buscó salida entre la penumbra... estaba... completamente sola; ... "sus" hombres, habían salido. (176-7)

Eventual e irónicamente, aunque la mulata aprende a leer y escribir, su desarrollo queda impedido al grado que su brío se torna en sumisión como mujer y en abandono como revolucionaria. Esta transformación, en que la coronela anonadada se deja afectar por el rubio profesor, abandonando la Revolución y convirtiéndose en esposa sumisa y madre abnegada, se abre a diferentes interpretaciones.

A primera instancia, este destino final de Angustias podría interpretarse simplemente como la reafirmación de que, a fin de cuentas, no hay lugar para una coronela mulata en el México revolucionario. Aunque se ha luchado, el triunfo es efímero pues al fin del recorrido se encuentra el status quo: la coronela mulata es prescindida de su participación heroica en la Revolución y robada de su pensión por el intelectual traidor; la mujer queda encasillada a la domesticidad, sirviéndole al esposo que la desprecia; y la sociedad regresa a la paz y el orden tradicional. Se cumple así la sentencia de la india Crescencia en que Angustias deja de "ser mocha" para hacerse "hembra completa" con el hombre que ha de quebrantarla (198). Dicho final, al parecer incongruente con el carácter revolucionario que muestra la protagonista en el resto de la novela, es sustituido por uno memorable en la película del mismo nombre.

La directora de cine Matilde Landeta no acepta el destino de sumisión de Angustias en la novela y asigna a la protagonista otro destino en la película. De esta manera, Angustias ahora se muestra llena de moños y vestida de muñequita ante el profesorcito, pero al final es capaz de sobreponerse al desprecio del profesorcito siguiendo su vida como revolucionaria (Landeta). Explica Landeta que la sumisión hace de las mujeres madrecitas abnegadas que se dejan humillar.[18]

Empero, la crítica del statu quo se inclina a una nueva lectura de la novela dentro de su contexto histórico de la Revolución y como producto tácito del periodo cultural posrevolucionario. En el hilo narrativo se refleja el pensamiento etnológico de la obra de Rojas y su compromiso social para con los de abajo. Con la obstaculización final del desarrollo negro en la novela, Rojas demuestra, además, su desilusión del movimiento revolucionario fallido.

De modo implícito, se concreta esta desilusión a medida que "las mesnadas de los endurecidos intereses" con sus "armas y técnicas modernas" se imponen "contra una trinchera de corazones", "incendiando los jacales y las cosechas" y encauzando a "las chusmas rebeldes a las montañas". La mulata misma presencia el discurso triunfante de Pérez Gómez, ahora comisionado del gobierno que llega a tomar la plaza en Cuernavaca. Escucha la proclama del científico mientras que:

> Poco a poco... se fué acercando... hizo entonces un esfuerzo supremo y pudo descifrar a medias *el último concepto*... "La Revolución, ciudadanos, no la hacen los ignaros; la Revolución es hija de los pensadores, de los preparados... Nosotros propugnamos un movimiento libertario *de orden científico*, en donde *la acción de la masa quede subordinada a* los dictados de los que saben, de *los que entienden y no al apetito de los muertos de hambre. Hay que aprovechar* racionalmente esta conmoción, *en servicio de toda la gran familia mexicana*". (Rojas, 182-3; énfasis mío)

Más aún, se establece un nexo entre la trayectoria final de la Revolución y la de la mulata al yuxtaponerse textualmente el devenir de la Revolución con los acontecimientos personales de Angustias quien se repite a sí misma:

> "...[D]onde la acción de la masa quede subordinada", ... queriendo penetrar en el significado de aquel concepto. Ya cuando creía tener la solución veníale a la mente otra frase no menos transcendente: aquella que, silbante, salió horas antes de los finos labios de Manuel de la Reguera y Pérez Cacho: "...mi unión con usted sería considerada como una cruza..." (183)

Ni la Revolución, ni Angustias, llega a su pretendido destino. Así como los más aprovechados, el científico entre ellos, corrompen los ideales de la Revolución subyugando al pueblo, la mulata se somete al "dominio" racista y machista de Manolo, suprimiéndola como agente activa —de la Revolución como coronela, de la identidad nacional como mulata y de la sociedad como mujer.[19]

La crítica dirigida a la antes revolucionaria mulata por "resbalosa" que se deja dominar despreciadamente por el pretendiente menos digno, un hombre delicado, rubio y de clase alta, es análoga de la crítica dirigida a los muchos dirigentes de la Revolución que dejan sus ideales atrás por el beneficio propio. Así como Angustias se enamora de Manuel, lo rapta y se casa con él aunque la lleva a la caída del olvido, los líderes revolucionarios se embelesan con el poder adquirido, lo toman propio y lo reglamentan repercutiendo en los ideales de la Revolución.

En sí, la estructura circular de la novela marca la trayectoria del afromexicano en la ideología identitaria nacional y su trascendencia en el México posrevolucionario. Como a un principio, al final se describe a la mulata en el ambiente doméstico: "[E]lla, 'la de la casa chica', lavaba y cantaba... pero cantaba canciones ajenas: ... [d]entro de una cunita, un pequeño de piel obscura y ojos verdes escuchaba embelesado el dulce canto materno, que se trenzaba con los gorjeos del mirlo prisionero" (227-8).

Si al principio la mulata canta como el jilguero alegre y aunado a la naturaleza, al final su canto se trenza con el llanto del mirlo enjaulado. El niño como el mirlo, por ahora, sólo siguen la voz de la mulata.

Sin embargo, es entre el principio y el fin cuando se escucha la voz silenciada de la mulata. El texto de Rojas se abre al dialogismo racial y la significación de la negra revolucionaria en el devenir histórico de México. En el contorno revolucionario, la mulata y los pobres se lanzan a una lucha que temporalmente los hace dueños de su destino. Aunque los signos indiquen lo difícil del triunfo, se recalca la importancia de emprender el camino, de buscar otros senderos. En el cerro de El Jilguero escuchan los serranos en torno del coronel Concho su voz firme que les dice, "—Naiden debe negarle a la mulata su condición de jefa... Sin sus tamaños, ni yo, ni ustedes, nos hubiéramos decedido a entrarle parejo a los plomazos..." (224).

Precisamente por aceptar este reto y desafiar con sus acciones lo establecido, es que Angustias tiene vigencia como protagonista y como símbolo femenino afromexicano, pero, sobre todo, como alegoría de un movimiento que, como ella, quiso romper con la inercia y el estancamiento para dar cabida a todos en una nueva sociedad.[20] Aunque parezca inútil, hay que emprender el camino. Angustias así lo hizo.

NOTAS

[1] Sommers identifica acertadamente a Rojas como "exponente literario del nacionalismo mexicano" que pone sus estudios antropológicos y su obra literaria al servicio de los ideales nacionales (Sommers 47).

[2] La herencia africana fusionó con las culturas occidental e indígena aportando su contribución propia a la construcción nacional. Afirma Aguirre Beltrán que "[e]l ejemplo de Morelos vale para afirmar que penas y amenazas no fueron capaces de impedir el soborno de los curas párrocos y que por esta vía pasaron a la casta euromestiza un número desconocido de negroides" (1946, 274). Aunque no se explicita en los textos, la ideología presente en ellos ha sido una combinación, por una parte, de la llamada por los ideólogos del Estado, de la "Revolución Mexicana" (Gómez).

[3] Velázquez Gutiérrez observa sobre los cuadros de castas que "las mujeres de rostros azabachados" contrastaban con los postulados morales de la época en cuanto al papel de la mujer. Agrega que "[s]us dones mágicos, su extravagante manera de vestir, sus lascivos ademanes y su temperamento altivo y audaz, aunque muchas veces es presentado por los ejecutantes de estas obras como 'poco deseables' y 'peligrosos', revelan que quizá algunas mujeres de origen africano se resistieron a acatar su condición de sumisión y segregación, tanto de esclavas como de mujeres" (Velázquez Gutiérrez 38).

[4] Ver análisis del personaje negro en la novela de Fuentes realizado por Hernández Cuevas.

[5] Rojas crea a la protagonista Angustias recreando la vida real de Remedios Farrera, coronela de la Revolución (Benítez 3; Macías 74).

[6] En su estudio sobre estereotipos de la mulata en la literatura, Mejía afirma que la mulata surgió de un activo mestizaje iniciado durante la Colonia, dando además un estereotipo de exuberante sexualidad dentro del contexto del placer como "amante o prostituta, no se la concibe como esposa del blanco ni del negro, tampoco se la incluye dentro de una práctica religiosa-cristiana, ya que su belleza y su atractivo han sido asociados a lo diabólico" (Mejía 1).

[7] Ver Menton, 299.

[8] La tendencia realista de usar el lenguaje arcaico de la población da mayor verosimilitud al texto (Aguirre Beltrán 1989).

[9] En su artículo "Los Deportados" (agosto 1931) publicado en la revista *Crisol*, Rojas ya se ocupaba críticamente del tema de la discriminación.

[10] El racismo tratado en la obra literaria de Rojas complementa documentos históricos que concretan la conciencia europeizante de los dirigentes nacionales. En 1927, se hace efectiva la prohibición de la inmigración de *negros*, sirios, libaneses, armenios, palestinos, turcos y chinos, para evitar "la degeneración de la raza" (el énfasis es mío, Yankelevich 1187).

[11] Irwin comenta que *La negra Angustias* y *Balún Canán* como exploraciones de mujeres masculinas van más allá de una simple expresión de ansiedad sobre el feminismo para demostrar la masculinidad en la mujer como posibilidad cultural en México (Irwin 189).

[12] En sus estudios sobre protagonistas negros superiores a otros negros y a los blancos, orgullosos de su identidad, revolucionarios y de espíritu rebelde como Angustias, Jackson escribe sobre la variedad de personajes negros en la novela latinoamericana y de las variadas interpretaciones y perspectivas del blanco que presentan los autores. Hace hincapié, además, en el reconocimiento enfático hecho por la *Hispanic American Historical Review* en 1947 sobre las contribuciones de negros fuera del Caribe en la historia latinoamericana, (Jackson 86-88).

[13] La campaña cultural posrevolucionaria borra al negro, en ese pasado y para el futuro, al fijar lo étnico en el indio y el europeo solamente. Vasconcelos, como director de dicha campaña, "deja a los afromexicanos fuera de la conciencia nacional". Tal es el impacto de dicha campaña que, en el transcurso de la presente investigación, se observó que la población en general y la academia siguen mal informadas e ignaras sobre la existencia y el reconocimiento de los negros en México. Además, ha de considerarse que, durante la época colonial, el hecho de que muchos afroamericanos pudieran haberse registrado como mestizos, castizos e incluso españoles era común (Del Valle 85).

[14] Ver Poniatowska, 24-5.

[15] La empresa Casasola ha compilado un gran número de fotografías de la época, las cuales ha publicado en varias ediciones de la *Historia gráfica de la Revolución*.

[16] Irwin parece pasar por inadvertido este mérito de *La negra Angustias* al afirmar que Angustias es mexicana, "but every bit an outsider… not a mestiza, nor even an india, but a black woman" y concluir que "México is not without an *African* immigrant *population*, but it *is not* a population in any way *visible* in Mexican high cultural production, and *is completely absent from explorations of lo mexicano* (Irwin 206; énfasis mío).

[17] Breymann observa que el grupo de científicos filósofos-políticos ha sido acusado de dirigir y apoyar el régimen de Díaz. Y explica:

> Actually, however, a study of the origins of the *científicos* reveals a background of criticism and opposition to the Díaz philosophy of government. This is a sharp contrast with the widely-held conception of a grafting and selfish oligarchy supporting an unpopular and decadent administration for personal gain. Much of the confusion concerning the true nature of the *científicos* stems from a change about 1903 in the objectives, program, and composition of the group, and its relationship to President Díaz. (Breymann 1)

[18] Ver Millán, 401.

[19] Cabe aquí subrayar que tanto Rojas como Campobello, la única autora de la novela de la Revolución, también son soldaderos. Poniatowska comenta que Campobello "va con la impedimenta, y los intelectuales de su época la usan o la menosprecian. Martín Luis Guzmán recibió el archivo de Francisco Villa que Nellie puso en sus manos y escribió así su *Memorias de Pancho Villa*. En 1940, Nellie publicó su libro *Apuntes sobre la vida militar de Francisco Villa*, que no tuvo resonancia, no por falta de méritos sino porque la autora no podía vencer su doble condición: mujer y mexicana" (Poniatowska, p. 27). La novela de Rojas carece de resonancia también, a pesar de la publicidad agregada a su obra por la película del mismo nombre dirigida por Landeta.

[20] Recientemente, se llegan a observar esfuerzos de conciencia de la negritud en México, entre ellos CONACULTA y su Museo de las Culturas Afromestizas en Cuajinicuilapa, Guerrero (Hoffman, 2008, 2006; Flores Dávila, 2006). No obstante, la obra de Rojas permanece como preámbulo de una literatura que subraya la importancia de crear un nuevo idioma del verdadero mestizo.

OBRAS CITADAS

Aguirre Beltrán, Gonzalo. "Oposición de raza y cultura en el pensamiento antropológico mexicano." *Revista Mexicana de Sociología* 31.1 (enero-marzo 1969): 51-71. *JSTOR*. Web.

———. *Obra antropológica VII. Cuijila: Esbozo etnográfico de un pueblo negro*. México: Fondo de Cultura Económica, 1989.

———. *La población negra de México*. México: Ediciones Fuente Cultural, 1946.

Althoff, Francis D., Jr. "The Afro Hispanic Speech of the Municipio of Cuajinicuilapa, Guerrero." Tesis doctoral. University of Florida, 1998.

Benítez, Fernando. "Francisco Rojas González, primer premio de literatura." *El Nacional* 15 octubre 1944: 3.

Breymann, Walter M. "The 'Científicos': Critics of the Díaz Regime, 1892-1903." *Proceedings of the Arkansas Academy of Science* 7 (1954): 91-97. Web.

Casasola, Gustavo, ed. *Historia gráfica de la Revolución, 1900-1940*. México: Royce Editores, S.A. de C.V., 1992.

Del Valle Pavón, Guillermina. "Transformaciones de la población afromestiza de Orizaba según los padrones de 1777 y 1791." *Pardos, mulatos y libertos: Sexto encuentro de afromexicanistas*. Ed. Adriana Naveda Chávez-Hita. Jalapa: U Veracruzana, 2001. 79-97.

Flores Dávila, Julia I. *Los Afrodescendientes en México. Reconocimiento y propuestas para evitar la discriminación*. México: Colección Estudios, 2006.

Fuentes, Carlos. *La muerte de Artemio Cruz*. México: Fondo de Cultura Económica, 1962.

Gallegos, Rómulo. *Doña Bárbara*. Buenos Aires: Espasa-Calpe, 1947.

Gómez, Yuridia. "El papel de la ideología dominante en los libros de texto gratuitos de ciencias sociales." Tesis de licenciatura. México: UNAM – FCPS, 1989.

Hernández Cuevas, Marco Polo. *African Mexicans and the Discourse on Modern Nation*. Dallas: UP of America, Inc., 2004.

Hoffman, Oddie. "México negro: ¿eslabón perdido o veta por explorar? Los estudios afromexicanistas hoy." III Congreso de la Asociación Latinoamericana de Población, Argentina, 24-26 septiembre 2008. Web.

———. "Negros y afromestizos en México: viejas y nuevas lecturas de un mundo olvidado." *Revista Mexicana de Sociología* 68.1 (enero-marzo 2006): 103-35. Web.

Irwin, Robert McKee. *Mexican Masculinities*. Minneapolis: U of Minnesota P, 2003.

Jackson, Richard. "Miscegenation and Personal Choice in Two Twentieth-Century Novels of Continental Spanish America." *Hispania* 50.1 (marzo 1967): 86-88. *JSTOR*. Web.

Landeta, Matilde, dir., adapt. y prod. *La negra Angustias*. 35 mm, 85 min., b/n. México, D.F.: TACMA, 1949.

Macías, Anna. "Women and the Mexican Revolution, 1910-1920." *The Americas* 37.1 (julio 1980): 53-82. *JSTOR*. Web.

Mejía Núñez, Guadalupe. "La mulata en la expresión artística." *Sincronía* otoño 2002. Web.

Menton, Seymour. "*La negra Angustias*, una doña Bárbara *mexicana*." *Revista Iberoamericana* 19.38 (abril-septiembre 1954): 299-308.

Millán, Márgara. "En otro espejo. Cine y video mexicano hecho por mujeres." *Miradas feministas sobre las mexicanas del siglo XX*. Coord. Marta Lamas. México: Fondo de Cultura Económica, 2007.

Poniatowska, Elena. *Hasta no verte Jesús mío*. México: ERA, 1969.

———. *Las soldaderas*. México: ERA, 1999.

Rojas González, Francisco. *La negra Angustias*. México: EDIAPSA, 1948.

Salas, Elizabeth. *Soldaderas in the Mexican Military: Myth and History*. Austin: U of Texas P, 1990.

Sommers, Joseph. *Francisco Rojas González: Exponente literario del nacionalismo mexicano*. Trad. Carlos Antonio Castro. Xalapa: U Veracruzana, 1966.

Vasconcelos, José. *La raza cósmica*. México: Espasa-Calpe Mexicana, S.A., 1994.

Velázquez Gutiérrez, María Elisa. "'Orgullo y despejo'. Iconografía de las mujeres de origen africano en los cuadros de castas del México virreinal." *Pardos, mulatos y libertos: Sexto encuentro de afromexicanistas*. Ed. Adriana Naveda Chávez-Hita. Jalapa: U Veracruzana, 2001. 25-38.

Yankelevich, Pablo. "Explotadores, truhanes, agitadores y negros. Deportaciones y restricciones a estadounidenses en el México Revolucionario." *Revista HMex* 57.4 (2008): 1155-99. Web.

Memorias de una soldadera, de Madero a los cristeros
HASTA NO VERTE JESÚS MÍO, DE ELENA PONIATOWSKA

Emil Volek

ARIZONA STATE UNIVERSITY

> Así como hay hombres, también hay mujeres,
> que cargan sus pantalones, aquí está una de ellas…
> aquella mujer valiente,
> que como era buena también era mala;
> valor tenía suficiente.
>
> (Corrido)

Al comenzar la década de los sesenta, Elena Poniatowska (1932) era una joven periodista y escritora relativamente poco conocida, autora de unos cuentitos para niños (*Lilus Kikus*, 1954), de muchas entrevistas (de los toreros a los escritores) y de unas divertidas crónicas de la contemporaneidad urbana del D. F., quien vivía a la sombra de su tía, la extravagante y algo excéntrica poeta Guadalupe Amor (a quien recordará con cariño en *Las siete cabritas*, 2000). Al despuntar los setenta, se convertiría en el ícono de la intelectualidad mexicana contestataria al sempiterno régimen del PRI. La improbable transformación se debe a dos libros que le ofrecen el azar, la época y el oficio de periodista, pero también su carácter y el trabajo preparatorio de las dos décadas anteriores. El primero, *Hasta no verte Jesús mío* (1969), es una obra híbrida, entre testimonio y novela, y el segundo, el más conocido, es el montaje testimonial *La noche de Tlatelolco* (1971).

El primero hace revista de la historia mexicana de la primera mitad del siglo XX a partir de los recuerdos personalísimos de una mujer de pueblo, Josefina Bórquez, que Poniatowska encuentra por casualidad en la imprenta del periódico donde trabaja. La escritora se siente atraída por su lenguaje, se le aproxima, empieza a conversar con ella y pasa a entrevistarla; esta relación se convierte tanto en el libro como en una larga amistad (véase su artículo en *Vuelta* y numerosas entrevistas). El segundo, sabemos, se enfoca en el traumático verano/otoño de 1968.

Hasta no verte Jesús mío marca la transición de la periodista de la "zona rosa", donde parecía destinada por su linaje de la alta sociedad, a la intrépida escritora "comprometida" con los temas sociales candentes, capaz de desafiar repetidamente el *establishment* del poder en el México de entonces y de hoy. En el comienzo de los sesenta, Poniatowska tiene la suerte de colaborar brevemente con el conocido antropólogo Oscar Lewis, cuyo trabajo *Los hijos de Sánchez* (1961), en la línea del estudio de la "cultura de la pobreza" urbana, irritó tanto al *establishment* mexicano. La joven periodista le ayuda a editar otra investigación antropológica, hecha a base de grabaciones, esta vez del campo: *Pedro Martínez, la vida de un campesino de Tepoztlán* (para unos detalles jugosos sobre este antropólogo paradigmático de los "subalternos", ver Steele 92). De esta manera, Poniatowska no sólo se familiariza con el trabajo antropológico, sino que también "se conscientiza", se siente tocada por los documentos sobre la indescriptible pobreza existente en México (Poniatowska, *Vuelta* 10).

Cuando el azar la conecta con Josefina, Poniatowska pone lo aprendido en la práctica. A diferencia de Lewis, "el gringo de la grabadora" (García Flores 12), quien era bastante paranoico además (Steele 92, García Pinto 181), Josefina no es para ella sólo un objeto de estudio con quien simpatizar en teoría pero mantenerse lo más lejos posible en la práctica. En realidad, Poniatowska siempre tenía mucha empatía con las mujeres de pueblo, probablemente porque, al llegar a México en 1942 de la Francia en guerra, ella creció y se "mexicanizó" con las nanas que trabajaban para su familia (Jörgensen); de manera que Josefina, poco a poco, llega a ocupar el lugar de la nana y también el de la madre ausente (muy *busy* con sus compromisos en la sociedad; en la familia de Poniatowska se hablaba francés e inglés). En el trabajo con Lewis y con Josefina, la joven y ciertamente algo romántica escritora absorbe, como una esponja, el coraje de los pobres ante la vida en su país, que para ellos no ha cambiado con la Revolución. La aristócrata se "mexicaniza" (Poniatowska, *Vuelta* 8). Con el paso del tiempo, tiene lugar algo como la transferencia en la terapia: la entrevistadora asume el dolor de la entrevistada y se convierte en su *alter ego*. Sólo que Poniatowska es un *alter ego* de los pobres potenciado por su condición y la capacidad de actuar con miras a un público mayor.

Josefina no es una persona fácil. Se resiste, y a veces no quiere hablar. Es rebelde, rencorosa, anárquica. Cuando al fin la escritora se gana su confianza, Josefina "se suelta" y hasta cambia de lenguaje (*Vuelta* 9): deja de cuidar su lengua y empieza a utilizar un idioma coloquial popular rico, imaginativo y contundente, lleno de "tacos" y de picardías que pueden herir sensibilidades "delicadas". A lo largo de unos cuatro años, Poniatowska acumula mucho material, en gran parte reconstruido (ya que Josefina se niega a hablar a la grabadora), y necesita organizarlo. Josefina se niega también a que en la obra se utilice su nombre verdadero.

Definitivamente, el modelo antropológico utilizado por Lewis se va al traste. Pero la ficción abre caminos que liberan a Poniatowska de la obsesión con la superficie documentalista y le permiten una reconstrucción más imaginativa y más profunda tanto de la historia narrada como de la persona central de su libro. Así surge el personaje de ficción, Jesusa Palancares. El título que Poniatowska pone a la creación final juega con el nombre de la protagonista también de otra manera, ya que "Jesús" no sólo se refiere a la reciente obsesión de ésta con la Obra Espiritual, una secta popular al margen de la Iglesia Católica, sino que también alude a su etapa de alcoholismo ("hasta no verte Jesús mío" se decía popularmente antes de "apurar" la copa). Poniatowska describe su trabajo de edición textual en esta fase de la siguiente manera:

> Maté a los personajes que me sobraban, eliminé cuanta sesión espiritualista pude, elaboré donde me pareció necesario, podé, cosí, remendé, inventé. (Poniatowska, *Vuelta* 10)

> Hice muchos diálogos para aligerar el texto; puse imágenes y construí capítulos. Por eso se trata de una novela y no de una cosa antropológica. (García Flores 13)

Por todas estas consideraciones, Poniatowska prefiere llamar el resultado de su trabajo organizador "novela testimonial" (*Vuelta* 10). El primer borrador, confiesa, atenuaba el lenguaje del personaje; pero al volver con Josefina para mostrarle lo que había hecho, la escritora se dio cuenta de que en esta forma, el lenguaje le falló al personaje y al relato, que su lenguaje necesitaba escucharse con toda su tal vez cruda pero siempre rica autenticidad. El lenguaje "del otro" (planteado como un tema fundamental del estudio por Mijail Bajtin y su grupo) reclama sus derechos, porque el idiolecto de Josefina/Jesusa va más allá de la fonética, más allá de unas palabras o palabrotas estratégicamente colocadas, más allá de los giros del lenguaje coloquial o regional que celebraba la novela costumbrista. Su lenguaje lleva en sí las imágenes, las percepciones, la cosmovisión y la visión social del estrato popular de la población con sus valoraciones a veces crudas, pero que son siempre imaginativas respuestas a su ambiente, contundentes aún en su extremo "realismo". Este lenguaje es su mundo y es inseparable de él. *Se podría decir que el lenguaje así restituido es el segundo protagonista del relato.*

Repasemos rápidamente la parte de la obra que muestra a la protagonista en la Revolución e intentemos escuchar su voz.

LA INFANCIA

 a familia de Jesusa era de un pueblo de Oaxaca. Se muere su madre cuando Jesusa apenas tenía cinco años (*Hasta no verte* 19). Su padre trabajaba en lo que se ofreciera, y según las temporadas, traía y llevaba a la familia entre Tehuantepec y el puerto Salina Cruz.

Desde niña Jesusa era, según dice, "muy hombrada", le gustaba jugar a la guerra, a las pedradas (*ibid.*). "Ninguno de mi casa fue como yo de peleonero" (23), reconoce. También hacía la vida imposible a las mujeres que el padre traía para vivir con ellos, y lidiaba "con maña" con aquellas que querían atraparlo en un matrimonio. Celebra con satisfacción que era "figurosa en eso de las maldades" (20). Freud se habría alegrado del "complejo de Electra".

Jesusa aprendió algo de trabajos domésticos con la madrastra Evarista, cuya familia administraba una prisión. Hasta dormía con una reclusa que era supuesta múltiple asesina y que sufría de ataques de ansiedad. Pasan juntas un terremoto (el de 1911), y unos días después, aparentemente, a la prisionera la salva milagrosamente el Niño de Atocha: la saca de la prisión y la deja aquella misma tarde lejos de Oaxaca, en Zacatecas… A lo mejor, la prisionera se escapó en la confusión del terremoto y Jesusa ajusta la memoria según sus creencias posteriores, donde el Niño de Atocha y el "espiritualismo" desempeñarán un papel clave (Poniatowska, *Vuelta* 7-8).

Jesusa observa comportamientos, acumula sabiduría popular (curaciones, explicaciones de terremotos —se cura ella sola de las viruelas—; *Hasta no verte* 51) y lo expresa todo en un lenguaje inigualable.

En aquel tiempo, su padre anda con los maderistas, pero la Revolución parece estar lejos. La niña trabaja en varias casas como sirvienta. Va creciendo, y la vida se hace más peligrosa para una mujer. Cuando en una trifulca de naipes muere su hermano Emiliano, quien acompañaba al padre en sus andanzas revolucionarias, éste se acuerda de su hija, la busca y se la lleva consigo en sustitución del hermano: así empieza su aventura de soldadera en la Revolución. Entretanto, el maderista se ha hecho carrancista. La suerte los arroja a Guerrero. Mientras que su comandante, el malogrado general Jesús Carranza, hermano del entonces presidente constitucionalista Venustiano, se encamina hacia México y hacia su muerte (en diciembre de 1914), el entierro de Emiliano demora a sus familiares, quienes se van luego con otra compañía para Acapulco y se ven involucrados en la lucha contra los zapatistas quienes defienden su territorio en la contienda entre las facciones revolucionarias.

El relato presenta tres ciclos de vida de Jesusa en la Revolución: en Guerrero, contra los zapatistas; en el norte, contra los villistas; y, más tarde, en distintas campañas contra los cristeros.

SOLDADERA CON SU PADRE: POR LAS TIERRAS DE GUERRERO

Jesusa describe el *modus operandi* de las soldaderas que acompañaban a sus hombres: por lo general, las mujeres no están pendientes del combate; la tropa las manda de avanzada para que vayan preparando la comida mientras los hombres pelean con el enemigo. En los pueblos, éstas son recibidas según y cómo: bien en los pueblos carrancistas, mientras que la gente de los pueblos zapatistas se esconde en el monte. A veces encuentran comida a medio preparar, y ni un alma cerca (*Hasta no verte* 66-67).

Cuando se topan con el enemigo, las mujeres tratan de confundirlo. Se desprende del relato que las soldaderas carrancistas son tratadas correctamente por los zapatistas. A veces, éstos les advierten que habrá balacera y cuidan de que se pongan a resguardo. Jesusa cuenta un episodio en especial, cuando Zapata en persona, todo un caballero y disfrazado de indio pobre, va a entregarlas personalmente a ella y a otras mujeres a su padre y a sus maridos, para garantizar con su palabra y persona que no se les ha tocado para nada, "que no vayan a sufrir con sus maridos" (74-77).

Entretanto, la hija del comandante, "la señorita" Lucía, "jalaba parejo en todo" con la tropa: estaba en el combate, atendía a los heridos y, a la noche, vigilaba el campamento y rezaba su rosario (80-81).

La lucha contra los zapatistas fue desigual, cuenta Jesusa, porque ellos conocían el terreno y libraban una audaz guerra de guerrillas. Comenta ella: "eran vivos, valientes... aunque fueran unos indios patarrajada, sin un petate en que caerse muertos" (78). En ese trajín pasan ocho meses.

Jesusa observa la Revolución, que más que "revolución" es "la bola", como se la llamaba popularmente, y con mucha razón. Ve cómo los maderistas o los zapatistas se hacen carrancistas y cómo se las agarran unos con otros, sin más motivo que el machismo irascible, susceptible de ofensas menos pensadas. "Así fue la revolución, que ahora soy de éstos, pero mañana seré de los otros, a cha-quetazo limpio, el caso es estar con el más fuerte, el que tiene más parque..." (71), comenta lúcidamente sobre aquellos súbitos cambios "ideológicos".

Mientras tanto, va deteriorando la relación con su padre, ya que éste se dedica más a sus mujeres que a su hija, que ya es "grande". Tendría en aquel momento unos catorce años. Jesusa está harta de la lucha y quiere volver a su tierra.

VIDA MARITAL

En aquel tiempo, empieza a asediarla un joven oficial dos años mayor que ella. Quiere casarse con ella. Jesusa se resiste, es muy "perra". El joven la lleva para hablar con su padre, pero éste se enfada, porque piensa que el "matrimonio" ya está consumado, como era la costumbre en aquellos tiempos revoltosos. Jesusa quiere irse, pero no hay una buena manera que lo haga. El comandante de la tropa, que hace las veces de padre, decide, prudentemente, que mejor se la entrega a su "marido" que a una tripulación de marineros de un barco de carga, que la llevaría de Acapulco a Oaxaca...

¿Qué decir de su vida marital? La noche de bodas la pasa sola, encerrada en casa, ya que su marido se fue a festejar... y no apareció por dos semanas. Luego, cuando la "ocupaba", no la dejaba ni desvestir, sólo le bajaba un poco los pantalones. Su marido no era de "apapachar", nada de besuqueos o caricias. "Era hombre muy serio", dice Jesusa, "nunca anduvo haciendo esas figuretas. Él tenía con qué y lo hacía y ya" (*Hasta no verte*, 86).

Pedro Aguilar, como se llamaba su marido, vaya sorpresa, era mujeriego, y las luchas que Jesusa tenía con las mujeres de su padre se repiten con las de su marido. Este también empieza a pegarla, después de que ella, en una de sus lar-gas ausencias, abre con otra mujer una cantina donde se la pasaban en grande (89-90). Pedro, como buen macho, era muy celoso y también muy "delicado" (97). Por delicadeza, no la golpeaba delante de la gente, sino que la llevaba aparte, bajo el pretexto de "que le fuera a lavar los pañuelos". De esta mane-ra, al escuchar la orden de ir a "lavarle pañuelos", ya sabía que la esperaba una nueva golpiza.

La cosa llega a un punto que Jesusa no aguanta más: la próxima vez ella también lleva su pistola para "lavar pañuelos". Cuando el marido la amenaza, Jesusa le contesta, no sin un toque de ambigüedad: "Saque lo suyo que yo traigo lo mío" (99). La confrontación introduce cierta paz y entendimiento en el matri-monio: "Pedro se volvió más bueno desde que lo balacié" (101), dice.

Poco a poco, Jesusa se da cuenta de que Pedro reacciona así por las malas lenguas de algunas soldaderas, que han puesto sus ojos en él y le dicen calum-nias de ella. Y también empieza a justificar sus infidelidades: son las mujeres las que lo siguen como "perras calientes"; él tiene "un chinguero de coscolinas" en torno suyo. Y Pedro, como buen macho, "cumple" con todas, porque "como hombre no le quedaba más remedio que cumplirles" (105). "¿Qué buscan las cabronas?", se pregunta. Y se responde: "Todas tenemos el tafiruche igual" (108).

Más tarde, cuando pasan una larga temporada en el norte, acampados en la sierra de San Antonio Arenales, Pedro hasta se pone a leerle libros durante las largas noches (114). Parece que el matrimonio ha llegado a un punto de maduración, de comprensión mutua y de paz. En ese momento, Pedro perece en una emboscada de los villistas. Jesusa no ha cumplido dieciocho años.

SOLDADERA CON SU MARIDO

on Pedro, la vida de soldadera de Jesusa cambia drásticamente. Pedro es de la caballería. La sube a caballo, aunque ella nunca lo había hecho antes, y que aprenda "a la brava". Pedro también se la lleva consigo al combate para cargar su máuser. Con él, Jesusa aprende a "andar entre los balazos" (*Hasta no verte*, 91). Le avisa también que "cuando él la viera perdida", primero la mataría a ella (se sobrentiende que antes que dejarla al enemigo). Por aquel entonces el padre de Jesusa muere en un encuentro con los zapatistas y ella ya no tiene a nadie más sino a su marido.

De Guerrero pasan a la capital donde el destacamento se adiestra para la campaña en el norte, contra Villa. Por el tiempo que se ha mencionado, dos campañas de ocho meses cada una contra los zapatistas, tiene que ser a mediados de o en la segunda mitad de 1916.

El traslado al norte en el tren militar va a paso de tortuga y tarda meses, ya que los villistas dinamitan a cada rato las vías férreas (94-95). No importaba si era un tren militar o de civiles. Implícitamente se contrasta el tratamiento de las mujeres por Zapata y por Villa: "Si el tren era de pasajeros también lo volaba y se apoderaba del dinero, y de las mujeres que estaban de buena edad... Eso no es de hombre decente" (95). Jesusa no tendrá una buena palabra para "el centauro del norte".

El marido la lleva a los combates aparentemente sin el permiso explícito de sus superiores y la viste de hombre para que se hicieran la vista gorda (109). Ella traía pistola y rifle, como se usaba en la caballería. En el combate, ella cargaba el máuser del marido, pero también disparaba su propio fusil. No sabe decir si mató a alguien. Poco a poco, Jesusa se acostumbra a las balas y hasta empieza a gustarle la euforia del combate, "pero me duró poco el gusto", dice (110).

De vez en cuando, el ejército acampa por largo tiempo y los soldados se hacen amigos de la gente. La vida se vuelve casi apacible. En una ocasión, como están cerca de Coahuila, de donde es Pedro, van de visita a su abuela. Pero tienen que salir volando, ya que a Pedro lo persiguen de la hacienda por un antiguo robo de caballos para la Revolución. Cuando le avisan que vienen a prenderlo, Pedro, entonces capitán del ejército constitucionalista, pregunta incrédulo: "Pero ¿cómo? Yo creí que las cosas habían cambiado con la revolución..." Sólo para escuchar la respuesta: "La revolución no ha cambiado nada. Nomás estamos más muertos de hambre…" (125-26).

A la vuelta, aparecen los villistas en la región. En el ataque malogrado contra ellos, cerca de Ojinaga, muere Pedro. La retirada lleva el resto de la tropa al lado norteamericano, donde son desarmados e internados por un mes. Al volver a México, el general le ofrece a Jesusa el mando de la tropa de su difunto marido. Pero ella se niega. Dice que "andaba en la bola siguiendo a mi marido más de a güevo que de ganas" (132). Parece que la revolución no es para ella.

LA DESMOVILIZACIÓN

esusa piensa volver a Tehuantepec, pero en la ciudad de México le roban todas sus pertenencias y dinero, y ella tiene que quedarse en la capital. Una amiga la lleva al Palacio Nacional para gestionar su pensión de viuda; allí Jesusa tendrá una memorable confrontación con el presidente Carranza, ya que éste se niega a firmar su documento, alegando que ella es muy joven para pensionarla. Su odio a Carranza sólo iguala al odio a Villa. Este le quitó al marido, aquél, el reconocimiento de su participación en la Revolución.

Jesusa dice que ya había conocido a Carranza antes, que lo vio "muy cerquita" en la toma de Celaya "donde le mocharon el brazo a Obregón" (*Hasta no verte,* 136). Según ella, al ver lo duro del combate, Carranza se echó a correr.

Es un recuerdo objetivamente imposible, ya que las batallas de Celaya tuvieron lugar en abril de 1915, y además, Obregón no perdió el brazo en Celaya sino más tarde, en Santa Ana. O sea, Jesusa habría tenido que salir para la capital junto con el malogrado hermano de Carranza y no podría haber tenido el tiempo de las campañas en Guerrero. Pero este "recuerdo" inexistente es explicable por su odio al entonces presidente constitucional donde, tal vez, media también el conocimiento previo de su hermano Jesús, asesinado en las disputas entre los constitucionalistas y los convencionistas (éstos llamados por la Convención de Aguascalientes del otoño de 1914 que desconoció a Carranza como presidente de la república).

Vivencias vividas y no vividas se mezclan libremente en la realidad de la memoria personal de Jesusa. Al mismo tiempo, el personaje acude a su autoridad de "testigo ocular" para "implantar" estos recuerdos falsos en su testimonio de la realidad. Su discurso no deja lugar a dudas de que "vio" lo que está relatando. En Jesusa, estos recuerdos postizos vienen de su rencor por el maltrato que percibe de parte de los revolucionarios, a los que odia cordialmente. En el testimonio latinoamericano, la "desmemoria" responde más bien a los rigores políticos de la época que han informado el polémico canon del género. (Para la política de la voz y de la memoria en el testimonio, ver mi estudio "Los entramados".)

Para Jesusa, Carranza es simplemente un mal ladrón. "A mí esos revolucionarios me caen como patada en los… bueno como si yo tuviera güevos.

Son puros bandidos, ladrones de camino real, amparados por la ley. … ¡Puro revolucionario cabrón!" (*Hasta no verte* 137).

Resume Jesusa casi a manera de epílogo el relato de la Revolución:

> Y aquí estoy ya nomás esperando a que den las cinco de la mañana porque ni siquiera duermo y nomás se me revela todo lo que pasé desde chiquilla, cuando anduve de guacha y sin guarache, haciéndole a la revolución como jugando a la gallina ciega, recibiendo puros trancazos, cada vez más desmadejada en esta chingadera de vida. (148)

Y dice en otro pasaje iluminador: "Yo creo que fue una guerra mal entendida porque eso de que se mataran unos con otros, padres contra hijos, hermanos contra hermanos; carrancistas, villistas, zapatistas, pues eran puras tarugadas porque éramos los mismos pelados y muertos de hambre" (94).

Es obviamente una perspectiva posterior, una que el personaje formula décadas después. En su visión, sin embargo, encontramos un curioso punto ciego: la Guerra de los Cristeros (1926-1929).

Jesusa no ha cumplido dieciocho años y no sólo en ese momento ha terminado su matrimonio y su vida en la Revolución, sino, en cierto sentido, la vida misma, aunque ella siga viviendo, pero sin rumbo, año tras año a la deriva, viviendo una especie de vida póstuma. Sin embargo, la vida le tiene una sorpresa: estalla la revuelta de los cristeros. El amor a la balacera resulta más fuerte que las atracciones de la vida en paz (juergas, bailes que compensan las chambas de poca monta…).

LOS CRISTEROS EN LA HISTORIA Y EN LA MANIPULACIÓN SIMBÓLICA

> Te doblas y haces arco, Plutarco
> con tus leyes impías, Elías
> y aunque la cara me ralles, Calles
> vales una caca seca, tu Plutarco Elías Calles
>
> (Rima popular entre los cristeros)

La Guerra de los Cristeros es un episodio todavía indigesto, poco entendido y mayormente reprimido o disimulado de la historia de la Revolución Mexicana (para un breve resumen de los hechos, ver Krauze 349-56, y más en la obra clásica de Meyer, *La Cristiada*). Es un bocado difícil tanto para la historia oficial como para los intelectuales progresistas hasta la actualidad quienes, en gran parte, se han identificado con el relato oficial de la Revolución como puerta al México moderno, y sólo se diferencian del mismo en las sutilezas, a veces indescifrables, que sus ideologías del momento marcan como caminos por seguir dentro de aquella supuesta modernidad (ver mi "Argirópolis"). Es un Auschwitz mexicano, preparado por casi un siglo del jacobinismo liberal, más inmediatamente por los ciclos de violencia crecientes desatados por la Revolución y, finalmente, creado por gusto precisamente cuando la consolidación de la Revolución promete empezar a traer los primeros frutos de la paz.

La trampa está tendida por unos artículos de la Constitución de 1917, artículos tan absurdos en su extremismo que a nadie se le ocurría ponerlos en la práctica, hasta que, en 1926, lo hace no sólo con saña sino también con malicia y cinismo el entonces presidente Calles (él tiene que obedecer la ley draconiana autoimpuesta hasta más allá de la ley misma). Tenemos delante la típica trayectoria de las ideas de la modernidad ilustrada que emergen, radicalizadas, con retraso de cien y doscientos años, cuando unos juegos intelectuales *risqués*, saboreados en su primer momento por una mínima élite entre aristocrática e intelectual, son puestos en la práctica en masa por un estado (que tira a) totalitario.

Históricamente, las tensiones entre la iglesia y el estado se remontan al Medioevo, pero recrudecen especialmente en la época moderna, cuando el estado impone sus distintos aspectos burocráticos totalizadores. El antecedente inmediato para la tragedia mexicana fue el *Kulturkampf* en Alemania entre 1871 y 1891. En confrontación con la Iglesia Católica (dominante en los Estados del Sur y en los territorios habitados por los polacos, entonces parte de Prusia), el "canciller de hierro" Bismarck intentó subyugar la iglesia al estado y así homogeneizar el recién unificado *Reich* en torno a la Prusia protestante y germánica. Mientras la "arrogancia del poder" aumentaba la presión, hasta forzar el exilio de muchos sacerdotes o ponerlos en prisión, la iglesia maniobraba astuta y conciliadoramente, se defendía pacíficamente (organizando resistencia no violenta, el retiro de los sacramentos) y se organizó políticamente. El extremismo persecutorio de la *religión* católica alborotó hasta a los conservadores protestantes, con el tiempo, disminuyó la paranoia del canciller y mermó su apoyo político; total, empezó a buscarse una salida "elegante" del lío autoinfligido, que se prolongó por más de una década, hasta encontrar un *modus vivendi* en 1887 y empezar a desmantelar las leyes represivas (¡la última, en 1953!).

La iglesia mexicana, ella misma involucrada en la larga lucha con las leyes de la "Reforma", se inspiró tempranamente tanto en el "renacimiento católico", propugnado por el papa Pío IX (1846-1878), como en el ejemplo de la iglesia en Alemania. Su activismo social será replicado, entre otras formas, en la proliferación de agrupaciones sociales, en la organización sindical de los obreros y de los campesinos y en una gran actividad editorial y del periodismo. Podría pensarse especialmente que el trabajo de organización sindical en México se estaba anticipando a las propuestas declaradas por la "Teología de la Liberación" de la segunda mitad del siglo XX, aunque los resortes disimulados de ésta eran más bien de corte marxista. Los éxitos tempranos no dejaron de crear conflictos: por ejemplo, cuando en las elecciones libres de 1912 los católicos ganan unos cien escaños, los liberales alborotados fuerzan a Madero a "meter la mano" y reducir el número a veintitantos. Se hacía obvio que los gobiernos que salían de la Revolución no eran exactamente democráticos, si no peores. También durante el conflicto de los años veinte, las maniobras institucionales tanto del gobierno como de la iglesia seguían de cerca el modelo probado del *Kulturkampf*. Con la diferencia de que en México intervino el pueblo de manera imprevista y que aquello que en Alemania fue un *bürgerdrama* de la clase media que no se olvidaba de ciertas cortesías compartidas, en México tomó matices de un baño de sangre salvaje.

Bajo Calles, la "modernidad" y la "liberación de las conciencias" serán llevadas al pueblo raso a punto de pistola, de torturas, de violaciones y de la "tierra quemada" por unos obcecados y fanáticos "desfanatizadores". Los resultados son inimaginables e inexcusables. El hecho de que la intelectualidad mexicana hasta ahora ha buscado todo tipo de pretextos para no distanciarse de este capítulo monstruoso de la Revolución, indica los límites del proyecto mismo que la izquierda latinoamericana tuvo en el siglo XX, y en gran parte sigue teniendo, para el continente.

Veamos algunos motivos para aplicar tortura y pena capital sin juicio: practicar el culto clandestino, proteger a algún sacerdote, guardar el Santísimo Sacramento, conservar en casa imágenes y reliquias religiosas, usar insignias prohibidas, gritar "Viva Cristo Rey", estar de luto sin permiso, llevar escapulario, rezar el rosario, interceder ante las autoridades para evitar una ejecución, reclamar el cuerpo de la víctima, velarlo, enterrarlo (Meyer, *Grandeza mexicana* 29).

Calles se propone nada menos que extirpar de un plumazo el catolicismo de México. Y lo dice sin ambages. En fin, para él la religión —en la mejor tradición ilustrada— es "el opio del pueblo" (como lo había formulado oportunamente Carlos Marx) y es un freno a la modernización del país. Y bien pensado, el catolicismo fue llevado al país por extraños.[1]

Las primeras reacciones ante tamaño atropello son sorprendentemente tímidas y pacíficas: peticiones organizadas, boicot de las actividades económicas patrocinadas por el gobierno, actos de desobediencia civil, o sea, resistencia no violenta. Siguen intentos de negociación, ya que nadie puede creer en la enormidad de lo que se está proponiendo. Tenemos así, inicialmente, una serie de paralelos con las prácticas fomentadas en aquel entonces en la India por Gandhi o, más tarde, con el movimiento de los derechos civiles en los EE. UU. de los años sesenta. Sólo que Calles no cede ni está dispuesto a negociar. Piensa en desmantelar la institución de la iglesia y subestima totalmente la reacción del pueblo. Como buen liberal, tiene además en mente el fantoche de la iglesia de la Colonia; no quiere ver los resultados del activismo social de la Iglesia Católica de las últimas décadas tanto en el campo como en la ciudad.

En el otoño, la desesperación de la gente común y corriente lleva a provocar las primeras protestas armadas, y al empezar el año 1927, las protestas masivas son ahogadas en sangre; hacia la mitad del año, el levantamiento en armas se expande ya por medio México.

Es totalmente erróneo hablar de "campesinos reaccionarios" que se oponen a la Revolución. Los cristeros no anhelan la vuelta del "antiguo régimen", no tienen siquiera un programa político. No son aliados de la hacienda, como se les imputa impunemente. Tampoco se oponen a la reforma agraria per se, con la salvedad de que "los agraristas" beneficiados tienen que enlistarse en la cruzada del gobierno. En realidad, en una gran parte del movimiento, los cristeros son los antiguos zapatistas (éstos sí celebrados en los manuales de la Revolución y en las historias de la literatura). Defienden su humanidad, siempre precaria en las condiciones infrahumanas de la vida en el campo. Son rancheros, mujeres, niños, viejos, quieren vivir en paz con sus familias y sus santitos (¿es un delito?). El hecho de cerrar las iglesias, profanarlas, romper los vitrales, los cuadros y los santos, ¿modernizó tal vez a México? ¿Mejoró en lo más mínimo las condiciones de la vida? Fue la Revolución la que abrió las compuertas a sus impulsos "ilustrados" más irracionales y empezó a devorar a sus hijos y a la gente misma que pretendía beneficiar.

La Revolución fue una gran maestra de la violencia y del embrutecimiento ante el sufrimiento humano (especialmente el de los "otros"). De manera que, ahora, todos entran en la lid bien instruidos, y con ganas. Un fanatismo provoca otro. En las palabras de Luis González, "Fue una guerra sangrienta como pocas, el mayor sacrificio humano colectivo en toda la historia de México" (Krauze 353). La historia oficial ve en los cristeros masas manipuladas por la alta jerarquía eclesiástica, los intelectuales progresistas, unos campesinos fanatizados por los curas obscurantistas (para una imagen paradigmática de éstos, ver la novela de Agustín Yáñez, *Al filo del agua*, 1947). Ningún intelectual que se precie, moderno o incluso posmoderno, ha sido capaz de reconocer que la gente en aquel momento defiende uno de sus derechos civiles fundamentales y que acude a la violencia cuando no se le abre otro camino.

Para retomar la polémica que ha marcado el discurso hispanoamericano desde la Independencia, podríamos decir que, en esta ocasión, la "barbarie" del campo (la ciudad, más controlada, se ha limitado a la resistencia y al apoyo estratégico de éste) defiende la forma de su espiritualidad y de sus valores culturales frente a la barbarie de la "civilización", que se ha olvidado de uno de los valores fundamentales de la Ilustración, la tolerancia. Si el México secular no se ha modernizado lo suficiente, no ha sido por la resistencia del catolicismo, sino por las limitaciones de los modelos de la modernización introducidos, por las limitaciones humanas de los introductores y por la explotación de las dudas acerca de estos mismos modelos en el giro culturalista que ha marcado con su herencia macondista la trayectoria intelectual de América Latina en el siglo XX (ver mi "Promesas" 148-53 y también "Argirópolis").

MISS MÉXICO VA A LA GUERRA

En este contexto de (di)simulación retórica, es elocuente la polémica en torno al atuendo "típico", ganador de un concurso, que la Miss México debía llevar para la competición de Miss Universo por celebrarse en México en mayo de 2007. Es interesante en especial la cobertura que le da al asunto *La Jornada*, el periódico de la izquierda intelectual mexicana, a lo largo de abril de 2007.

La diseñadora jalisciense, María del Rayo Macías Díaz, propuso un traje montado sobre los motivos de la guerra cristera, ya que, según ella, "somos descendientes de cristeros. Nos guste o no, es parte de lo que somos" ("México lleva la Cristiada a la pasarela de Miss Universo", 1 de abril, archivo digitalizado del periódico). El 6 se publica una nota incendiaria y algo incoherente por un tal Jorge Camil ("Franquistas y cristeros"), donde este sujeto editorialista, además de hacer comparación del atuendo con los franquistas contemporáneos, se imagina, con mucha risa, "a *Miss USA* con un traje 'típico' que incluyera imágenes de una reunión nocturna del Ku Klux Klan en el *Deep South*, con capuchas, cruces ardiendo y latas de cerveza". La distorsión no podría ser mayor en ambos casos, y la ignorancia de la historia, también. El 15 de abril interviene en la polémica toda una plana mayor de conocidos intelectuales mexicanos, desde Monsiváis hasta Loaeza ("El traje cristero, revanchismo de la derecha"). Lo menos ofensivo que se dice es que recordar los tiempos de los cristeros es "inconveniente" o "inoportuno", que la ocasión frívola banaliza el tema y que, en realidad, sólo desvía la atención de "los verdaderos problemas del país". Monsiváis intenta salir por la tangente con un chiste barato: "¿los mexicanos, todos, descendemos de los concursos de belleza?"

En realidad, si el diseño fuera "de mal gusto", como afirman casi unánimemente los "historiadores y analistas políticos" consultados por *La Jornada*, no habría ganado en la competición. La iconografía es tal vez un poco fuerte, pero no más que la historia que recuerda: "El vestido ganador está confeccionado en manta y muestra imágenes pintadas a mano: batallas; cristeros colgados de postes telegráficos; fusilados, como el padre Pablo García; mujeres en misas clandestinas; un templo donde varios cristeros fueron fusilados, y, por supuesto, la Virgen de Guadalupe" ("México lleva la Cristiada"). El montaje incluía un distintivo que llevaba la abuela de la diseñadora como parte de una organización de mujeres católicas citadinas que apoyaban la rebeldía. Eran las brigadas "Santa Juana de Arco", en las que al final de la rebelión participaron cerca de veinticinco mil mujeres (Meyer, *La Cristiada* III: 120-33).

El tema de los cristeros resultó demasiado polémico hasta a la altura del año 2007. El 17 de abril comunica *La Jornada* con satisfacción que el diseño será cambiado, y muestra un insípido pero alegre traje confeccionado sobre los motivos de las frutas del país…

En realidad, si un Octavio Paz plantea en *El laberinto de la soledad* (1950) que la Revolución Mexicana es un tipo de "vuelta a la madre", al México profundo, podría argumentarse que la vuelta histórica más auténtica se manifiesta precisamente en el episodio de los cristeros (sobre Paz ver mi "Anverso"). Ellos no luchan simplemente por la no reelección, menos por un caudillo, ni tampoco por un terruño o por cualquier otra ventaja material, sino que defienden los valores del ser humano tal como los sienten ellos. Para el intelectual moderno, quien asume sin cuestionarse que es la vanguardia obligatoria de la humanidad, es imposible entenderlo, y aún menos perdonar, cuando el "pueblo" no sigue sus dictámenes (recordemos que de tanto pensarse dios, el pobre Nietzsche se volvió loco).

LOS CRISTEROS DE JESUSA

 uando estalla la rebeldía, Jesusa está lista. Dice a su entrevistadora:

> La balacera es todo mi amor porque se oye muy bonita. Los primeros
> balazos, sí se oyen, pero el fuego cerrado ya no se oye. Nomás se ve
> la humareda, los humitos que salen de los distintos lugares. Sólo de
> acordarme me daban ganas de irme a la revolufia. (206)

Jesusa sale con el primer batallón y, a la vuelta, comenta con satisfacción:

> La requema de los cristeros fue balacera de a de veras. Balacera
> tupida. Y los colgados nomás se bamboleaban de los árboles... Eran
> indios tarugos que se daban en la madre los que se levantaron en
> armas para defender a la Virgen de Guadalupe... Y bala, bala y bala.
> Bala que das y bala que te pega. (206-07)

Jesusa va y viene con la tropa, vive pegada al cuartel, para estar al tanto de los movimientos de los soldados e irse con ellos cuando la avisan (213, 237). Pasa casi un año con la guarnición en Oaxaca. Aunque hace el trabajo en que se empeñan las soldaderas (216), ella no se siente como una; tal vez porque no sigue a ningún hombre en particular sino que va, por decirlo así, con "amigos" (206). Les hace compañía (220). Sin embargo, la gente no se fija en esas sutilezas y las mujeres locales la llaman despectivamente "señora de batallón", por no decir simple y llanamente "puta" (229). El estado de Oaxaca era uno de los centros menores de la rebeldía cristera. Hemos dicho que la organización de apoyo activo al movimiento se concentraba en las ciudades y en manos de mujeres. No sorprende entonces esta actitud hostil de las mujeres ante las "soldaderas". Antes, cuando la tropa se quedaba largo tiempo en un lugar, establecía lazos de amistad con la gente del lugar. No ahora, ni siquiera la propia familia de Jesusa le abre las puertas.

En estos movimientos, Jesusa recorre del oeste, al sur y al norte, todo el territorio en que había andado con su padre y luego con su marido. Ahora es un territorio de pocos amigos.

La imagen que Jesusa da de los católicos involucrados en la Guerra de los Cristeros viene de un odio visceral que ella tiene ante toda entidad organizada y que corresponde, en concreto, tanto a su distancia del catolicismo ortodoxo como a la propaganda antirreligiosa oficial. Por ejemplo, se sabe que Calles guardaba unos documentos comprometedores de amoríos entre los religiosos y unas damas sonorenses (Krauze 356). Jesusa magnifica estas acusaciones, acudiendo otra vez a la autoridad del testigo presencial:

> Yo no creo ya en los padres porque los he visto muy de cerquita... pasando
> la misa para mí ya no son más que hombres materiales, como todos los
> de la calle con todos sus defectos y hasta más, porque andan hambrientos
> de mujer... Por eso cuando Benito Juárez regresó a Oaxaca... lo primero
> que hizo fue vaciar los conventos... entró Benito Juárez con toda su escolta
> y agarró a los padres con las manos en la masa. Y a la cárcel. A las monjas

las echó para afuera. Luego ordenó que escarbaran los patios de los conventos, porque aunque él estaba chiquillo las veía bien chipotudas y luego de un día para otro se deshinchaban...

Por eso al escarbar encontraron muchas calaveritas, muchos huesitos de niño todavía blanditos... ¡A cuántas muchachas no las infelizan en los confesionarios! Que una confesadita y una tentadita, las empiezan a manosear y luego al dormitorio, como si estuvieran en un bule, o si no para más rápido a la sacristía. Por eso yo no los quiero. Aquí en la ciudad, en el Defe, han salido sus obras hasta en el periódico...

Las monjas me caen todavía más gordas aunque no estén embarazadas. Yo las he visto... (*Hasta no verte* 208-09)

Jesusa lo habrá visto, pero más bien en la revista mensual *El Soldado*, que se distribuía gratuitamente entre los militares, llena de burdas caricaturas que pintaban a los religiosos como obsesos sexuales (Meyer, *La Cristiada* II: 201). Su visión de los católicos corresponde, en realidad, punto por punto a la violencia discursiva de la propaganda oficial (ver Meyer 200-4). Sorprende que esta imagen se mantenga tan viva más de treinta años después. La Escuela de Frankfurt tendría en ello un buen ejemplo de la manipulación de los medios.

Los ciclos de violencia revolucionaria creciente marcan también a Jesusa. A los zapatistas los veía todavía en términos de igualdad, como seres humanos con quienes podía conversar, simpatizar y compartir; los villistas eran para ella odiosos enemigos, unos bandidos, pero todavía de alguna manera seres humanos, a pesar de todo, con quien luchaba de igual a igual. En cambio, la humanidad desaparece de la imagen de los cristeros; éstos son meros cadáveres que se bambolean al viento de los postes de telégrafo, o son los fantoches pervertidos de la propaganda oficial.

Al final de su transformación, Jesusa arremete contra todo y contra todos. Según ella, no hay hombres buenos ni mujeres buenas: "Todos somos malos sobre el haz de la tierra. En el hombre hay mala levadura" (209). También se nota en su vocabulario la enseñanza "espiritualista". Los "otros" eran unos indios tarugos, campesinos (vocablo utilizado por ella como insulto), guarachudos, mal comidos... Es interesante ver la distancia marcada en su discurso; Jesusa no se reconoce a sí misma, a pesar de compartir con ellos sus facciones indígenas (véase su foto, la única publicada hasta que sepamos, en Poniatowska, *Fem* 33).

Para Jesusa, no sólo los cristeros sino también los de los demás bandos revolucionarios son los "otros", a los que odia un tanto más (a los villistas) o menos (a los zapatistas). Como ella anduvo siempre con los constitucionalistas victoriosos, en cierto sentido es —a pesar de su amargura y sus rencores personales, y a pesar de su registro esperpéntico— la voz de la revolución oficial, tal como *Los de abajo* da la voz al predicamento de una de las facciones derrotadas (esta sensación del fracaso luego será atractiva intelectual y estéticamente para la "novela de la revolución"). Con ésta la va a unir sólo la sensación de la futilidad de la Revolución.

Este reconocimiento intelectual de la futilidad de la gesta revolucionaria, no obstante, no le impide desear volver "a la bola" en cualquier momento: "cualquier día me vuelvo a ir a donde se arme la bola, pero que haya balazos, muchos balazos, yo le entro a la lotería" (*Hasta no verte* 206, también 217 y 237). "Volver a la bola" es volver a la juventud, volver a experimentar la euforia de la "lotería" del combate, entre la vida y la muerte, *volver, volver...* como dice la canción. Parece que el peligro de muerte es la consolación de todos los seres descontentos y/o acomplejados. Escribe Ludwig Wittgenstein en su diario de la guerra: "If only I may be allowed to risk my life in some difficult assignment... perhaps the nearness of death will bring light into life". Pareciera que para estas almas en pena en plena vida, ganaron aquéllos que perecieron en la contienda.

Jesusa es una anarquista de espíritu. Por ejemplo, además de la Iglesia Católica, odia a los sindicatos, y cuando emerge el movimiento de los estudiantes de 1968, está también visceralmente en contra de ellos (Steele 94). En *Hasta no verte* Poniatowska registra aquélla, pero omite caritativamente esta actitud, tal vez en un intento de salvarla de sí misma ante los ojos escudriñadores de los lectores modernos. Obviamente, en el testimonio latinoamericano no todas las transgresiones son consideradas como iguales.

CONCLUSIONES

uando Jesusa vuelve definitivamente a la capital, cansada de su aventura cristera, poco queda por decir; la segunda parte de su vida, aunque sea cronológicamente la más larga, parece tener poco interés tanto para ella como para la entrevistadora, y abarca sólo la última quinta parte del texto. Termina *una novela* en la novela testimonial: una historia articulada en torno a la formación del personaje, un *Bildungsroman,* con la diferencia de que un *Bildungsroman* documenta la preparación de un joven para la vida; aquí la vida se acabó. Sigue una cotidianidad mediocre de una sobrevida. De la vida quedan sólo los recuerdos y vagos deseos de *volver.*

Lo que sigue en *Hasta no verte Jesús mío* rebasa la vida de una persona. Poniatowska reconoce que ha utilizado materiales no sólo ofrecidos por el "informe" de Jesusa, como lo llama en *Las soldaderas* (12) donde cita o parafrasea ciertos pasajes de la novela. Al cerrarse los ciclos de la Revolución, el relato autobiográfico adquiere más un sabor de la picaresca y también, en partes, de una enciclopedia de la cultura popular mexicana.

La visión de la Revolución que arroja *Hasta no verte Jesús mío* la sitúa en la línea de las obras canónicas de la novela de la revolución desde Azuela (*Los de abajo,* 1915), Rulfo (*El llano en llamas,* 1953, *Pedro Páramo,* 1955), Fuentes (*La muerte de Artemio Cruz,* 1961) y Ibargüengoitia (*Los relámpagos de agosto,* 1964), que van del espejo cóncavo del esperpento hasta la parodia; por la visión y experiencia femenina que ofrece, además, en la línea de Nellie Campobello (*Cartucho,* 1931) hasta Elena Garro (*Los recuerdos del porvenir,* 1963), y entre todas ellas ocupa un lugar muy especial.

El relato autobiográfico revela una serie de filtros. En primer lugar, la narradora en primera persona, Jesusa, recuerda su vida en la Revolución desde la distancia de treinta y hasta cincuenta años. Diversas experiencias se solapan o se contradicen en su relato. Al tiempo de la narración, la vieja Jesusa ya es en gran parte otra persona; y no sólo eso: en sus recuerdos se le interpone continuamente su obsesión religiosa con la Obra Espiritual, que ha conocido en los años veinte. El "espiritualismo", aclara Poniatowska (*Vuelta* 7-8), es la versión popular tardía del espiritismo (y la teosofía), que entusiasmaba a las elites hispanoamericanas en las primeras décadas del siglo XX.

Anotemos sólo que, en una dimensión, el espiritualismo popular, originado al margen del catolicismo, es una respuesta democrática a la Iglesia Católica rígidamente jerárquica (tal como lo es la expansión de las iglesias evangélicas en muchas comunidades indígenas y en los barrios populares hispanoamericanos). En otra, no se nos escapa la coincidencia de su emergencia en los años veinte con la persecución oficial de la Iglesia Católica y con los intentos de sustituir a ésta por un brebaje "mexicano".

La escritora-editora es, entonces, un segundo filtro: por un lado, elimina en lo posible las interferencias extemporales y, en este sentido, devuelve al personaje a sí mismo, tal como ella estaba en los años de la Revolución, y también destaca las características que la van a definir a lo largo de su vida. Esa fidelidad del personaje a la persona trae ciertas dificultades. Comenta Poniatowska:

> Quise hacer hincapié en las cualidades personales de la Jesusa, en aquello que la distingue de la imagen tradicional de la mujer mexicana... Llegué a la conclusión de que a mí no me tocaba hacer un análisis histórico del personaje. ¿Para qué? ... No milita en partido alguno, no hace política, no asiste a ninguna manifestación, a ningún mitin, no se adhiere a protestas, tampoco invade tierras. No puedo ponerla a hacer guardia bajo ninguna bandera rojinegra ni hacerla desfilar en las filas de un sindicato. ... Si yo la transformara en un Zapata de barrio traicionaría todas esas horas que vivimos juntas. (*Vuelta* 11)

Por otro lado, como en el mencionado caso de sus actitudes ante el movimiento estudiantil, la autora no resiste el impulso y "corrige" al personaje, omitiendo sus opiniones no tan "políticamente correctas".

Sea como sea, surge un personaje inimitable, diríamos algo "anárquico", por falta de una mejor clasificación. Algunos lectores, y lectoras en especial (Sommer), se quejarán de este personaje, porque no entra en sus deseados casilleros prefabricados. Jesusa, tal como la otra mujer indómita, la boliviana Domitila Barrios, se resiste a fáciles lecturas y asimilaciones "ideológicas".

A pesar de o por la multiplicidad de los filtros, Jesusa no está hecha de una pieza, y es un sujeto fragmentado, contradictorio. Lo que la literatura posmoderna se propone a veces afanosamente, aquí arroja el azar y el proceso de la elaboración semi-documental. El "sujeto" de Jesusa va emergiendo a partir de su palabra idiosincrática, a partir de sus personalísimos recuerdos fragmentarios, y la escritora-entrevistadora organiza los materiales dispersos, pero deja suficiente "margen" a la libertad de la persona y de su personaje. El lenguaje, dijimos, atrae la atención sobre sí mismo y se erige como el segundo protagonista de la narración.

La escritora como segundo filtro construye también un relato autobiográfico del personaje más o menos coherente y cronológico, enmarcado entre el comienzo *in medias res* y el final que están situados en el tiempo contemporáneo de la elaboración de las memorias (los sesenta). El trabajo creativo de editora convierte a la interlocutora en la autora de los dos avatares de Jesusa. Cierra la obra la memorable petición de Jesusa, dirigida a su interlocutora y autora: "Ahora ya no chingue. Váyase. Déjeme dormir."

NOTA

[1] La atmósfera de fervor y de renovación religiosa en México en los años veinte, la creación de una religión auténticamente mexicana, está recreada en los delirios esta vez antimodernos de D. H. Lawrence en *The Plumed Serpent* (1926), que refleja su doble estadía en el país en 1923. Ver los intentos de creación de una Iglesia Católica Apostólica Mexicana en 1925 (Krauze 349). La explosión de las sectas populares semi-religiosas en la misma década, como la Obra Espiritual, queda registrada en la novela testimonial que comentamos.

OBRAS CITADAS

García Flores, Margarita. "Elena Poniatowska: *Hasta no verte Jesús mío*". *Revista de la Universidad de México,* suppl. Hojas de crítica. 24.2 (octubre 1969): 12-15.

García Pinto, Magdalena. "Entrevista con Elena Poniatowska". *Historias íntimas. Conversaciones con diez escritoras latinoamericanas.* Hanover, NH: Ediciones del Norte, 1988. 175-98.

Jörgensen, Beth E. *The Writing of Elena Poniatowska.* Austin: U of Texas P, 1994.

Krauze, Enrique. *Biografía del poder. Caudillos de la Revolución Mexicana (1910-1940).* México: Tusquets Editores, 2006.

Meyer, Jean. *La Cristiada.* México: Siglo XXI, 1973. 3 vols.

———. *La grandeza mexicana.* Vol. IV de *La Cristiada.* México: Editorial Clío, 1997.

Poniatowska, Elena. *Hasta no verte Jesús mío.* México: Era, 1969.

———. "Hasta no verte Jesús mío". *Vuelta* 24 (noviembre 1978): 5-11.

———. *Las soldaderas.* México: Era/Conaculta, 2007 (orig. 1999).

———. "Testimonios: Jesusa Palancares". *Fem* 4.24 (agosto-octubre 1982): 33-35 [la foto de Jesusa p. 33, pp. 34-35, pasajes del final de la novela].

Sommer, Doris. "Hot Pursuit and Cold Rewards of Mexicanness". *Proceed with Caution, When Engaged by Minority Writing in the Americas.* Cambridge, Mass.: Harvard UP, 1999. 138-59.

Steele, Cynthia. "Elena Poniatowska. Entrevista". *Hispamérica* 18.53-54 (1989): 89-105.

Volek, Emil. "Las modalidades del Testimonio y *Hasta no verte Jesús mío* de Elena Poniatowska". *Literatura mexicana/Mexican Literature.* Ed. José Miguel Oviedo. Filadelfia: U of Pennsylvania, 1993. 44-67.

———. "Los entramados ideológicos del Testimonio latinoamericano: La Revolución anunciada, el oscuro objeto del deseo, el macondismo posmoderno/poscolonial, Menchú y Stoll." *Chasqui* 31.2 (noviembre 2002): 44-74.

————. "Anverso y reverso del laberinto: Octavio Paz, ¿fundador de Macondo?" *Memoria del XIX Coloquio de la literatura mexicana e hispanoamericana.* Ed. Alma Leticia Martínez-Figueroa. Hermosillo: U de Sonora, 2005. 35-49.

———— "Promesas y simulacros en el baratillo posmodernista: saber y ser en las encrucijadas de una 'historia mostrenca'." *Treinta años de estudios literarios/culturales latinoamericanistas en Estados Unidos. Memorias, testimonios, reflexiones críticas.* Ed. Hernán Vidal. Pittsburgh: Instituto Internacional de Literatura Iberoamericana, 2008. 129-64.

————. "From Argirópolis to Macondo: Latin American Intellectuals and the Tasks of Modernization." *Latin American Issues and Challenges.* Ed. L. Naciamento y G. Sousa. Nova Science Publishers (2009, forthcoming).